PRAISE FOR LISTEN, LEARN & LOVE

"I hope reading this book will ignite a hunger to hear first-hand from family and ward members, neighbors and colleagues, their personal experiences of what it feels like to be gay, lesbian, bisexual, transgender or queer in our church and communities. And in becoming witnesses to the joys and challenges of each life, that all of us will resolve to make room in our hearts and homes for the varied paths and choices each individual makes as they journey toward physical, emotional and spiritual wholeness."

—TOM CHRISTOFFERSON, AUTHOR OF *THAT WE MAY BE ONE: A GAY MORMON'S PERSPECTIVE ON FAITH AND FAMILY*

"As we come to know each other's stories, see one another as the Savior does, we can truly become as the Good Samaritan, helping others along the sometimes challenging path of life. *Listen, Learn & Love* opens a window to the lives of our LGBTQ brothers and sisters, and their families. Greater understanding paves a path to Zion."

—GANEL-LYN CONDIE, BESTSELLING AUTHOR AND SPEAKER, HOST OF *REAL TALK CFM*

"In this book, Richard creates a safe place for anyone to learn how to listen and love with more understanding and compassion. Reading this can gently, but powerfully, coax us all to a higher plane of Christianity."

—STEVEN SHARP NELSON, THE PIANO GUYS

"As the mother of a gay teenage son, I've asked myself, 'How do we embrace our gay child and embrace the gospel we love?' *Listen, Learn & Love* answers that question with a treasure trove of personal stories, quotes from Church leaders, and invitations to follow the Savior's example and better keep our baptismal covenants to bear, mourn, and comfort. I recommend this book to every parent, church member, and church leader. This book has the potential to save testimonies, families, and even lives."

—BECKY EDWARDS, SPEAKER, BLOGGER, LIFE COACH, AUTHOR

FOREWORD BY STEVE YOUNG

Listen Learn & Love

FOREWORD BY STEVE YOUNG

Listen Learn & Love

Embracing LGBTQ Latter-day Saints

RICHARD H. OSTLER

CFI
AN IMPRINT OF CEDAR FORT, INC.
SPRINGVILLE, UTAH

ISBN 13: 978-1-4621-3577-6

Published by CFI, an imprint of Cedar Fort, Inc.
2373 W. 700 S., Springville, UT, 84663
Distributed by Cedar Fort, Inc., www.cedarfort.com

Library of Congress Control Number: 2020942523

Cover design by Shawnda T. Craig
Cover design © 2020 Cedar Fort, Inc.
Edited by Trina Caudle, Alison Palmer, and Kimiko Hammari

Printed in the United States of America

10 9 8 7 6 5 4 3 2 1

Printed on acid-free paper

To my wonderful parents,
Don and Barbara Ostler,
who raised me in a loving home
where they taught
the gospel of Jesus Christ.

CONTENTS

Foreword

I became aware of Richard Ostler in 2016 when I read his supportive messages about LGBTQ Latter-day Saints during his service as a YSA bishop. Since that time, we have become close friends and speak frequently about how to better meet the needs of LGBTQ Latter-day Saints as they walk a difficult road.

Richard has met with hundreds of LGBTQ Latter-day Saints to understand their perspectives. He has sat with them in their pain, heard and validated their stories, and been willing to learn from them. He sees their contributions to our church and society, and chooses to be a voice of support. He started a podcast and organization, where I am on the advisory board, called Listen, Learn & Love. The goal of both is to amplify LGBTQ Latter-day Saint voices so we can better understand their unique journey and provide more support.

This book is a groundbreaking extension of that same goal, as he has put so much into the tender walk to bring others' experiences to a wide audience. It is more than just a single story but a compilation of hundreds of stories from LGBTQ Latter-day Saints and LDS parents of LGBTQ children. Reading stories changes hearts, builds more empathy, and offers new insight to provide better encouragement. These stories take you on a journey to answer both simple and difficult questions.

His book is consistent with the four pillars of the law of love that are near and dear to my heart: long-suffering, gentle persuasion, love unfeigned, and meekness. I encourage every LDS member and local leader to read this book and share it with others. It will give you valuable insights to better meet the needs of LGBTQ Latter-day Saints and use their gifts to strengthen our congregations and families. I also encourage our LGBTQ members to read it. It will give you more hope, perspective, and understanding. I hope this book will help us better come together as Latter-day Saints to help everyone feel welcome, needed, and included within the body of Christ.

—Steve Young

INTRODUCTION

We need to listen to and understand what our LGBT brothers and sisters are feeling and experiencing. Certainly, we must do better than we have done in the past so that all members feel they have a spiritual home where their brothers and sisters love them and where they have a place to worship and serve the Lord.

—PRESIDENT M. RUSSELL BALLARD[1]

The purpose of this book is to help members of The Church of Jesus Christ of Latter-day Saints implement President Ballard's vision to more fully include our LGBTQ[2] members, helping them feel hope and find belonging in our church and society as they walk a difficult and unique road. The book is supportive of the Church, its leaders, and its doctrine. The aim is to guide humble consideration of how we can "do better than we have done in the past" to meet the spiritual and emotional needs of our LGBTQ members and utilize their gifts to strengthen our church.

I was led to minister specifically to LGBTQ individuals after several experiences, the most impactful being my time as a bishop in a young single adult (YSA) ward.[3] During my time as bishop, I met with LGBTQ members, listened to them, and tried to understand their perspective. My view shifted from seeing LGBTQ people as a separate group to seeing them as my fellow Latter-day Saints. I learned to set aside my assumptions to better fulfill my stewardship responsibility to minister to them, to help ease burdens instead of adding to them, to help them come unto Christ, and to encourage their unique and needed contributions to our church.

The name of this book, *Listen, Learn & Love*, is the same name as the podcast and website I started to provide a platform for LGBTQ Latter-day Saints to share their stories.[4] This book is an extension of that same goal. As we listen to, learn from, and love our LGBTQ members, we are better able to "touch their cross" and embrace them, as taught by Fiona Givens in reference to LGBTQ Latter-day Saints: "Every Latter-day Saint who wishes to help bear another's burden must touch that person's cross to understand the nature and depth of the pain being carried."[5] I also hope the stories and principles outlined here will help all Latter-day Saints increase their testimony of the restored gospel, become more like Christ, and have better tools and insights to help meet the needs of LGBTQ Latter-day Saints.

This book is also for LGBTQ Latter-day Saints. By sharing stories from other LGBTQ members and their insights into the gospel of Jesus Christ, it aims to provide more hope, peace, and perspective so that LGBTQ Church members feel that they "have a spiritual home where their brothers and sisters love them." For Latter-day Saints barely hanging on to your membership in the Church, I hope this book helps you feel like you can stay. We need you because of your unique perspectives, gifts, and contributions. And you, like all of us, need the gospel, teachings, ordinances, and covenants in our lives. And for those who have stepped away from the Church, I hope the principles highlighted will help reinforce your relationship with God and feel a greater degree of unity and connectedness with Latter-day Saints.

If Church members can collectively learn to better minister to LGBTQ individuals and create a stronger sense of belonging, we can increase the chances that more LGBTQ members will be able to stay in the Church and offer us their voices and gifts. When an LGBTQ member does step away, however, my hope is that family circles will stay together, united in love, communication, and support. A core belief in our church is the importance of maintaining a strong family, and I believe this goal still stands even if a family member steps away from the Church (more in chapter 10). I also hope this book provides principles and awareness to reduce tension between people who stay in the Church and people who leave the Church; we are, after all, all members of the human family.

Most of the content of this book comprises the individual experiences of LGBTQ members and Latter-day Saint parents of LGBTQ children. These perspectives often go unheard in our congregations and thus are overlooked, but both of these groups are earnestly seeking personal revelation, and hearing their perspectives is crucial. Many Church members express love for our LGBTQ members but are not fully aware of the struggles they go through. Understanding others' experiences creates empathy and allows us to reach out to others. I've had the blessing to meet with hundreds of our LGBTQ members, and each of their stories is unique. I'm honored to introduce their stories to a wider audience. They are some of my heroes.

I hope and pray that as you read their stories, insights will come to your mind and heart on how you can more fully love and include the LGBTQ Latter-day Saints within your circle of influence.

Before we begin, it's important to understand the terms within this book. These are labels that some Latter-day Saints apply to themselves to describe what they experience in terms of their sexual orientation and gender identity. I've learned that each LGBTQ member, if desired, chooses their own label, and that taking on a label is not against the Church's teachings (for more on labels, see chapter 5).

These are various terms we will be using, with a brief description of the person to whom the term applies: [6]

- LGBTQ: lesbian, gay, bisexual, transgender, queer; those who are not heterosexual or cisgender
- Lesbian: female with sexual orientation to same sex
- Gay: male or female with sexual orientation to same sex
- LG: lesbian, gay
- LGB: lesbian, gay, bisexual
- Same-Sex Attraction: male or female with sexual orientation to same sex
- Bisexual: male or female with sexual orientation to both sexes
- Transgender: person whose gender identity or gender expression does not match their biological sex
- Gender Dysphoria: distress a person feels when their gender identity does not match their biological sex
- Cisgender: person whose gender identity matches their biological sex
- Non-binary: person whose gender identity is not exclusively masculine or feminine
- Cishet: person who is both cisgender and heterosexual
- Queer: umbrella term for someone who is not straight and/or not cisgender, or is questioning[7]
- Pansexual: person who is attracted to people regardless of their gender
- Asexual: person who is attracted to no one

In this book, I will generally use gay instead of same-sex attraction, but we should let each person, if desired, choose their own label—and we should remember our primary identity is a beloved child of Heavenly Parents. There are many who use the same-sex attraction label and many who use the gay label. We shouldn't try to convince either group to adopt the label of the other group but instead honor individual choices.

ENDNOTES

1. M. Russell Ballard, "Questions and Answers" (devotional address, Brigham Young University, Provo, Utah, November 14, 2017), speeches.byu.edu/talks/m-russell-ballard/questions-and-answers/.
1. For a complete definition of terms, please refer to the end of the introduction.
3. YSA wards include unmarried individuals between the ages of eighteen and thirty.
4. See listenlearnandlove.org/. Listen, Learn & Love podcast is available on all major podcast platforms. Episodes can also be found at listenlearnandlove.org/podcasts.
5. Tad Walch, "God Loves Every Single Person, Speakers Tell LGBT Mormons at Affirmation Conference," *Deseret News*, September 20, 2015, deseret.com/2015/9/20/20572717/god-loves-every-single-person-speakers-tell-lgbt-mormons-at-affirmation-conference#members-of-affirmations-2014-leadership-team-attend-the-this-is-the-place-international-conference-at-the-university-of-utah.
6. For a more complete glossary of terms, see "General Definitions," Education & Training, Lesbian, Gay, Bisexual and Transgender Resource Center, University of California, San Francisco, lgbt.ucsf.edu/glossary-terms, accessed February 3, 2020.
7. The word *queer* used to be a highly offensive term but is now used by many in a positive way as an umbrella term for those who identify somewhere in the LGBTQ spectrum or who are questioning their gender identity or sexual orientation.

CHAPTER 1

A DESIRE TO HELP OUR LGBTQ MEMBERS

A major milestone in my story of wanting to help our LGBTQ members came in September 2013, when my wife Sheila and I were called to serve in a young single adult (YSA) ward in which I would serve as bishop. We were called to an area of the Salt Lake Valley that was outside of our home ward area, and we didn't know a single member of the congregation. I prayerfully chose counselors from the area, and we were sustained, set apart, and started our assignment. We served with some of the finest adult leaders and YSA members we've ever met.

Learning the Principles of Effective Ministry

Since social media is a key component of communication today, at the beginning of my service in the ward, I asked the previous bishop how he used Facebook to interact with the ward members. He said, "I friend request everyone." I had become fairly good at using Facebook the year before when I had tracked down former missionaries for my thirty-year mission reunion, so I followed his advice and sent friend requests to everyone on the ward rolls. Though many young single adults are transitory, never staying in one place for too long, this ward was largely stable. And with members staying in the ward for long periods, over time most accepted my friend requests (as did even some of their nonmember friends). Facebook became one of the key tools I used to reach and minister to those who did not attend weekly Church meetings.

Once I was connected to ward members on social media (Facebook, Twitter, and Instagram), I sent introductory direct messages (DMs) to those not attending. Most didn't respond right away, but some gradually opened up, and we had meaningful conversations online without ever meeting in person. Some responded in a time of crisis since they could scroll back through their messages and contact me.

Eventually two streams of YSAs were meeting with me: those who actively attended Church meetings (who worked through the executive secretary to get on my calendar) and the social media group who were less active (with whom I booked meetings directly). My executive secretary and I shared a Google calendar so we both could book appointments.

The less active group fascinated me. This was the first time I had priesthood responsibility at the ward level for those who were less active, and I spent considerable time listening to their stories. I realized that for the most part, this group considered The Church of Jesus Christ of Latter-day Saints to be their spiritual home, even though they did not actively attend Church meetings (for a number of reasons I had not previously fully considered).

The longer I served as bishop, the more I felt impressions from Heavenly Father to listen to the YSAs' stories and develop the maturity to resist my typical toolbox of suggestions (read, pray, go to church) to resolve their questions. It often took multiple visits of asking follow-up questions and resisting the urge to turn the conversation back to me (and my suggestions) for an individual to fully share their journey. I took notes of the spiritual promptings I felt and circled back to them when the members finished telling their story and I felt I understood their perspective. I did not sit behind the bishop's desk but at the side, facing the other person in the chair across from me. Sitting face to face created a feeling of equal footing, allowing more open communication.

I also learned to validate how someone felt, even if I didn't feel the same way. Validating others' feelings and being fully heard by a trusted leader can often be deeply healing. If people had concerns about the Church (about its history or stance on current issues, for example), affirming that their feelings were real and understandable didn't deepen any wedge between them and the Church and, in fact, usually did the opposite. Being heard, understood, and validated are deeply powerful principles of good ministering (see chapter 7 for more on this topic).

Once I fully understood their road, I had an increased ability to offer specific spiritual suggestions based on their unique circumstances. Further, a priesthood blessing would often be the most helpful after I understood the totality of their situation because I was more open to spiritual impressions from Heavenly Father that addressed the content of our conversations. While my goal was to help each YSA come closer to Christ through our restored Church, sometimes I'd let the young single adults set the agenda. A few had no immediate desire to return to Church activity but wanted my help, mentorship, and insights, as well as, on occasion, Church services to overcome significant challenges (financial problems, family issues, addictions, unemployment, educational challenges, and so on). My relationship with these members and my role in their lives was not conditional on Church activity. I felt at peace that this was consistent with Christ's example, and being in these individuals' lives as a trusted leader allowed me to talk with them about their return to church if the right circumstances arose. I was far from a perfect leader, but I did my best.[1]

Wiping My Hard Drive Clean: Reconstructing My Views on LGBTQ Issues

In my efforts to reach out to those who were less active, I connected with a couple of gay men in our ward. I remember one man answered my Facebook message with, "Let's meet." Starting in early 2014 we met weekly for several months as he told me of his life as a gay Latter-day Saint. I felt prompted to do a lot of listening. The Spirit told me the best way I could help him was to try to understand, as fully as I could, the road he was walking. This was the first time I had listened to a gay Latter-day Saint, but it wasn't the last.

One foundational experience that opened my heart to our LGBTQ friends was in early 2012. While in the Jordan River Temple, I felt a strong prompting to organize a thirty-year mission reunion for Ellis and Katie Ivory, who presided over the England Manchester Mission from 1979 to 1982. They had been in their thirties when leading the mission and were still very much alive thirty years later. I contacted them, and we agreed to have a reunion that fall. My self-assigned job was to find all of our missionaries, invite them to the reunion, and encourage them to join a new Facebook group for our mission. I was joined in this effort by a former companion, Tom Puck, who had kept a mission list and made the entire event possible.

I will never forget the day I found Blane van Pletzen, a convert from South Africa and one of our best missionaries. I learned from his Facebook page that he was an Episcopal priest and in a same-sex marriage. I thought, "Well, that isn't what we taught in England." I figured he wouldn't come to the reunion and wondered if I should even send him a friend request. As I scrolled further on his page, I noticed that for his congregation, he had posted links to the Easter and Christmas performances of the Tabernacle Choir. I realized he still had a soft spot for the Church. I sent him a message about the reunion, and he responded that he'd love to attend with his husband, Scott, who was also a Latter-day Saint returned missionary.

At the reunion, President and Sister Ivory extended the hand of kindness to Blane and Scott, who joined Sheila and me at our table. The Ivorys led by showing friendship, kindness, and a desire for them to feel welcome at the reunion. While they are concerned about any of their missionaries living outside the teachings of the Church, they demonstrated that no one is outside the circle of their love. I believe the reunion was divinely inspired to bring us back together to support each other and share our love for the gospel.

A couple of years later, I was in New York and arranged to visit Blane on a weekday in his parish church. As I drove into the parking lot, I was a little uncomfortable, as if by being there I was somehow compromising my beliefs. I said a brief prayer, and my uneasiness faded as I remembered Christ's example of spending time with *all* of Heavenly Father's children. After giving me a tour of his church, Blane took me up to the parish organ, high above the empty seats. I could easily imagine the chapel full of worshipers singing. Blane surprised me when he sat at the organ and spontaneously played a familiar Latter-day Saint hymn. It was a beautiful moment.

I could see the goodness in Blane and how he was helping people in his congregation. I had assumed that those who left our church and were in same-sex marriages had abandoned their belief in God and wanted the Church to fail. My experiences with Blane, however, taught me that the situations of those who leave the Church are less black and white than I had originally concluded and that each situation is unique. My heart was softened toward LGBTQ members who had left the Church. Getting to know someone on an individual level reframed my perspective. Dr. Brené Brown[2] has said, "People are hard to hate close up. Move in."[3] I found this statement to be true as I met with more people outside my normal circle.

The November 2015 Policy Statements

The November 2015 policy statements, particularly the section which denied baptism to children of those in same-sex marriages, were unsettling to me.[4] They seemed inconsistent with Christ's teaching to "suffer little children to come unto me, and forbid them not: for of such is the kingdom of God" (Luke 18:16). Prior to the statements, a few YSAs told me of hopes for a kinder and gentler LGBTQ message from the Church, without a change in doctrine. I was working hard as I met with and prayed for them to stay in the Church. The policy statements made my assignment more difficult, and I did have one YSA bring me a notarized letter of resignation a few weeks later.[5] All of this increased my desire to better understand our LGBTQ members by talking directly with them and listening to their stories.

The day after the policy statements were made, I posted a message on Facebook, sensing some of my YSAs, their friends, and others in my circle might have concerns: "I will be on my knees to better understand the LDS Church's policy statement for children in same gender marriages. I love, support and sustain my leaders. That being said, today my heart is heavy for my dear friends, some of the best people I know, in or connected to the LGBT community—or anyone feeling pain from these statements. I pray for peace and comfort to each of you."[6]

During this time, I was informally teaching a man the gospel. He asked about my feelings on the policy statements. I was honest and told him I was unsettled about them. He felt the same way and later shared that my Facebook post was key to his decision to continue investigating the Church; he felt he didn't need to have a perfect understanding or testimony of every aspect of the Church. I also believe his respect for and trust in me increased because I was honest. I eventually invited him to meet with the missionaries, extended an invitation to be baptized, and had the honor of performing his baptism.

The policy statements provided me and others with an opportunity to learn how to minister to members when they have concerns about something within the Church. If someone bravely opens up to us as fellow Church members, family members, or local leaders, how do we handle these honest concerns? Do we validate their feelings, even if their feelings are not held by the majority of Church members? Or do we potentially add to their burden by comparing them to the elect who will be deceived at the last days, or to the tares in the parable of wheat and tares (see Matthew 24:24 and Matthew 13)? Or do we ask them to just have more faith? I believe we need to give them the benefit of the doubt that they are doing their best to come unto Christ and stay committed members of the Church.

My home stake president, David Sturt, hit a ministering "home run" when I expressed my concerns with the policy statements. Though he didn't share my concerns, he gave me permission to have a "fallen domino or two" as I continued to make my way forward as a faithful Latter-day Saint. He created needed space for me. He didn't ask me to change my feelings or give me a spiritual checklist of things to do that would somehow align my feelings with the policy statements. I never gained a testimony of the policy statements. But I have many dominoes standing with deep roots that keep me a believing and committed member of the Church. Some of these dominoes are the doctrine of Heavenly Parents who love me, the plan of happiness, the restored priesthood, a modern-day prophet, the truthfulness of the Book of Mormon and its ability to help me come unto Christ, the power of temple covenants, and the Atonement of Jesus Christ.[7]

All these experiences resulted in a deep impression in late 2015 that I needed to wipe my hard drive clean, so to speak, of all my previously held notions about LGBTQ people. I didn't know which of my conclusions were accurate and which were not. I realized that the vast majority of my conclusions about LGBTQ individuals had come from cishet (cisgender and heterosexual) people, and I should listen to and learn from LGBTQ individuals to see them how Heavenly Father sees them. A cholesterol test gives me specific numbers to inform me about my cardiovascular health. But there's no easy way to measure my levels of homophobia or transphobia—attitudes I may have inadvertently picked up—or to gauge how my previous assumptions and resulting actions might have added to the burdens of others. Moreover, as a bishop, I had stewardship responsibility for all members of my ward and knew there were likely closeted LGBTQ members in my congregation. I wanted to say and do things that lifted their burdens and pointed them to Christ. So I decided to start from scratch. Just as we wipe a computer's hard drive to eliminate corrupt files, I mentally tried to remove everything I thought I knew and decided to learn about LGBTQ people from themselves and through spiritual impressions from Heavenly Father.

This principle also applies to other groups we might form opinions about without taking the time to personally know people in that group. I call this tendency the "trap of unearned opinions." It is easy, for instance, for me to think I know the feelings of Black teenagers, undocumented workers, women, people who are incarcerated, or people who have left the Church. However, it takes discipline and humility not to form an opinion until listening to an individual's experience. When we do that, we not only acquire more accurate insight into their lives but also learn that each person within a group is unique and has their own views and characteristics. As we learn directly from them, we can lighten their burdens instead of potentially adding to them with uninformed opinions.

In April 2019, the November 2015 policy statements were reversed. The news was covered in an article by the *Deseret News*, which marked a new and kinder tone toward our LGBTQ members. The remarks in the *Deseret News* article from Church members and leaders provide insights on how we should treat others: "The very positive policies announced this morning should help affected families," President Dallin H. Oaks said. "In addition, our members' efforts to show more understanding, compassion and love should increase respect and understanding among all people of good will. We want to reduce the hate and contention so common today. We are optimistic that a majority of people—whatever their beliefs and orientations—long for better understanding and less contentious communications. That is surely our desire, and we seek the help of our members and others to attain it."

The *Deseret News* article continued, quoting Tom Christofferson, a gay Latter-day Saint and brother of Elder D. Todd Christofferson: "'The big message to me is that this continues to be something that the brethren are seeking further light and knowledge on, and I'm really grateful for that.' . . . He said his mind was on friends and others who stopped associating with the Church after November 2015. 'I'm thinking of them today and hoping that they will feel that this removed the impediment that they had seen to their continued engagement,' he said. 'I hope many will want to come back and worship with us again.'"

Regarding the removal of the policy statements, Tom added:

> I think this is a recognition of the prayers of so many people that there could be a way to have a more welcoming place in the Church

> for LGBTQ people. . . . And simultaneously it is, in my mind, an indication of that continued wrestle that prophets have to know what God would have them do in this time, today, and with the increased understanding we have about the nature of what it means to be gay, that we don't have all the answers that we would want. But what this clearly says to me is that there's an opportunity to continue to be more welcoming to people wherever they are in their lives.

The *Deseret News* article also quoted the reaction of former NFL quarterback Steve Young: "We've all been looking for things to get better for our LGBT brothers and sisters, and the policy rescission is a tremendous step forward. To have that go away allows for some really productive conversations to take place inside of families, and to try and keep families together and create space for people."

A few of my thoughts were also shared in the article: "Our LGBTQ members have a difficult road, and I feel these adjustments help us better mourn, comfort and bear their burdens as they make their way forward."[8] I have hope the reversal of the November 2015 policy marks the turning of a page in the Church's relationship with LGBTQ members. This book is intended to support the positive messages shared by President Oaks, Tom Christofferson, and others and to further encourage us to be kinder to LGBTQ loved ones.

The reversal of the policy statements was painful for many of our LGBTQ members. At first this surprised me, but as I listened, I better understood. One LGBTQ Latter-day Saint described it as a scab that had healed but was then ripped off. Another said it was like someone setting your home on fire and then that same person heroically returning to put out the fire. These are powerful visual analogies of the pain some LGBTQ members are feeling. Instead of dismissing their pain, we should honor how these good LGBTQ members are feeling. Doing so may help them stay in the Church and receive the associated blessings. We can validate their feelings while still supporting and sustaining our leaders and remaining a faithful Latter-day Saint.

Hearing Stories from My LGBTQ Friends

During this time, my desire to learn more about our LGBTQ members increased, and I started proactively reaching out to LGBTQ friends and parents of LGBTQ members. I contacted a high school friend, Doug Balli, and his husband, Rob Blackhurst, and invited them to dinner. I was Facebook friends with Doug but hadn't crossed paths with him in decades. However, I had seen them a few months earlier in the Amsterdam airport, when Sheila and I were returning home from a vacation, but I hadn't initiated a conversation. I was embarrassed for not saying hello because I lacked the skills and confidence to have a conversation with a couple in a same-sex marriage.

Doug and Rob agreed to dinner, and we had a wonderful evening together before I had to leave to go to the bishop's office for a night of interviews. They told me about their journey as gay men and how they found each other, support from their family, their careers, and counseling with other LGBTQ people (especially closeted Latter-day Saint youth). I learned so much from them, including that sexual orientation is not a choice (see chapter 3), heard several painful experiences, and felt my new hard drive being programed with accurate information. I later posted a photo of our dinner on Facebook because I wanted to publicly show that a person could be an active Latter-day Saint and have LGBTQ friends.[9]

I anticipated that some would not respond well to my Facebook post and would leave negative comments. That didn't happen; however, what did happen was dramatic and unforeseen. Several cishet YSAs (including some who were not active) reached out to me, concluding that if the bishop could love LGBTQ people, he could also love them. They seemed to feel safe opening up about difficult issues for the first time and trusted that I would talk with them without being harsh or overly judgmental and help them come unto Christ. I've reflected on this experience many times and have concluded that if parents and local leaders want to create a culture where people feel safe confiding in them, publicly saying kind things about and being with individuals or groups of people on the margins goes a long way. This is exactly what Christ did during His ministry (more on this in chapter 2).

I started to share kind things on social media about LGBTQ Latter-day Saints and posted videos and statements from the Church's official LGBTQ website.[10] As I did this, I received hundreds of messages from LGBTQ members and parents with LGBTQ children. Many asked to meet and share their stories with me. I was honored to hear them, and I tried to have an open heart to let their experiences sink in and be part of my new framework. Knowing I was a bishop, several mothers of YSA-aged LGBTQ members asked if their child could be in my ward. I saw their heartfelt desire and prayers for their LGBTQ children to have a safe place. Unfortunately, I was unable to fulfill any of these requests since the individuals did not live in the ward's boundaries. But trying to follow the example of Jesus, who ministered without boundaries, I still met with many of these young people, not as a bishop, but as a trusted adult who would listen and try to point them to Christ.

In June 2016, three months before Sheila and I were released from our YSA calling, I saw an Instagram post from Alyson Paul, the mother of a gay Latter-day Saint teenage son. I had never met Alyson; her husband, George; or their gay teenage son, Stockton. Instagram is usually a happy place where we post our finest moments, but the caption under Alyson's photo of her son read: "I lost my son yesterday to suicide. He is a beautiful young man with so much to give. My son is gay. He was a square peg trying to fit in a round hole and as such suffered immensely. We can do better recognizing differences and loving others unconditionally. My challenge to you all is to choose love."[11]

I was stunned and devastated. Here was a mother posting about the suicide of her child the day after the tragic event.[12] As I read those words and looked into the young man's face in his photo, I received a spiritual impression that there is a gap between our restored Church and its ability to fully meet the needs of its LGBTQ members, including some like Stockton who "suffer immensely." I felt impressed to step into that gap and help minister to our LGBTQ members. This ministry is not, however, to be an activist, not to make suggestions to the general councils of the Church, not to advocate for changes in doctrine, and not to criticize Church leaders, whom I sustain and support. I also do not wish to develop a following or make it about me. I believe that the mission reunion, developing social media skills, and my YSA assignment were divinely guided to create the foundation for this ministry.

I want to help close this gap by fostering more understanding of our LGBTQ members. To do this, I strive to amplify their voices so we can better recognize their contributions, help meet their needs, better understand their difficult road, and offer healing whenever possible. I'm grateful to many others who have gone before me and are also working to help fill the gap. My efforts and this book are dedicated to Stockton and all our LGBTQ members. All proceeds from this book go to the Stockton Powers Memorial Scholarship.[13]

One of the first things I did after receiving this impression from Heavenly Father was to add "LGBTQ Ally'" to my Facebook, Twitter, and Instagram profiles. What is an ally? For me, it is using my privilege—those things I was born with that I didn't earn—to bring voice to our LGBTQ members. Although this book is told from my perspective and is based on my experiences, being an ally is not about me but rather about helping another group to be seen, understood, embraced, and ultimately thrive. The purpose of this book is to foster better understanding about our LGBTQ members, to step out of the way, and to let them shine. I like the visual imagery of the last verse of Simon and Garfunkel's song "Bridge over Troubled Water" to describe my service: "Your time has come to shine," and my role as an ally means that "I'm sailing right behind."

> Your time has come to shine
> All your dreams are on their way
> See how they shine
> Oh, if you need a friend
> I'm sailing right behind
> Like a bridge over troubled water
> I will ease your mind[14]

ENDNOTES

1. While social media was a key component of my ministry, I don't want to suggest it is necessary to be an effective leader. Each leader has his or her own strengths, and building on one's strengths is often the best approach to bless others.
2. Dr. Brené Brown is a research professor at the University of Houston, where she holds the Huffington Foundation—Brené Brown Endowed Chair at the Graduate College of Social Work. Brené is also a visiting professor in management at the University of Texas at Austin McCombs School of Business. She has spent the past two decades studying courage, vulnerability, shame, and empathy and is the author of five number-one *New York Times* best sellers: *The Gifts of Imperfection, Daring Greatly, Rising Strong, Braving the Wilderness*, and her latest book, *Dare to Lead*, which is the culmination of a seven-year study on courage and leadership. uh.edu/socialwork/about/faculty-directory/b-brown/.
3. Brené Brown, *Braving the Wilderness: The Quest for True Belonging and the Courage to Stand Alone* (New York: Random House, 2017), 63.
4. Aaron Shill, "LDS Church reaffirms doctrine of marriage, updates policies on families in same-sex marriage," Deseret News, Nov 5,

2015, deseret.com/2015/11/5/20576115/lds-church-reaffirms-doctrine-ofmarriage-updates-policies-on-families-in-same-sex-marriages

5. She agreed to let me keep her resignation letter in my desk drawer as we continued to meet. We met for several weeks, and she ultimately decided to not resign from the Church.
6. Richard Ostler, "I will be on my knees to better understand the LDS Church's policy statement," Facebook, November 6, 2015, facebook.com/richard.ostler.5/posts/10206998938885074.
7. For further information on ministering to those with questions, please read my brother David's book: David Ostler, *Building Bridges: Ministering to Those Who Question* (Salt Lake City: Greg Kofford Books, 2019).
8. Tad Walch, "Church to allow baptisms for children of LGBT parents, updates handbook regarding 'Apostasy,'" *Deseret News*, April 4, 2019, deseret.com/2019/4/4/20670097/church-to-allow-baptisms-blessings-for-children-of-lgbt-parents-updates-handbook-regarding-apostasy#-file-the-church-office-building-in-salt-lake-city.
9. Richard Ostler, "Wonderful dinner with my friends Doug Balli and Rob Blackhurst," Facebook, November 25, 2015, facebook.com/richard.ostler.5/posts/10207094352990367.
10. churchofjesuschrist.org/topics/gay and churchofjesuschrist.org/topics/transgender, accessed April 2020.
11. Alyson's Instagram post: instagram.com/p/BHNhAekgRgJCrCEV-ofKsRyW5NRnSA-Ag-ZFZ3s0/
12. Stockton's obituary: russonmortuary.com/obituary/Stockton-Powers
13. For more information on this scholarship, see standingforstockton.com/.
14. "Bridge over Troubled Water," track 14 on Simon and Garfunkel, *The Concert in Central Park*, Warner Brothers, 1982, simonandgarfunkel.com/track/bridge-over-troubled-water/.

CHAPTER 2

USING CHRIST'S TEACHINGS TO SUPPORT LGBTQ LATTER-DAY SAINTS

In the summer of 2018, Sheila and I watched several young men carry others across the Sweetwater River to dry ground. We were on our stake-sponsored pioneer trek at Martin's Cove, Wyoming, and the young men were reenacting the moment in 1856 when Latter-day Saints answered Brigham Young's call to rescue the Willie and Martin handcart companies, who were starving and stranded in icy cold weather. I was reminded of those men from the past who honored their baptismal covenants to help those in severe physical distress.[1]

I have often thought that our baptismal covenants have both a vertical and a horizontal aspect. The vertical aspect is our covenant that reaches up to God, in which we strive to obey the commandments, follow our leaders, and maintain a relationship with our Heavenly Parents. The horizontal aspect is the covenant that stretches outward to our families and fellow humans, and it includes bearing their burdens, mourning with them, and comforting them. The Sweetwater rescue represents both aspects—the rescuers followed their leaders (vertical) and saved others (horizontal).

In introducing the two great commandments, Christ teaches both the vertical and horizontal aspects of our covenants: "Thou shalt love the Lord thy God with all thy heart, and with all thy soul, and with all thy mind, and with all thy strength: this is the first commandment. And the second is like, namely this, Thou shalt love thy neighbor as thyself. There is none other commandment greater than these" (Mark 12:30–31).

Upon first reading these verses, it may seem that these two commandments are not coequal. "Love thy neighbor as thyself" is listed as the *second* great commandment and may thus appear to be subordinate to the first commandment. Latter-day Saint scripture, however, seems to place loving our neighbor as an equal and central focus of our covenants. For instance, in Moses 7:33, these two great commandments are listed in the reverse order: "Unto thy brethren have I said, and also given commandment, that they *should love one another*, and that they should choose me, their Father" (emphasis added).

In the Book of Mormon when extending a baptism invitation, Alma begins with the horizontal aspect of our covenants—that is, to bear, mourn, and comfort—in order to join the fold of God: "Behold, here are the waters of Mormon . . . and now, as ye are desirous to come into the fold of God, and to be called his people, and are willing to bear one another's burdens, that they may be light; Yea, and are willing to mourn with those that mourn; yea, and comfort those that stand in need of comfort" (Mosiah 18:8–9).

These scriptures do not suggest that one commandment is more important than the other. They indicate that the vertical and horizontal aspects of our baptismal covenants are actually the same great commandment: to love and serve our fellow human beings *is* to honor and obey God. There is no need to set up a false dichotomy in our minds that to fully love and follow God, we need to stop loving some of His children. After all, the Lord has said, "Inasmuch as ye have done it unto one of the least of these my brethren, ye have done it unto me" (Matthew 25:40).

In my own life, I worry that my focus on these two aspects has been out of balance. At times, I've focused almost exclusively on commandment-keeping and my relationship with God without considering my responsibility to others. When I do this, I falsely think I can make my way to exaltation in isolation, without reaching out and serving others. I now realize that interacting with and lifting the burdens of others are critical parts of my covenants as a committed Latter-day Saint. The road to heaven includes reaching out and bringing others with me. Our doctrine teaches that there is no scarcity of salvation or exaltation. There is room for everyone. I also find that when I'm serving others, it becomes easier to strengthen my relationship with God and keep the commandments. This is consistent with the words of Elder Marvin J. Ashton: "The best and most clear indicator that we are progressing spiritually and coming unto Christ is the way we treat other people."[2]

A quote mentioned earlier from Fiona Givens helps me visualize the horizontal aspect of my baptismal covenants: "Every Latter-day Saint who wishes to help bear another's burden must touch that person's cross to understand the nature and depth of the pain being carried."[3] We must listen, ask questions, show empathy, and validate others' burdens if we want to truly help those who are hurting. We need to resist simple platitudes (like "these trials are all for your good" or "it will work itself out in the next life") that keep us emotionally safe but prevent us from understanding the depth of another's pain, which is one of the first steps to provide healing.

We also should avoid judgment when reaching out to others. Thomas Merton, a Catholic Trappist monk, teaches: "Our job is to love others without stopping to inquire whether or not they are worthy. That is not our business and, in fact, it is nobody's business. What we are asked to do is to love, and this love itself will render both ourselves and our neighbors worthy."[4]

Elder Dieter F. Uchtdorf has also emphasized the importance of the horizontal aspect of our baptismal covenants:

> We could cover the earth with members of the Church, put a meetinghouse on every corner, dot the land with temples, fill the earth with copies of the Book of Mormon, send missionaries to every country, and say millions of prayers. But if we neglect to grasp the core of the gospel message and fail to help those who suffer or turn away those who mourn, and if we do not remember to be charitable, we "are as [waste], which the refiners do cast out" . . .
>
> . . . To put it simply, having charity and caring for one another is not simply a good idea. It is not simply one more item in a seemingly infinite list of things we ought to consider doing. It is at the core of the gospel—an indispensable, essential, foundational element. Without this transformational work of caring for our fellowmen, the Church is but a facade of the organization God intends for His people. Without charity and compassion we are a mere shadow of who we are meant to be—both as individuals and as a Church. Without charity and compassion, we are neglecting our heritage and endangering our promise as children of God. No matter the outward appearance of our righteousness, if we look the other way when others are suffering, we cannot be justified.[5]

One of my institute teachers taught that before the breakup of Christ's original church, faith was expressed in how a person treated others, not in a statement of belief or creed. He suggested that in Christ's day, if you asked someone who had been listening to His sermons and following His example the question "What is it to have faith?," you'd get answers about treating others—especially those marginalized by society or deemed unworthy by those in power—with love and empathy. The way people treated others was a manifestation of their faith.

After Christ's death and the breakup of His church, faith became more of a statement of doctrinal beliefs that differentiated one Christian church from another. Our church's articles of faith follow this pattern, focusing on our beautiful restored doctrine, rather than on actions toward others. Only the thirteenth article of faith, which mentions "doing good to all men," talks about how to treat others. Yet as Christ's church continues to be restored through our modern-day prophets, we can find recurring instances when we have been taught that as followers of Christ, we are obligated to serve and take care of others. Brigham Young's command to rescue the handcart companies and the recent call from our leaders to minister to refugees are just two of many examples.

Behaving kindly toward other people is a consistent value across all world religions. Latter-day Saints refer to this value as charity, the pure love of Christ (see Moroni 7:47). In other religions, it is often referred to as benevolence or compassion. Even outside of religion, people refer to the "golden rule," which is to treat others the way you would like to be treated. I believe that our Heavenly Parents knew most of Their children would spend their entire lives outside our restored Church, and they wanted this value to be a foundational principle across all religions and traditions, regardless of what other doctrines or creeds were taught.

Love and kindness are exemplified in the life and teachings of our Savior. I believe Christ knew that we'd need the foundational and timeless parables contained within the New Testament to navigate complex issues of our day, including ministering to LGBTQ Latter-day Saints, as well as to women, undocumented workers, minority races, and any other group that often faces a hard road. His teachings reinforce that it is important not only to love God and keep His commandments but also to have charity and love our neighbors as ourselves. Latter-day Saint leaders have called us a "peculiar people" because of our ability to stand out. We can continue to be known as a peculiar people because of the Christlike way we treat others.[6]

Following is a review of six stories from Christ's life or teachings that showcase the importance of ministering to the one. These stories provide a doctrinal foundation to better minister to our LGBTQ members. Perhaps we can use these examples from Christ in our family and Church discussions to explore better ways to minister to LGBTQ Latter-day Saints.

I hope when we think about and pray for the gathering of Israel, we will receive promptings on what we can do and say to help our LGBTQ members feel welcome and included, for they too are part of Israel. These six stories help us understand that Christ wants us to gather people. We are called to be gatherers, not sifters. We leave that up to Him.

The Pool of Bethesda

Hanging on a wall in our home is a print of Carl Bloch's painting *Christ Healing the Sick at the Pool of Bethesda.*[7] Based on John 5, the painting depicts a group of individuals, many with visible infirmities, gathered at the edge of a pool. Christ's association with these individuals, who had been ostracized by society, was an act of cultural defiance. But there He was. In the painting, He gently lifts the edge of a makeshift canopy to reveal a man, presumably suffering from a physical infirmity. Christ looks directly at the man and extends His hand toward him. The painting's design encourages our eyes to follow Christ's extended arm, which leads to this man.

As I have looked at the man in the painting, I have wondered who he is and why he's alone. My sense is that he feels shame; perhaps he feels unworthy even among the most marginalized people. I've also wondered how this man felt knowing the Savior saw him. Who do you see when you look at the man beneath the canopy?

When I see this painting, I think of individual LGBTQ Latter-day Saints such as a gay woman or a transgender man. Just as the man beneath the canopy may appear broken on the outside, many of our LGBTQ members feel broken on the inside. It's not a physical brokenness, but the brokenness that comes with feeling shame—because of things they've heard and negative comments they've internalized—about their sexual orientation or gender identity.

In the New Testament, Christ teaches about how those gathered at Bethesda should be treated: "Inasmuch as ye have done it unto one of the least of these my brethren, ye have done it unto me" (Matthew 25:40) and "The last shall be first, and the first last" (Matthew 20:16). Do we view people who are LGBTQ as being on the margins of our families and Church community? Are they, in other words, "the last"? If so, these teachings from Christ indicate just how important and special these individuals are. If we want to serve God, we should serve our LGBTQ brothers and sisters.

I pray we can look at Christ's example at Bethesda and strive to follow His admonition to "follow me, and do the things which ye have seen me do" (2 Nephi 31:12).

The Good Samaritan

Most of us are familiar with the story Jesus Christ told of the good Samaritan. A Jewish man is robbed, beaten, and left bleeding on the street. Nobody stops to help him, but then a Samaritan comes along. The Samaritan cleans the man's wounds and carries him to an inn. This act of kindness is even more remarkable because at the time Christ told this story, the Jews had "no dealings with the Samaritans" (John 4:9). As the Samaritan is leaving the inn, he pays the innkeeper to watch over the man until he recovers. As a modern audience, we look upon the Samaritan as a hero and a true disciple of Christ. But this story would have been shocking in Christ's day since this was a story about showing kindness to someone perceived as an adversary or outsider to the Jews.

The person delivering aid was not a priest, a temple worker, or one of the beaten man's own countrymen—he was an individual who Christ's listeners would have considered unclean and unworthy. Christ tells this parable to answer the question, "Who is my neighbor?" (Luke 10:29). The answer? Everyone—even those, and especially those, who we, with our limited view, consider unworthy.

How do we look at LGBTQ Latter-day Saints? Some of the LGBTQ Latter-day Saints I know, like the Samaritan, exhibit superior moral behavior even when despised by some around them. When I first stepped into this space to minister to LGBTQ Latter-day Saints, I thought my job was to help save them. But in reality they are saving me by helping me be a better disciple of Christ as they teach me about compassion, charity, service, and kindness. I'm grateful for this parable that teaches me that my LGBTQ friends are my "neighbors" and worthy of my aid, friendship, support, and understanding.

The Canaanite Woman

Sometimes we get caught up in the false notion that salvation or exaltation is scarce—that there's only space for a select few at the Savior's table. If we believe that exaltation is limited, we may be tempted to look around to figure out who is and who is not on the covenant path, concluding that some are unworthy of exaltation. However, our doctrine teaches us to leave judgment to our Savior and His perfect understanding; we should instead turn our focus to our own worthiness and recognize that there is room for everyone in God's kingdom. This beautiful concept is one of the reasons I like the account of the Canaanite woman in Matthew 15.

The Canaanite woman comes to the Savior to beg Him to take mercy on her daughter, who is "grievously vexed with a devil" (Matthew 15:22). At first, Christ doesn't seem to respond to her. His disciples tell Him to send her away, concluding, I imagine, that because she is a Gentile, she is not worthy of the Savior's time or His miracles. Instead of sending her away, however, Christ engages her in conversation. The woman worships Him and continues to ask for His help. In spite of all the times this woman has been told no, in spite of the judgment from Christ's disciples that she is not worthy, the Savior makes the Canaanite woman's daughter whole that same hour because of the woman's "great faith" (Matthew 15:28).

Everything about this woman represents someone on the margins of society during Christ's time. She is a woman, a Canaanite, and a Gentile. Yet Christ heals her daughter. When I read this account, I like to place myself in the shoes of the disciples. These individuals, like most of us, were followers of Christ, but they still erred in their judgment. If those who daily walked with the Savior could make such a mistake, couldn't I as well? I ask myself, "Who is the Canaanite woman in my life? Who have I incorrectly concluded—consciously or subconsciously—would be sent away by Jesus?"

When I think of these questions, I re-evaluate my responsibility to LGBTQ Latter-day Saints. Christ didn't define His ministry by "who's in" and "who's out," even when the people surrounding Him encouraged that He make that distinction. Christ was frequently criticized for making room at His table: "The Pharisees and scribes murmured, saying, 'This man receiveth sinners and eateth with them'" (Luke 15:2). But He did it anyway. We can follow Christ's example and make room at our table by helping those on the margins—those who have been made to feel insignificant—feel welcome in our congregations, families, schools, and workplaces. Like Christ, we can talk to these individuals to better understand them, even if there are others around us who suggest we do otherwise.

The story of the Canaanite woman teaches us that there is no scarcity of salvation in Christ's gospel. Perhaps one of the reasons this account exists for our day is to teach us to open our hearts to LGBTQ individuals—and others on the margins—and follow the Savior's example of not judging but extending a welcoming hand of friendship, love, and support. In doing this, we can help heal and give hope to our LGBTQ members, which is exactly what Christ did for the Canaanite woman.

The Roman Tax Collector

The fact that Christ made room for those who were often rejected—sometimes literally putting Himself in the same room as them—is evident in his treatment of Zacchaeus, the chief publican (or tax collector). Publicans were reviled by the Jews. They were considered greedy, and many of the Jews resented them for their relationship with the Romans. When Christ sees Zacchaeus watching Him from the treetops, He does not point at him and cry, "Sinner!" as some did. Instead, Jesus invites Himself over to Zacchaeus's home.

After Christ announces that He will visit Zacchaeus, the Jews murmur that "he was gone to be guest with a man that is a sinner" (Luke 19:7). But let's look at how Zacchaeus responds to Christ and what Christ's invitation means to him. Zacchaeus receives Christ "joyfully" and tells Him, "Behold, Lord, the half of my goods I give to the poor; and if I have taken any thing from any man by false accusation, I restore him fourfold" (Luke 19:6, 8). After Zacchaeus feels seen and welcomed by Christ, he offers to make amends to anyone he has deceived. After he feels seen and welcomed, we see the goodness of his heart.

Some have referred to Christ's interaction with Zacchaeus as "table fellowshipping," the act of helping others feel a sense of belonging and worth by breaking bread and spending time with them. It's a practice we can adopt in our treatment of others whom the world—and often our own communities—have left little room for. What would happen if we literally opened our front doors and made more space at our kitchen tables for our LGBTQ neighbors? What if we, like Christ, sought them out as friends? How might our relationships with our LGBTQ brothers and sisters change if we behaved less like the judging crowd and received them joyfully? To do so would honor the part of our covenants that asks us to be *with* others in times of both sorrow and joy. To do so would extend the pure love of Christ.

The Lost Sheep

In discussing this parable, I don't want to imply that LGBTQ people as a group represent the lost sheep. Rather, this parable is about individual people who stray and, more important, Christ's role as the shepherd and how we can follow His example.

In the story, the shepherd cares for a flock of one hundred sheep. One sheep, however, goes missing. The shepherd knows his sheep well enough to know why the one left and where to find it. He physically leaves all ninety-nine of the others to find the lost one. The shepherd "goeth into the mountains" to seek the sheep that is lost (Matthew 18:12). The word *mountains* is interesting here. I believe it illustrates the work that is required on our part to go to the rescue of others. As the shepherd, Christ didn't stand at the edge of the flock and call out to the one. He left and actively sought the missing sheep. He didn't ask the ninety-nine why the one left. He knew the one well enough to know why it left and where to find it.

An elders quorum president once told me of an experience he had visiting a member of his ward who didn't attend Church meetings. After building a genuine friendship of trust with this good man, the president asked him why he didn't attend. This man told him, with tears in his eyes, "I've lived in this ward for over twenty years, and no one has ever asked me this question." This man was touched by one Church member's desire to understand him, and a genuine friendship was established. How can we minister to the "lost sheep" if we don't know why they left? Christ is able to minister to lost sheep because He truly knows them. He understands their needs. How can we minister to our LGBTQ members who have left if we don't have some understanding of what brought them to where they are?

I wish I had understood this principle earlier in my life. I was once a home teacher for a member of our ward who was not active. During our visits, we would have a nice conversation and end with a prayer. Both of us seemed to be going through the motions, and neither of us brought up the elephant in the room: why he didn't attend church anymore. If I could go back in time and redo this visit, I'd try to first develop a genuine friendship with this man in order to earn his trust. Then I could ask about his feelings toward the Church, and he could feel safe responding to the question. If I had known the reasons he didn't attend church, perhaps I would have had better insights into how to more effectively minister to him.

Since that time, I've sat with hundreds of our LGBTQ members who have left the Church, and it's been eye-opening to hear their stories. Many of them still have strong testimonies of the restored gospel, but our LG members describe living with a double bind: they feel as if they must choose between full fellowship in the Church and their desire for a life partner.

I first met with an LGBTQ person who had resigned from the Church while I was serving as a YSA bishop. In our meeting, I didn't sense rebellion, an evil spirit, or a desire to turn away from God. Yes, I was concerned that this person was not following Church teachings, and I asked if he would consider returning to the Church. Even though my invitation to return was declined, I asked if he would like a blessing, which is what I usually did when concluding a visit with ward members. I was surprised when, with tears in his eyes, he said yes. As I gave that blessing, I felt the depth of Heavenly Father's love for him and His desire for this young person to stay close to Him. Afterward I reflected on how well Heavenly Father knows all His sheep, how aware He is of the difficult road they walk, and His love for them as they move forward.

Mary and Martha

One of the simplest but most profound of Christ's teachings comes by way of His example. Having traveled for several days, Christ receives word from Bethany that His friend Lazarus is sick. Upon turning back and arriving in Bethany, He learns from Lazarus's sisters, Mary and Martha, that Lazarus has just passed away. Most of the town has gathered to comfort the sisters.

Martha rushes to the Savior when He arrives and tells Him, "Lord, if thou hadst been here, my brother had not died. But I know that even now, whatsoever thing thou wilt ask of God, God will give it thee" (John 11:21–22). Although grieving, she has faith that things will be okay, and Christ speaks to that faith. He sits with her and discusses the Resurrection with her, comforting her about life after death. He asks if she believes Him. Martha responds with a powerful affirmation of her faith: "Yea, Lord: I believe that thou art the Christ" (John 11:27).

At the end of their conversation, Martha goes to find Mary and bring her to the Savior. Mary is at home being comforted by her neighbors. When Martha tells Mary that Christ would like to see her, she leaves, with all of her neighbors following her.

When she sees Christ, Mary falls at His feet. She doesn't tell Christ she has faith that things will work out; she doesn't ask Christ about the Resurrection. She simply weeps for her brother, and those who are with her weep also. Seeing Mary's pain and the pain of her friends, Christ "groan[s] in the spirit" and is troubled (John 11:33). He asks to see where they've laid Lazarus, and then He weeps. The Savior has full knowledge that Lazarus will live again—His role in the plan secures that—but He still weeps with Mary and her friends. He's there to mourn with and comfort Mary and Martha. He puts everything else on hold to be with them in their time of grief.

Many of our LGBTQ members are carrying heavy burdens that cause them to cry out and weep. They are in pain, they feel alone, and they don't have answers. Are we reaching out to them in their times of need, or are we ignoring them? Are we addressing their pain with platitudes about the next life when "everything will work out," or are we holding and validating their current pain? Are we, like the Savior, ministering to them according to what they most need to heal?

Christ knew when the individuals He ministered to, like Mary, needed someone to cry with and when they, like Martha, needed someone to teach them. He fed them when they needed food, and He spent time with them when they needed time. He was the perfect example of bearing, mourning, and comforting because He centered His life around serving others. We speak of Christ's life and ministry, but really His whole life was ministering.

By studying the ways Christ engaged with individuals, including those who were ostracized by others, and by studying His teachings, we can learn the best ways to minister to LGBTQ individuals. We can begin to see them the way our Heavenly Parents see them. We can meet the horizontal aspect of our covenants and become a little more like Christ. Most importantly, we can share His love for them.

Peter Taking the Gospel to the Gentiles

We can learn an important lesson about how to treat LGBTQ people from Peter's interaction with Cornelius in Acts 10. Before Jesus ascended to heaven, His final instruction to His disciples was to teach the gospel to and baptize all nations (see Matthew 28:19, Mark 16:15). Despite this commandment, the Apostles did not extend those teachings to the Gentiles. The Jews, including the disciples of Jesus at that time, believed the Gentiles (non-Jewish peoples such as Romans, Greeks, and so on) were unclean, and they refused to associate with them. To change this attitude, the Lord gave specific visions to both Cornelius, a Gentile, and Peter, the church leader.

An angel appeared to Cornelius and told him his prayers and offerings were accepted by God and that he should find Peter and bring him back to his house to further instruct him. From this vision, Cornelius—a Roman centurion and Gentile, not of the Lord's covenant people—knew by revelation that God heard and accepted his prayers and offerings, even though the church members did not believe the Lord would respond to him.

In Peter's vision, he saw the heavens open and a vessel filled with all kinds of animals, birds, and other creatures that the law of Moses forbade him to eat. A voice commanded him to kill them and eat. This rattled Peter and he declined; he had never eaten anything impure or unclean. The voice said, "What God hath cleansed, that call not thou common" (Acts 10:15). Peter had this vision three times but he still didn't understand what it meant.

While Peter was still pondering this vision, Cornelius's servants arrived asking for him. The Spirit told Peter to meet the men and go with them. When they arrived at Cornelius's house, Peter had the temerity to remind poor Cornelius that it was against his religion to associate with or visit a Gentile. But Peter finally seemed to be gaining a comprehension of the vision, as he also told Cornelius that God told him he should not call anyone impure or unclean.

Interestingly, it wasn't until Peter had spent two nights and two days traveling with Cornelius's most trusted servants (imagine the conversations they must have had), and then spent time face to face with Cornelius and his family in their home, hearing their story and experience, that Peter understood the full meaning of the vision that had previously been an enigma to him: that God loves and accepts all His children, even Gentiles. "God is no respecter of persons" (Acts 10:34). He doesn't show favoritism to any particular group of people. As Peter taught them the gospel of Christ, the Holy Ghost fell on everyone there. Peter's companions were actually "astonished" that Gentiles such as Cornelius and his family could receive the Holy Ghost.

I, too, was once astonished to see the Spirit of Christ and the Holy Ghost in the countenances of my LGBTQ brothers and sisters. Like Peter with the Gentiles, I once believed my LGBTQ brothers and sisters were unworthy or outside the reach of God's influence. Like Peter, it wasn't until I actually spent time with them face to face, listening to their stories and learning what they have experienced that I could actually love them, see what rich spiritual gifts they have been blessed with, and recognize how much they can offer if we only welcome them in. Let us not treat them as the ancient church once treated Gentiles.

Let us not be afraid to associate with them and enter their homes. Let us instead travel with them, listen to them, learn from them, and love them as God loves them.

ENDNOTES

1. "Remembering the Rescue," *Ensign*, August 1997, churchofjesuschrist.org/study/ensign/1997/08/remembering-the-rescue.
2. Marvin J. Ashton, "The Tongue Can Be a Sharp Sword," April 1992 general conference address, churchofjesuschrist.org/study/general-conference/1992/04/the-tongue-can-be-a-sharp-sword.
3. Tad Walch, "God Loves Every Single Person, Speakers Tell LGBT Mormons at Affirmation Conference," *Deseret News*, September 20, 2015, deseret.com/2015/9/20/20572717/god-loves-every-single-person-speakers-tell-lgbt-mormons-at-affirmation-conference#members-of-affirmations-2014-leadership-team-attend-the-this-is-the-place-international-conference-at-the-university-of-utah.
4. Thomas Merton to Dorothy Day, quoted in Stephen Hand, Catholic Voices in a *World on Fire* (n.p.: Lulu.com, 2005), 180, as cited in "Thomas Merton," Wikiquote, accessed February 4, 2020, en.wikiquote.org/wiki/Thomas_Merton.
5. "Transcript: President Uchtdorf Address to the Salt Lake City Inner City Mission," *Newsroom*, The Church of Jesus Christ of Latter-day Saints, December 4, 2015, newsroom.churchofjesuschrist.org/article/president-uchtdorf-transcript-salt-lake-inner-city-mission.
6. John A. Widtsoe, "Why Are the Latter-day Saints a Peculiar People," *Improvement Era*, September 1942; reprinted in *Ensign*, April 1988, churchofjesuschrist.org/study/ensign/1988/04/i-have-a-question/why-are-the-latter-day-saints-a-peculiar-people.
7. Carl Bloch, *Christ Healing the Sick at the Pool of Bethesda*, 1883. Brigham Young University Museum of Art, image available at Gospel Media, The Church of Jesus Christ of Latter-day Saints, accessed February 6, 2020, churchofjesuschrist.org/media-library/images/pool-of-bethesda-carl-bloch-83121.

INTRODUCTION FOR CHAPTERS 3, 4, AND 5

One day during my study of the Book of Mormon, I read, "For he that *diligently seeketh* shall find; and the *mysteries of God shall be unfolded unto them*, by the power of the Holy Ghost" (1 Nephi 10:19, emphasis added). I've read this scripture many times, but this time I pondered about our LGBTQ Latter-day Saints. I thought, "God's LGBTQ children are a mystery to me." I wondered how they fit into the plan of happiness and why Heavenly Father would create some of His children to be LGBTQ. This scripture reminded me that if I "diligently seeketh" for an answer, by the "power of the Holy Ghost" I could perhaps find some answers for this particular "mystery."

This scripture also encourages us to be humble and teachable—more open to learning what God knows and wants us to understand. This principle is consistent with what Elder Uchtdorf taught in a 2012 worldwide leadership training:

> Brothers and sisters, as good as our previous experience may be, if we stop asking questions, stop thinking, stop pondering, we can thwart the revelations of the Spirit. Remember, it was the questions young Joseph asked that opened the door for the restoration of all things. We can block the growth and knowledge our Heavenly Father intends for us. How often has the Holy Spirit tried to tell us something we needed to know but couldn't get past the massive iron gate of what we thought we already knew?[1]

One of my favorite institute teachers, S. Michael Wilcox, has shared a similar perspective: "In some matters, it is better to be intellectually uncertain rather than superficially sure. This will still leave us with a great deal to be certain about, while maintaining a humility to learn."[2]

President Hugh B. Brown taught the same concept at a BYU commencement address: "We have been blessed with much knowledge by revelation from God which, in some part, the world lacks. But there is an incomprehensibly greater part of truth which we must yet discover. Our revealed truth should leave us stricken with the knowledge of how little we really know. It should never lead to an emotional arrogance based upon a false assumption that we somehow have all the answers—that we in fact have a corner on truth, for we do not."[3]

Part of diligently seeking is learning the latest the Church is teaching about our LGBTQ members and listening to them and their families. In both religious and secular circles, LGBTQ individuals have often been unaccepted and persecuted. As a result, their voices and insights have been stifled in past eras. Thus we may hold several assumptions that were once widely shared but have been challenged and rejected only in recent years. Both society and our church are consistently receiving new light and understanding on LGBTQ issues, so if we want to better understand and minister to others, it is important that we pay attention and be willing to question and, when necessary, put aside old, incorrect conclusions or false statements.

Perhaps some of us have held onto certain conclusions because of a desire to keep everything in a nice, tidy box. If we can explain why people are LGBTQ with a simple answer, we are kept emotionally safe. Such conclusions may even feel right because they are in harmony with what we already believe about life and the gospel. This line of thinking, however, may make us complacent, preventing us from feeling a responsibility to learn more and help meet the needs of our LGBTQ members.

Chapters 3–5 discuss false statements and conclusions that many LGBTQ Latter-day Saints and their parents would like us to reconsider:

Chapter 3: False Statements on Why People are LGBTQ
Chapter 4: False Statements About LGBTQ People
Chapter 5: False Statements on What LGBTQ People Should Do

Most of the statements are discussed in the context of personal stories. Many of the stories and information found herein were gathered through two private Facebook groups that I created in 2019, each with more than one hundred members. One group includes Latter-day Saint parents of LGBTQ children, and the other group consists of LGBTQ Latter-day Saints. As I planned and drafted this book, I posed questions to each group, wanting to bring in their voices as much as possible. You will find their responses throughout these and other chapters. Some participants' names have been changed so they would feel more comfortable being honest and telling their full story.

Given the qualitative nature of this project, the individual responses found here are not meant to reflect the entire LGBTQ experience. Due to the makeup of the Facebook groups and because all responses were voluntary, I received more responses from some groups than others. For instance, from parents with LGBTQ children, I received more responses from mothers than fathers. And among LGBTQ members, I received more responses from gay men. I'm sensitive that lesbian, transgender, nonbinary, pansexual, bisexual, intersex, asexual, and other experiences are often overlooked. Already members of a marginalized group, they may feel further marginalized by this underrepresentation. All LGBTQ stories are equally valid, and I've tried to bring in as many stories as possible. Even if a response is from one LGBTQ perspective, I hope the insights shared will give us ideas to better meet the needs of *all* LGBTQ individuals. I pray we may all learn from reading each response. For each LGBTQ respondent, I've added their preferred label in the LGBTQ+ spectrum.

In some discussions, instead of featuring responses from individuals in these Facebook groups, I quote from other sources that highlight LGBTQ experiences, including interviews that aired on the podcast I host, *Listen, Learn & Love*. These participants' names have not been changed since the podcasts are public. I have also used other resources such as Church statements, personal observations, public blogs, Facebook posts, and outside studies to address these myths. Because of differences in the amount of available material, the discussions for some issues are longer than for others; readers should not infer, based on the length of the discussions, that some false statements are more important than others.

I'm glad you will be reading the stories of LGBTQ Latter-day Saints. These stories have changed my heart. I am indebted to all who participated in these two groups and who have been on the podcast. They are strong and courageous. I wish every Latter-day Saint could read every answer within the Facebook groups. I've prayed and fasted to know which responses to include in this book to best help Latter-day Saints better minister to our LGBTQ members.

Some of the stories may stretch us and encourage us to set aside past assumptions. One reader may find a few of these points challenging while another does not. A reader may readily accept some conclusions but wonder about others. For me, growth comes from being a little uncomfortable. If anything feels uncomfortable, I encourage readers to lean into that feeling, don't dismiss it, ask more questions, and continue to "diligently seek."

While I believe that rejecting these statements does not compromise any Church doctrine, I recognize that what I am calling a "false statement" may be something that some readers and LGBTQ Latter-day Saints believe and do not feel a need to set aside. That is okay. If we disagree on specifics, that's also okay. The goal of this book is not to come to uniform conclusions, but rather to have a faithful conversation about this sensitive topic as we all try to better meet President Ballard's challenge "to listen and understand what our LGBTQ brothers and sisters are feeling and experiencing."

I'm sure there are other false statements that I have not listed here, but I hope these chapters give us tools to better come together as families, friends, and congregations. I believe that by dispelling false ideas, we will come closer to enacting God's doctrine to love one another, which helps us better meet the needs of LGBTQ Latter-day Saints.

ENDNOTES

1. Dieter F. Uchtdorf, "Acting on the Truths of the Gospel of Jesus Christ," Broadcasts, The Church of Jesus Christ of Latter-day Saints, accessed February 11, 2020, churchofjesuschrist.org/broadcasts/article/worldwide-leadership-training/2012/01/acting-on-the-truths-of-the-gospel-of-jesus-christ.
2. S. Michael Wilcox, *Who Shall Be Able to Stand? Finding Personal Meaning in the Book of Revelation* (Salt Lake City: Deseret Book, 2003), ix.
3. Hugh B. Brown, "An Eternal Quest—Freedom of the Mind" (devotional address, Brigham Young University, Provo, Utah, May 13, 1969), brightspotcdn.byu.edu/33/b4/85f307924e4ca01512072c8c8ba5/an-eternal-quest-freedom-of-the-mind-hugh-b-brown.pdf.

CHAPTER 3

FALSE STATEMENTS ON WHY PEOPLE ARE LGBTQ

False Statement 1:
They choose to be LGBTQ.

This is the idea that someone chooses their sexual orientation or gender identity. In meeting with hundreds of LGBTQ individuals, I have not found a single person who told me that they chose to be LGBTQ. Further, it is almost incomprehensible that anyone would choose to have a sexual orientation or a gender identity outside of societal norms. It's a brutal road.

I like the Mackintosh family story, featured on the Church's official website with this exchange between Scott, an active Latter-day Saint father, and his gay son, Xian:

> **Scott:** So I started letting him have all the ammunition that I'd saved up. I just blurted out with, "Xian, why would you choose this? Why?" And he just looked at me, and he just chuckled. Not a laugh like in-your-face but just a chuckle. It caught him so funny, and he said, "Dad, I didn't choose this."
>
> **Xian:** "Why would anyone choose this?" And I think that's when he [Scott] kind of started to understand.
>
> **Scott:** Once that hit me, the pain, the suffering, all the jokes that I'd told him, all the mean comments, all the times that I said something snide about somebody else to the whole family, and him sitting in the backseat, sitting there thinking, "My dad has no idea that he's talking about me." All those times just came flooding back

> to me. The pain my son had gone through. From that time on, it's been an about-face. It's been a change. I just put my arms around my son and loved him.[1]

Scott's "light bulb" experience led to this interaction, a parenting home run. Despite inadvertently causing past hurt, Scott listened to his son and accepted a new framework—one that allowed Xian to feel the love and support from his family.

A few years ago, when discussing this topic with a YSA stake president, he told me of a high councilor who stated that homosexual people choose to be gay. This wise stake president wanted the high councilor to reconsider his opinion and asked, "When did you choose to be straight?"

In the past, some Church leaders made statements about this being a choice. The Church no longer teaches that anyone, LGBTQ or straight, chooses their sexual orientation. Avoiding speculation that being lesbian or gay is a choice, President Oaks presented the Church's current view on why some people are LGBTQ: "The Church does not have a position on the causes of any of these susceptibilities or inclinations, including those related to same-gender attraction. Those are scientific questions—whether nature or nurture—those are things the Church doesn't have a position on."[2]

President Ballard also teaches that individuals do not choose to have same-sex attraction: "Let us be clear: The Church of Jesus Christ of Latter-day Saints believes that the experience of same-sex attraction is a complex reality for many people. The attraction itself is not a sin but acting on it is. Even though individuals do *not choose to have such attractions*, they do choose how to respond to them. With love and understanding, the Church reaches out to all God's children, including [those with same-sex attraction]."[3]

As I've visited with LGBTQ Latter-day Saints, they have reported how painful it is to hear, especially from someone in authority such as a parent or leader, that being gay is a choice. Armed with these Church statements, we should no longer add to the burdens of LGBTQ Latter-day Saints by saying sexual orientation is a choice.

Recent scientific research also indicates that sexual orientation is not a choice. However, the central aim of this book is to present the voices of LGBTQ individuals so that we as readers can learn to listen and love better. Extensively discussing scientific findings is therefore beyond the scope of this book, and I also recognize that scientific findings do not always come to the same conclusion. If you'd like to learn more about the science, you might start with an article at listenlearnandlove.org/articles called "Sexual Orientation Is Not a Choice,"[4] which is a summary of the latest science studies concluding sexual orientation is not a choice.

As mentioned, this book has responses from LGBTQ Latter-day Saints and their parents to address many of the topics included. Below is the first of those responses.

VANCE BRYCE (GAY MAN)

No. No, I did not [choose to be gay]. I live in a small town (USA), where the worst thing you can be is gay. Why would I choose to be the worst thing in my community? I love the scriptures, the temple, my family, and my Heavenly Parents. Why would I choose what seems contrary to what I love?

I prayed with real intent to be straight every day and night for over a decade which turned out to be impossible. I *didn't* choose to be gay. I fasted, then starved myself to try to be straight. Would I have gone without food for seventy-two hours at a time if I secretly wanted to be gay?

I went to therapy to learn "coping skills" like how to change my body language to be more manly, learning to love watching football (which did work by the way), bonding with my male friends, and trying to come up with reasons why it was my mom and dad's fault that I was gay. This therapy was awful, and it drove a wedge between me and my entire family. We believed I could be sealed to them forever if I could find a way to be straight. It looked like I was failing. I wasn't trying hard enough. I didn't love them enough to change and live with them forever. It was the most frustrating time of my life. Would I have chosen to be gay and separate myself from my family, whom I love more than anything?

When I was twenty-two, I was offered a [five-figure] treatment plan to make me straight. That guy was sure slick. My dad said it was worth the money. I was done. I knew that [five figures] wouldn't do anything. I had tried too many things that should have worked. The "doctor/salesman" said, "I can't cure you if you don't want to change. It sounds like you don't. You secretly like being gay." I'd never been angrier in my whole life. This kook was going to tell me who I was? No way. (He created his "treatment" to cure his son, and they are estranged, by the way).

I prayed about how to tell my dad that I refused to go. I knew what it would look like: I had given up. I liked being gay. I had wasted everyone's time. I had failed.

The website mormonsandgays.org [now churchofjesuschrist.org/topics/gay] came out that month. Finally. Finally. Finally. My Prophet allowed a website to say that some of us are born gay. And it was a good thing, too. It was my "ram in the thicket." I had tried everything, except giving my life. I was prepared to make myself straight by killing myself before my parents spent that [five figures]. I was ready to give my life. So many of us have. So many have killed themselves to be like you. So many have squashed down who they are to be like you. We weren't meant to be like you—we were meant to be like God.

The release of that website saved my life. Don't let anyone tell you that people don't make life and death decisions based on Church policy, because we do. I did. The release of that website was a huge relief for my dad and me. It healed our relationship. After I told him that he needed to go to the website, he grumbled a little. A few days later he woke up wide awake at 4:00 a.m. with an intense impression that he needed to go to the website. He did. He watched every video and read every word. He called me and told me that we had been wrong, that he had been wrong. I was no longer the rebellious son who chose to separate myself from our family because of lust. I was his loving son, God's son, trying to do the best I could in an impossible situation.

If you think people choose their sexuality, you are wrong. Pray about it. Ask Heavenly Father if homosexual people choose to be gay. Ask Heavenly Father if gay people are evil. Ask to see me as God sees me, and not as man sees me. Ask if we are good. Ask if we are Their [Heavenly Parents'] children, too. Ask if They love us just like They love you. If you ask with real intent, you will know that we are children of God, embodying God's exquisite beauty, strength, and insight. We are eternal beings of light, truth, and reason. Stop making us in your own image. Humble yourself, be curious, be open to learning how God would have you minister to and accept ministering from us. Did I choose to be gay? No. God did. Man made me out to be some ugly, evil, disfigured thing. Heavenly Father revealed to me that I am his eternal, worthy, complete son.

JERRY CHONG (GAY MAN)

When asked to describe myself, I let people know that I have known from the age of six that I was different, that there were no environmental influences that made me gay but that I was born gay. I let them know it's taken time to accept and understand this part of me. I tell them I do not need to change in order to be happy. I tell them I have found peace knowing that Heavenly Father has a purpose for me and that the Savior loves me.

JOHN GUSTAV-WRATHALL (GAY MAN)

I "chose" heterosexuality for about fourteen years (how long it took from the time I was first aware of same-sex attraction until I finally came out as gay). If our sexuality was something we could choose, homosexuality would be virtually nonexistent. Most of us, especially if we grew up in conservative religious settings (Latter-day Saint, Catholic, Evangelical, Pentecostal, Jehovah's Witness, Muslim, Orthodox Jew) fought [same-sex attraction] with everything we had. I'd actually love to see some of my heterosexual brothers or sisters engage in the same exercise. . . . Try "choosing" homosexuality and see how well it works for you.

False Statement 2:

They are LGBTQ because they use pornography. Being LGBTQ is an addiction, like pornography, alcohol, or illegal drugs.

Sexual orientation or gender identity should not be compared to drugs, alcohol, or pornography. Those are temptations of the world that need to be overcome by all people, regardless of their orientation; addictions to them are a result of choices. Sexual orientation or gender identity, on the other hand, are inherent traits. Being LGBTQ does not need to be "overcome," just like being left-handed, having green eyes, or having red hair do not need to be overcome.

Many people have talked about being LGBTQ as if it were an addiction to drugs or alcohol, but the most persistent comparison is to pornography. Ben Schilaty shares in his blog: "I wish more Latter-day Saints could see the hearts of their LGBT brothers and sisters instead of condemning them. My experiences with being open about my sexuality have been overwhelmingly positive. However, there was that active woman who emphatically accused me of being addicted to pornography because that was the only way someone would develop such deviant thoughts as same-sex attractions."[5]

This woman's statement made Ben feel unwelcome and misunderstood. We shouldn't try to manufacture a back-story so we can blame someone for being LGBTQ. It is an example of why, according to President Ballard, "we must do better than we have done in the past so that all members feel they have a spiritual home where their brothers and sisters love them and where they have a place to worship and serve the Lord."[6]

During my time as a YSA bishop, I had hundreds of interviews with men and women working to distance themselves from pornography. They are some of the strongest people I know, and helping them to overcome their problems was one of the most sacred parts of my service.[7] Pornography has the potential to destroy marriages. It needs to be solved. It's been my experience, however, that pornography is a window into someone's sexual orientation, but it's not something that changes sexual orientation.

It is time to stop linking pornography to sexual orientation or gender identity. We may have previously thought that pornography was the reason people became LGBTQ because it helped us find a way to explain why someone isn't cishet. But that belief is incorrect and adds to the burdens of our LGBTQ Latter-day Saints, preventing us from effectively ministering to them.

On my podcast, I interviewed Mikel Eldredge, a Latter-day Saint father in Houston, Texas, and his son Joe. Mikel shared that one night in April 2014, he woke up, sensing a possible intruder.

> It was a very memorable night. I was lying in bed. It was late, and I felt a complete and total feeling come over me that something wasn't right, like the door was unlocked or I had an intruder in my home. And I recognized that as a possible threat to my family. I then turned over to my wife [and] told her I was going to go do a sweep of the house. I went to . . . my side table and grabbed my nine-millimeter. I realized it's one of my kids out of bed, and it was Joe because Joe had given up his bed that night to my mom. And once I realized it was my child, I put the safety back on.
>
> Joe was sixteen, and I saw that he was watching male pornography, and quickly he turned the phone over. We had a conversation. The conversation kind of went like this: "Whatcha doing?" "Nothing." "Can I see your phone?" "Sure." Joe's face went into the pillow. I found out what was on the phone. I handed the phone back to him. I didn't delete [anything]. . . . I just turned to him, and I said, "When you're done, come up and talk to me and Mom." And I turned around, and I walked back upstairs and put away the gun [and] climbed back in bed with my wife. [I] let her know that Joe was coming up to talk to us and that I had just found him viewing pornography, and [after] what seemed like forever, Joe came up and sat on the end of the bed, which

was not the place where I wanted him. He broke down crying. I didn't want him there as he started crying, so I pulled him into the bed in between me and Wendy and got him under the covers, and we just held him for hours, for hours. And at that point he came out to us that he is gay. I didn't know what to do at that point other than just hold him and love him.

Joe then described his point of view:

> Up to this point, I had kind of realized that I was gay when I was probably eleven or twelve and got into pornography. But [I] didn't ever have the courage to tell Mom and Dad because, you know, every Sunday School teacher would come up to Mom and Dad [saying,] "Oh, my goodness, your children are just perfect. They know all the answers, and they're just so reverent." And I had this expectation that I'm just the good Latter-day Saint kid, and I didn't want to ruin that. I didn't want to ruin that perspective that my family had of me, and so when Dad discovered me viewing the gay pornography, I was absolutely terrified but at the same time entirely relieved because finally I could talk about [it]. I could get the courage to talk about it because otherwise I don't know when I would have come out to them. Probably would have been right before I went on my mission, out of desperation—I'm not sure.
>
> So there was a good amount of time after Dad went up before I followed him up, and I don't exactly remember what happened there. It was just a rush of emotions of relief and terror. . . . Walking up those stairs was surreal, which is why that whole night feels like a dream. Because finally my life was heading towards repentance and improvement and coming more unto my Savior. . . . Then sitting at the edge of their bed, feeling that separation, which is I am sure why the Spirit told my dad . . . to bring me in and to hold me. [It] was exactly what I needed—to feel that my parents loved me . . . no matter [what]. And that's been a mantra from them that they have always told me—no matter what happens, . . . they're there for me.[8]

Yes, this is a story about pornography, which is a serious problem that needs to be addressed. I respect Mikel, Wendy, and Joe for their courage to share their story—it is one of the finest parenting stories I've ever heard. Credit goes to Mikel for following a spiritual prompting that led to the chance for Joe to come out as gay and for this family to come together in love and support. Joe later served a successful mission in New Zealand. No one feels Joe "became" gay because of pornography, just like no one would feel their sixteen-year-old-son "became" straight because he viewed heterosexual pornography.

MARION McCLELLAN (MOTHER OF GAY SON)

Addiction and being LGBTQ are not the same and should never be compared or brought up in the same lesson or conversation. Being gay is not a choice, as taught at churchofjesuschrist.org/topics/gay/. Addictions all begin with a choice, usually several. Addictions can be recovered from. Being LGBTQ does not go away, as it is an innate part of a person's nature. Addictions are something extremely damaging and undesirable; being gay is not.

CALEB JONES (FATHER OF GAY SON)

Pornography, drugs, and alcohol can lead to disconnection from self and others; LGBTQ identities are about seeking connection with self and others. The comparison comes from past pathologizing of LGBTQ people.

CAROL M. COLVIN (MOTHER OF GAY SON AND BISEXUAL DAUGHTER)

Being LGBTQ is not the same as or similar to anything! People who try to compare it to addiction are desperately searching for a way to make being queer a problem for the queer person to overcome instead of an opportunity for them to expand their souls with more charity. Also, an alcoholic or a drug addict or someone unable to stay away from porn has to actually try the thing they are addicted to in order to become an addict. Queer people are queer even if they remain celibate or don't take hormones or don't undergo gender reassignment surgery. It's impossible to be addicted to something you've never tried.

LISA KNAPP (MOTHER OF GAY SON)

This is a sensitive topic for me. I have a son who is gay. He is a wonderful, loving, compassionate, loyal, kind, generous human being. He helps others and is basically the ideal child to have.

My ex-husband is addicted to pornography. He was abusive, cruel, and selfish. The deeper he got into his addiction, the more this behavior increased. Ultimately his addiction escalated, and after he visited a brothel in Nevada for the purpose of gratifying his addiction, due to his infidelity, I prayerfully filed for divorce and obtained a protective order.

> There is no comparison between my son and my ex-husband. My son is wonderful, and his dad is destructive. It comes back to knowing people by their fruits. Having a son who is gay and meeting so many LGBTQ+ friends and allies have brought nothing but good fruit. My LGBTQ+ loved ones are some of the best and most compassionate, kind and genuine people I know. My life has been greatly enriched by interacting with these beautiful children of God. Being married to a porn addict for almost three decades showed me toxic fruit I'm still working to purge from my life. I have been diagnosed with betrayal trauma and PTSD as a result of the behavior resulting from the pornography addiction, how that spilled into all aspects of our relationship, and how he treated me. Many, if not all, of my children also have lasting effects from the trauma in the family dynamic.
>
> Comparing being LGBTQ+ and pornography addiction isn't even comparing apples to oranges; it is comparing a delicious fruit (choose your favorite) to a venomous cobra or something equally deadly and, in fact, is triggering to my trauma.

False Statement 3:

They are LGBTQ because they were sexually abused as children.

In episode 41 of the *Listen, Learn & Love* podcast, Jerry Chong talks about being a gay man in Canada investigating the Church. As he got closer to deciding that he would get baptized, he told the missionaries he was gay. He received a witness of the truthfulness of the gospel and decided to be baptized. Before proceeding with his baptism, Jerry was asked to meet with the mission president to discuss his being gay. The mission president asked him if he had been molested and turned gay as a result. Jerry was horrified by this line of questions from someone he had just met. Jerry felt that people do not ask such personal questions of people they do not know. He had never been a victim of sexual abuse. This leader believed that people who are gay became so in response to sexual abuse, and Jerry almost didn't join the Church. He spoke with his bishop and was reassured that the mission president's assumption was not part of the teachings of the gospel of Jesus Christ. Jerry is currently an active, faithful member of the Church, holds a calling as second counselor in his branch presidency, and is a temple ordinance worker in Calgary. He has held LGBTQ inclusion and sensitivity training meetings with leaders in many stakes in and around Calgary.

This is not to be critical of the mission president (or of myself, since I once held the same assumption) but to point out how important it is to be up-to-date with the latest information on LGBTQ issues and to put prior conclusions aside. I've met with hundreds of LGBTQ Latter-day Saints, and in the course of honest discussions, a few have mentioned prior sexual abuse, including same-sex abuse. But during my YSA service, I also met with a few men who experienced same-sex abuse and are still straight.

The Church teaches: "Some people have been abused during the early years of life or have engaged in sexual experimentation at a young age. If this has happened to you, please understand that abuse by others or youthful experiences should not create a present sense of guilt, unworthiness, or rejection by God or His Church. Innocent mischief early in life *does not predispose a youth toward same-gender attraction as an adult*."[9]

The frequency of news reports is evidence that sexual assault and abuse are more common than many of us may have realized and often happens to those who are the most vulnerable. We should strongly condemn all sexual abuse and recognize the difficult road survivors of sexual abuse walk and the need to love, support, and minister to them. If we believe or promote this myth, we may discourage individuals from sharing their personal hardships (if they in fact wish to discuss them) for fear that they will be judged unfairly.

A few of my LG friends who are survivors of same-sex sexual abuse are no longer trying to figure out exactly why they have same-sex attraction or if it is connected to sexual abuse. They just know that their sexuality is part of who they are, and they are trying to make the best decisions they can going forward.

My friend Patrick Risk bravely shared his story of sexual abuse from a male relative in episode 172 of the *Listen, Learn & Love* podcast:

> There really are things that happen to us in life, things that really don't always make sense, things we didn't ask for or that aren't always fair, things that really change us. They change our perspective of the world. . . . I decided to do this podcast in the hopes that by discussing my experience, it might help illuminate the dark corners—we so often like to hide these things we wish would disappear. It's my belief that that which is born in the dark flourishes there. So it's really only by bringing it into the light that we're finally able to gain that perspective to see the proper place to put the experience in, those experiences that we long to get rid of. . . .

I was sexually abused as a child from age six to twelve. It was a male cousin that's ten years older than me. In the ashes of that stolen innocence and the brokenness of my wounded soul, I've often asked the time-worn question of, "What if?" If I hadn't been abused, what would I be like now? Would I not have had an eating disorder and the various impacts from that? Would I not have missed out on so many opportunities I let pass by because of immobilizing fear and anxieties? Would I be married already with children, or [would] my marriage have worked out? Would I not have same-sex attraction? Believe me, I have gotten lost on that endlessly winding and never-progressing road of "what if?"

About a year ago, I had that wakeup call to the "what if?" dream cycle that I found myself stuck in. I falsely assumed that by answering the "what if?," I could change the "what is" of my reality. In other words, if I could relate my same-sex attraction to my abuse, then that would magically solve the problem. It would go away. Maybe I was right. Maybe the abuse did cause my same-sex attraction. It only seems logical that a young boy having repeated sexual experiences in abuse by a man, from six to twelve years of age, is obviously going to create some confusion for that boy and that man.

But what I finally realized is that "what if?" didn't really matter. It's in "what now" that I really needed to place my focus. I don't know what I would have been like without the abuse. I can't change that. What I can do is determine what I'm going to do now because of the experience. With all the new pieces added to my puzzle of life, I'm going to have to figure out how to fit them in. This is going to completely change the picture, but that doesn't mean the end product won't be just as beautiful. What's more, it will be entirely unique, a one-of-a-kind picture created by a thousand pieces of experience.

So in case anyone has missed this big revelation, for the first time publicly and without hiding behind the explanation of "what if?," I'm acknowledging "what is." I have same-sex attraction.

As many know, being a devout member of The Church of Jesus Christ of Latter-day Saints, that doesn't make this easy. It makes my future even more uncertain and creates a thousand more questions. But by acknowledging it, I can now bring into the light that which has been hidden in the dark, and in that light is where I think I'll find a way.

In an unequivocal declaration, I affirm my testimony of God and His eternal plan of happiness. Despite not fitting the general mold of membership in the Church and the challenges that this will present in my life, but acknowledging with added appreciation those that experience this, I recognize and never will judge individuals that walk their

> own individual path. We are each figuring this out in our own way and God will surely help us in our discovery. He will meet us where we are, and He will walk with us to where we need to be.
>
> No matter how your story began, you get to write its ending. Circumstances do not dictate our existence. Yes, they impact and mold our present, but they do not determine our future—we do. "What if" means nothing when answered with the defining question of "what now?" That's entirely up to us.

Patrick is one of my heroes. He showed great courage and vulnerability in sharing some of his journey. His counsel is instructive to all of us as we try to move forward after difficult experiences and use the power of the Atonement of Jesus Christ to heal from the pain that comes into the lives of the innocent.

In my podcast I frequently share this quote by Henri Nouwen, a Catholic priest: "A minister's service will not be perceived as authentic unless it comes from a heart wounded by the suffering about which he speaks. The great illusion of leadership is to think that others can be led out of the desert by someone who has never been there."[10]

Patrick knows the desert of being a survivor of sexual abuse. That is a brutal desert I know nothing about. Patrick is now a "wounded healer" and can authentically lead others out of the desert, offering hope and healing. In some ways we can all be wounded healers, learning empathy from our past hardships and drawing on our journeys in our individual deserts to help us become more effective ministers to others.

I've always loved Elder Jeffrey R. Holland's talk "Like a Broken Vessel," about his journey with emotional health. He said: "In that regard I once terrifyingly saw it in myself. At one point in our married life when financial fears collided with staggering fatigue, I took a psychic blow that was as unanticipated as it was real. With the grace of God and the love of my family, I kept functioning and kept working, but even after all these years I continue to feel a deep sympathy for others more chronically or more deeply afflicted with such gloom than I was."[11]

Elder Holland and Patrick are bravely using their experiences to help and heal others. I admire their courage to share their difficulties. And as we know, our Savior Jesus Christ is the ultimate wounded healer since He knows the pain and suffering of all of our deserts.

Patrick's conclusions also provide a road map the rest of us can follow: we can choose to focus on the "what now." As Latter-day Saints, our "what now" is to let go of this idea that people are LGBTQ because of sexual abuse. By so doing, we will become better at not allowing a search for an explanation for the "cause" of being LGBTQ distract us from effectively ministering to our loved ones.

Another gay Latter-day Saint friend who is a sexual abuse survivor told me of the priesthood blessing he had received to "cast out the evil gay spirit." The blessing didn't change his sexual orientation, and it was an unsettling experience for my friend. I'm sure the person giving the blessing believed he was doing the right thing, but he unintentionally caused more harm than good. This should be instructive to us, encouraging us to try to reflect God's will in our ministry instead of doing what *we* think is needed to resolve a situation.

If an LGBTQ individual is a survivor of sexual abuse, perhaps the abuse happened because they were placed in vulnerable positions because of their sexuality, or maybe it is just a tragic indicator of the prevalence of sexual abuse. While there could be some correlation, as suggested by some stories in this section, correlation doesn't equal causation.

I asked the Facebook group of LGBTQ Latter-day Saints about sexual abuse and its relationship to their sexuality and gender. The last few responses are from parents of LGBTQ members. I'm grateful to the many people who shared their thoughts on this sensitive subject that can help us understand that sexual abuse as a cause of homosexuality is a myth that needs to be set aside.

SAM SKIDMORE (GAY MAN)

I have not been sexually abused. I am also gay. Two separate facts about my life. I have done a fair amount of research on LGBTQ+ psychology in my graduate degree, and there is no actual proof that sexual abuse causes homosexuality.[12] Yes, there are some correlated cases. There are also uncorrelated cases. More importantly than the lack of empirical evidence is the lack of compassion that generally encompasses this question. I have been asked before if I have been sexually abused. People tend not to believe my response, as though being abused is the only possible reason that I could be gay (outside of me choosing to be). While I understand that this helps them reconcile homosexuality with Church teachings, it minimalizes the individual. I think the question is unhealthy; instead of focusing on figuring out why a person is gay for one's own benefit, it would be much healthier for all involved if we focus instead on understanding one another and our journeys in an effort to support and sympathize as well as to empathize where possible.

JOEL MCDONALD (GAY MAN)

Sexual abuse happens far more often than is ever reported, and those who have experienced abuse are all along the spectrum of sexual orientation. Yes, there are those who are LGB who have experienced sexual abuse. Yes, there are those who are LGB who have not experienced sexual abuse. The same is true for those who are straight. I have never experienced sexual abuse, and I am gay. I have friends who have experienced sexual abuse and are straight. Sadly, the painful experiences of some within the LGB community are used to support a narrative that the cause of our sexual orientation is abuse or that we're otherwise broken. We're not broken.

JEFF CASE (GAY MAN)

I'm gay but was not sexually abused and had great parents. While childhood sexual abuse is positively correlated with homosexuality in adulthood, there's no causal link. More likely than abuse causing same-sex attractions, predators are good at picking out the boy who's on the outside, who lacks good connections, or who might seem effeminate. In NO WAY am I blaming the victim; I'm merely stating that predators learn to observe and groom young boys/young men whom they believe they are better able to control and manipulate. I worked in the sex-offender treatment program at the state prison and heard this frequently from inmates who abused young males.

BEN SCHILATY (GAY MAN)

I would just say that I've never been sexually abused. Which is true. Unfortunately, this is a part of the journey of many people, but it wasn't part of mine.

KARL MALCHUT (GAY MAN)

It took me awhile to accept myself, and I had to get past the sexual abuse to actually understand I was gay, but I had to separate the two because they are different.

BLAIRE OSTLER (BISEXUAL WOMAN)

I feel like the premise of the question [about previous sexual abuse] assumes we need to find a cause for homosexuality so it can be cured. I don't care what caused me to be attracted to women. I am attracted to women, and it's not bad.

Look at it this way—we don't put this much effort into understanding why you like grapefruits and why I like oranges. We don't care because it's not a problem. We can simply have a different fruit preference without it being something that needs to be cured.

What if we treated our gender preferences as benign as our fruit preferences? You probably wouldn't ask me about when I first realized I liked oranges or when I was first exposed to oranges or if I watch "orange pornography" or if I was made to taste oranges against my will at some young age. No. You wouldn't care what caused my liking for oranges because it doesn't need to be cured.

For me, I don't care what caused my attraction toward women because it doesn't need to be cured. It's a preference, not a disease.

STANLEY ALVEY (GAY MAN)

I have had a difficult time with this topic as a survivor myself. I was taught that I was same-sex attracted because I was abused as a child. I believed that until I returned from my mission. It gave me a sense of security knowing why I "turned out" gay. It gave me a reason; I was born straight, but because of the evil in my abuser and the ability Satan had to work through him, I became gay.

I came to understand that narrative was false when I finally accepted that I am gay because my Heavenly Parents created me that way. I shed all the hatred in my heart for God allowing it. I shed the hatred for myself. I finally figured out that I am not the product of the evil that happened to me as a child.

Yes, I was sexually abused as a child, but I did not "turn gay" because of that. I have been gay since my spirit was created, and I believe I will be gay for eternity. I have gained so much peace accepting that I am not a product of evil, but a product of my Heavenly Parents' love.

ANNIE HOLLIS (BISEXUAL WOMAN)

My experience is similar but also opposite, if that makes sense. As a fourteen-year-old, I was raped by a much older man at a youth Church activity, and it left me with a lot of PTSD. Especially [being] surround[ed] [by] men/being touched by men (even platonically). So when I came out to some people, I was questioned if I was actually attracted to women or if I was just afraid to be attracted to men because of what happened to me.

I would tell them that my assault absolutely affects my life in countless ways, but my sexuality is not one of them. I knew I was attracted to women when I was ten or eleven, and the abuse didn't even occur for several years after that. Abuse and assault play no determining factor in sexuality.

AUSTIN HODGES (GAY MAN)

When I was growing up and realized I was gay, I lied and said I was molested by a male classmate. (Never accusing someone by name, never telling anyone who it was because there was no one. . . . I realize how awful this is and how it detracts from real survivors' experiences.) I did this because of the belief that was pushed onto me that people are gay because they were molested by someone of the same sex. I said it because I didn't want it to be my fault, because there had to be a reason, and if the reason was "someone did this to me," then there was an explanation, and that explanation meant (to me at the time) that it wasn't my fault and that I wasn't broken and could be cured.

As I've grown up and learned to love myself, I have corrected that lie to all I told and have learned that being gay doesn't need a reason, someone to blame, or need to be "fixed." I was never molested, not even close. I am still gay. On the flip side, I have a male family member and a male best friend who have both opened up and told me about their sexual abuse from other males in their early childhood, and neither of them is gay.

MATTHEW AYDELOTTE (QUEER MAN)

I wasn't abused as a child, neither of my parents was distant, I had no experiences with porn at a young age—none of the stereotypical (and incorrect) reasons someone can "become" gay apply to me. Unfortunately I've had to explain that to people who assume something must have happened to me when I was younger, and they're generally surprised when I tell them that's not the case.

DAVID DOYLE (GAY MAN)

My father has asked me several times about being sexually abused—when did it happen, who did it, how many times? I do not have such abuse in my history. I hate that he assumes this must have happened. It limits our ability to communicate about this part of my life.

My father can't believe gay people just exist; they must be made. It feeds into the myth that gay people are a threat to children because this is the method we use to gain new recruits. And that homosexuality is a mental disorder in reaction to trauma.

CONNER TALON (GAY MAN)

This is something that has personally bothered me for years and is the only reason why I hated myself for being gay. I'm a survivor of sexual abuse, and my perpetrator is of my same sex and is gay.

For the longest time in Young Men and Sunday School, Church leaders would press on us that there are some gay people who are actually straight and confused because of the sexual abuse they experienced. This [was] drilled into me, and I HATED myself. I'd fast and pray and tried to be straight in hopes the feelings and attractions would go away.

When I came out to my mom and expressed these issues, she slammed all of them and said, "You were very gay before that happened." The abuse happened when I was seven. And according to my mom (and looking back), I was very gay growing up: I had a crush on Prince Eric, I wanted to be Ariel, my childhood crush was my neighborhood best friend growing up. So this statement is very false and detrimental—it only causes more problems than there needs to be.

MICHELLE KING WASDEN (MOTHER OF GAY SON)

I am saddened when people ask if my child was sexually abused as a child and that's why "he is the way he is." First of all, that is the most insensitive question ever and why would they ever think it was their business! And second of all, it is so misguided.

LIZ MACDONALD (MOTHER OF GAY SON)

When our son came out, one of our friend's first questions was, "So was your son molested?" I said no. The friend said, "As far as you know." In other words, she was effectively saying, "Your husband or someone else likely molested your gay son," which is untrue and added to our family burden.

DEBRA OAKS COE (MOTHER OF GAY SON)

I did have a son that was molested as a child—but it wasn't my gay son. It was another son that could easily have won the most heterosexual male award. The two [being gay and sexual abuse] are just not connected.

CHER PETERSON McCOY (MOTHER OF GAY SON)

My son's molester was not gay and molested at least thirty children, male and female. Did he "turn" my son gay? No. Did he damage him? Oh yes. I had a man in this same ward say to me that the only two reasons my son was gay was molestation or pornography. It is pathetic that he had to stay in the closet and deal with molestation at the same time. That he was to blame for the molestation and for being gay—this makes my blood boil.

False Statement 4:
They are LGBTQ because of a faulty parenting style.

In his book, Tom Christofferson relates that his parents believed for a time that they were the reason he is gay: "For a period, my father was convinced that I was gay because he had spent so much time traveling for work and had not been present often enough as I was growing up. My parents wondered what they could have done differently so that I would not be gay."[13]

Similarly, when I was growing up in the 1970s and 80s, I remember hearing that a person being gay was caused by an absent father and/or an overbearing mother. At the time, that somehow seemed logical, and it allowed me to easily explain away why people are LGBTQ instead of being open to better understand. I later learned that any link to parenting style and a child becoming LGBTQ is false.[14] Tom has mentioned to me that one reason he wrote his book is to help Latter-day Saint parents understand they didn't do something to cause their child to be LGBTQ.

The Church has also refuted this belief. In addition to President Oaks' statement that the Church has no position on the cause of homosexuality,[15] Elder Holland has specifically taught that parents are not the reason their children are LGBTQ. He said, "If you are a parent of one with same-gender attraction, don't assume you are the reason for those feelings. No one, including the one struggling, should try to shoulder blame."[16]

I should also add that many Latter-day Saint parents with LGBTQ children don't feel having an LGBTQ child is a trial, a burden, or something gone wrong. Yes, it can be a bumpy road. But they are glad they have an LGBTQ child, feel this is part of Heavenly Father's plan, and wouldn't change things if they could.

NECA ALLGOOD (MOTHER OF TRANSGENDER SON)

If that were true [that parents' actions cause their children to be LGBTQ], all my kids would be LGBTQ because they all grew up in the same family.

REBECCA SIMPSON CRAFT (MOTHER OF GAY SON)

We had a family member tell my husband, "You need to take that kid out riding motorcycles and shooting guns!" I think this is a variation on that idea that engaging in masculine hobbies would "fix" this more sensitive, bookish, artistic son. That's a subtle way of thinking that a more involved dad [and] doing manly stuff will prevent or cure a son's sexual orientation.

DEBRA OAKS COE (MOTHER OF GAY SON)

I think [blaming the parents] is an invitation to a family feud with each parent blaming the other. Besides, if it were true, many military kids would be gay. [Having an absent father and overbearing mother] is a good description of all military family dynamics.

TROY AND AUBRIE HUGGARD (PARENTS OF GAY SON)

We go over and over this together as far as raising our gay son. My husband always reflects on how he did the same activities (i.e., hunting, fishing, horseback riding) with our oldest, eighteen-year-old gay son that he does with our straight twelve-year-old son. They were the things that [my husband's] dad did with him too, and he thought they were natural for men to enjoy. When our oldest son didn't show much interest in them, [my husband] felt like he had failed [our son]. [My husband] now realizes that it was because [our son] was interested in less "masculine" things because of the way he was made and knows that it isn't his fault that his son is gay. I think somehow we believed this rhetoric about overbearing mothers and absent fathers. It wasn't until our son came out last year that we reflected on his upbringing and realized that this is a complete myth. I feel horrible for judging other parents of gay children based on this. It's absolutely false!

CAROL M. COLVIN (MOTHER OF GAY SON AND BISEXUAL DAUGHTER)

This myth is awful. Even my husband said something to me early on after our son came out, hinting that our son was gay because maybe I wasn't affectionate enough with him. It was hurtful. All of the theories about dysfunctional family relationships causing a child to be gay have been abandoned by science and by the Church.[17]

ANGIE WAITES LEAVITT (MOTHER OF GAY SON)

Why do I have one gay son and another straight son, both raised by the same father and mother? Believe me, our parenting styles didn't change. This idea has been discredited by all psychological/psychiatric professions. It came to be, in my opinion, because society thought that there was something wrong with being gay instead of recognizing that it is just one of many sexual variations.

HEATHER ROBERTSON (MOTHER OF GAY DAUGHTER)

Isn't this myth so sad? Wouldn't the adversary do all in his power to get us to blame each other and tear apart families?

EMILY EARL NELSON (MOTHER OF GAY SON)

There is a common myth that gay kids have overbearing mothers and absent fathers. I do consider myself a strong woman, but my husband could never be considered an absent father. He has been around more than most fathers. He has been loving and supportive and very involved. He has attended school events and activities. We have five sons, but only one of them is gay. So if we caused this, shouldn't they all be gay? There is nothing a parent can do that turns their child gay.

ANDREA PARKS (MOTHER OF GAY SON)

Homosexuality exists across cultures and even throughout the animal kingdom. There are very different family dynamics and parenting styles around the world—but that doesn't change the presence of LGBTQ kids. And its existence in the animal kingdom really challenges the parenting-styles theory.[18]

As long as we see being LGBTQ as something that is "wrong," we'll be looking for reasons why and how to prevent it. But if we can see it as a completely normal part of humanity and biology, that perspective changes the conversation and how we accept our LGBTQ brothers and sisters.

False Statement 5:
LGBTQ parents will have LGBTQ children.

While there may be some situations in which an LGBTQ parent has an LGBTQ child and perhaps there is a genetic link, the vast majority of all children are not LGBTQ. We shouldn't tell a child they will be LGBTQ or cishet because of the sexual orientation or gender identity of their parents.[19]

In episode 111 of the *Listen, Learn & Love* podcast, Bryan Fugal (a married father of three in his thirties) and his gay father, Lawrence (in his sixties), talk about their relationship. I asked Bryan: "One of the thoughts that may come to mind is, 'If I've got an LGBTQ parent, I'm going to be LGBTQ.' Did you ever go down that road as a ten-year-old?"

Bryan referenced a film he and his father were working on about growing up with a gay father:

> **Bryan:** I've thought of that, especially growing up in the nineties in Utah County. Calling somebody "gay" or a "homo" was usually done in a joking way and not usually meant as an offense, or if it was, it was just between guy friends or whatever. But to think about it seriously, which eventually you do discover or learn what being homosexual actually is, and the negativity that was associated with that, definitely made me concerned—my dad is gay; does that mean I'm gay? We go into that in the film a little bit too. The son character gets called a bad word which means homosexual, and he reacts to that in a fearful way, a little homophobic as his sexuality is getting challenged even as a young teen.
>
> **Me:** I'm glad you addressed that in the film.
>
> **Bryan:** It's pretty brief but it's there. Also, in the truck, the antagonist is teasing the dad character . . . and he says, "Well, the apple doesn't fall too far from the tree." Like father, like son, but using other stronger language.
>
> **Lawrence:** Bryan became pretty clear, and he's mentioned before, that he's not gay. [*laughs*] The apple did not fall close to the gay tree.[20]

Bryan loves his father and did the best he could during his teenage years to navigate having a gay father. But the conclusion that Bryan will be gay since his dad is gay is a myth and the associated teasing and bullying was not helpful, to say the least.[21]

EVAN SMITH[22] (FATHER OF GAY SON)

> The fact that so many gay teens aren't supported by their parents speaks to the falseness of the idea that parenting style makes kids gay. I also believe studies have indicated there are no significant differences on any measure between heterosexual vs. homosexual parents and the sexual orientation of their children.[23]
>
> At the risk of oversimplifying (and over-generalizing) the development of a complex biological characteristic, I think current science shows that inherited genetics (which can include

genes passed on from multiple generations) is around 25–30 percent responsible for someone being born gay.[24] Epigenetics (which is how gene expression is altered/hard-wired by environmental factors) in utero seems to be primarily responsible otherwise.[25]

CALEB JONES (FATHER OF GAY SON)

One clarification I give after explaining this is that children who have LGBTQ-affirming parents are far less likely to be closeted which can give the appearance of higher rates. But when that is controlled for, there are no higher rates of LGBTQ people regardless of upbringing.

MATT ROBERTSON (FATHER OF GAY DAUGHTER)

This myth is a logical consequence to another myth: that being LGBTQ is a choice or just something they know how to do. If this were the case, then it would logically follow that being in an openly accepting environment could make it more likely that a child would become LGBTQ. But the truth is the vast majority of LGBTQ kids are born to and raised by straight parents. That's just simple math because LGBTQ kids are in the minority by a long way.

An environment of unconditional love and acceptance around issues of gender identity and sexual orientation does not make it more or less likely that a child will be gay or transgender. Such an environment does make it much more likely that kids will be happy and well-adjusted, and much less likely that they will engage in self-harm or suicide. And this holds true regardless of whether our kids are gay or straight.

KATE CARPENTER (MOTHER OF GAY SON)

Well, I do have a gay friend whose father is gay and whose son is also gay (the father is in a mixed-orientation marriage), so I do believe there is a genetic component. However, if all kids were like their parents, no heterosexual parents would ever have gay kids. So it doesn't really hold up.

LISA WARBURTON GLAD (MOTHER OF TWO GAY DAUGHTERS)

I have an interesting situation that totally blows this theory out of the water. First of all, I am straight. My first marriage lasted five years; we had one daughter. My second marriage is going strong at thirty-one years, and we have two daughters. Years after the divorce, I found out that my first husband is gay. So two of my three daughters are gay/queer. I joke that God has a sense of humor: my gay husband gave me my straight daughter, and my straight husband gave me my two queer daughters.

JEFF CASE (GAY MAN)

Actually, heterosexual couples are the world's leading producers of LGBTQ children. While there is a genetic component to homosexuality (nothing identified yet regarding genetics and transgender identity that I've come across), it's a complex, polygenic issue.

BRITT JONES (GAY MAN)

Honestly, I wish this were true. I kind of oddly wish that at least one of my kids were queer in some form, in the same way that many dads who are University of Utah fans hope their kids will be too. It'll be something special (to me) that I would share with my kid(s). But it just isn't so, statistically, whether the kid is yours by birth or some other way (like adoption).

DALLIN STEELE (GAY MAN)

My parents are straight, so I see no logic in that statement. Neither of my parents are transgender but I have a transgender brother. So again it doesn't make sense.

SAM SKIDMORE (GAY MAN)

Although research suggests that LGBTQ+ parents do have LGBTQ+ offspring more frequently, this can't be blamed entirely on genetics, as two men or two women can't both contribute to making a child (that I know of). My assumption is that this slight increase in having LGBTQ+ children is that the child is likely raised in a more open-minded and LGBTQ+-friendly atmosphere. As such, children are more likely to be in tune with and open to their own sexuality.

False Statement 6:

Heavenly Father did not intend for anyone to be LGBTQ. Their sexual orientation is a mistake.

Before I started to meet with LGBTQ Latter-day Saints and listen to their stories, I assumed that Heavenly Father had not intended to create people as LGBTQ—that something unplanned had occurred to cause someone's sexual orientation or gender identity not to be cishet. Maybe it allowed me to make sense of the world and not have to ponder how

LGBTQ Latter-day Saints fit into the plan of salvation. Keeping everything in a nice, tidy box meant I didn't have to consider my responsibilities to this group of people.

However, meeting with LGBTQ Latter-day Saints caused my feelings to shift. As I began to "diligently seek" the "mysteries of God," I felt new insights "unfolded" to me (1 Nephi 10:19). I feel that everyone is created as our Heavenly Parents intended them to be created. I don't believe our Heavenly Parents see Their LGBTQ children and say, "Oh no, what went wrong?" I feel our Heavenly Parents are not capable of being surprised or making a mistake. Rather, I believe LGBTQ people are part of Heavenly Father's plan and part of the needed diversity that makes this mortal experience beautiful. They have unique gifts and provide needed contributions to the body of Christ.

When giving blessings to LGBTQ individuals, I've blessed some who, I believe, were noble spirits and who fought for and brought many to the Savior's plan—but who they are and their unique mortal missions are largely hidden from our current view. I've never had an impression during one of these blessings that someone's sexual orientation or gender identity needed to change.

Believing that everyone is created as intended puts us all on the same moral footing as we all work to come unto Christ and live His teachings. We know, of course, that only our Savior is truly perfect; we are all imperfect mortal beings. And though we may have been created just as God intended, we still must exercise agency and choose to follow the commandments, live the teachings of the gospel, and come unto Christ. But I don't believe our Heavenly Parents want any of Their children to look in the mirror and feel they are a mistake. Rather, we should all see ourselves as Heavenly Parents' wonderful children, created in Their image and worthy of Their love.

Now, I am not suggesting that these feelings or impressions I've had about LGBTQ individuals are Church doctrine are true for all LGBTQ Latter-day Saints. But I have felt these impressions deeply as I've ministered to our LGBTQ members, and I encourage others to try to see the LGBTQ people in their lives as noble spirits with a choice mission.

I like the words that Nephi taught to see everyone as "alike unto God": "And he inviteth them all to come unto him and partake of his goodness; and he denieth none that come unto him, black and white, bond and free, male and female; and he remembereth the heathen; and all are alike unto God, both Jew and Gentile" (2 Nephi 26:33).

In a 1979 speech at BYU, Elder Howard W. Hunter expounded on this verse:

"From this statement it is clear that all men are invited to come unto Him and all are alike unto Him. Race makes no difference; color makes no difference; nationality makes no difference." I would add that sexuality and gender identification make no difference.

Elder Hunter continued: "The brotherhood of man is literal. We are all of one blood and the literal spirit offspring of our eternal Heavenly Father. Before we came to earth we belonged to His eternal family. We associated and knew each other there. Our common paternity makes us not only literal sons and daughters of eternal parentage, but literal brothers and sisters as well. This is a fundamental teaching of The Church of Jesus Christ of Latter-day Saints."[26]

I love the words of Elder Uchtdorf: "While the Atonement is meant to help us all become more like Christ, it is not meant to make us all the same. Sometimes we confuse differences in personality with sin. *We can even make the mistake of thinking that because someone is different from us, it must mean they are not pleasing to God.* This line of thinking leads some to believe that the Church wants to create every member from a single mold—that each one should look, feel, think, and behave like every other."[27]

My prayer is that we embrace the belief that none of God's children are a mistake and the differences we see in those around us are not only okay but also necessary to our Heavenly Parents' plan.

TEMBER HARWARD (GAY MAN MARRIED TO A WOMAN)

Of course [being LGBTQ] is part of the plan! God has blessed us to have certain traits or experiences in mortality to help mold us into the exalted beings we are meant to become.

JAKE SHEPHERD (GAY MAN)

I don't know why this couldn't be part of the mortal plan. I feel we have a distinct plan from our Heavenly Father, our own "plan of salvation," if you will, [that differs] from [the plans of] all other individuals of God's kingdom. As I read my scriptures and my patriarchal blessing, and [as I] further my knowledge and testimony of the gospel of Christ, my testimony that I was preordained to have this put upon me strengthens.

Our mortality is filled with trials—this being one of them—[that] help us build empathy and love for others. I feel with empathy and love, [through] which Christ shared the gospel. As we use our own trials to reach out to others, they . . . could be great missionary tools to bring all sheep back to the flock someday. Some people may see being gay as a curse; some see it as a blessing; some see it as a gift. I choose to see it as a blessing and gift, since I know I am supposed to use it in a manner that is pleasing to my Heavenly Father and to help spread that gospel—to show that a gay man can find joy and happiness within the walls of any chapel, stake building, or temple that God has placed him in.

JOSEPH ELDREDGE (GAY MAN)

So it's not part of God's plan for someone to rely on Christ? A huge reason why I would never give up my queerness is because it is a powerful link to my Savior. The more queer people [that others] meet, the more they'll see the patterns. God is a god of patterns. He also creates us queer folk so we can teach others how to love more fully.

AUSTIN HODGES (GAY MAN)

I know that being gay is a gift from God. The lessons I've learned, the people I've grown close to, who I'm becoming, how I see the world, the empathy that I've learned, my testimony—lots of aspects of my life are influenced by being gay. [If I were not gay,] I wouldn't be the person I've grown up to be.

I truly believe this is God's design and purpose for me. I just wish I knew how I fit into the plan of salvation, knowing that I am meant to be gay. I have pondered and searched for an answer or some bit of direction for "where do I fit in now?" now that I know that I was created this way and was not designed to be straight.

DAVID DANIELS (GAY MAN)

We certainly don't know God's intentions. We don't know if it was random, although I think God gave each of us unique challenges that He felt would help us grow [and that] also give those around us a chance to love and support. He gave my parents two gay sons (out of seven kids). That's a fairly unique situation for any parent.

We are here to be tested but also to gain experience. God also knew we would all fall short in whatever our challenges are, and He gave us all a way back.

BLAIRE OSTLER (BISEXUAL WOMAN)

I believe I was created queer for a reason. It is my responsibility as a queer person to help teach others what it means to love, to really love one another, when loving each other isn't easy. My creation wasn't a product of "things going awry." It was deliberate. We can't learn to love one another as God does without loving each other through our differences. My queerness is a gift, not a mistake.

JEFF CASE (GAY MAN)

First of all, the plan of salvation is a concept that does resonate with me. As far as how sexuality fits into it, all conditions of this world and our bodies are deliberate elements of that plan. I believe that it is up to the individual to work out how their own orientation and identity fit into the master plan.

KATHERINE HERRMANN (TRANSGENDER WOMAN)

I think we are and always have been what we are. It's part of our intelligence. We weren't all perfect spiritual beings, so God gave us the gift of mortality and the forgetfulness of the veil, which gives us an opportunity to do something different. What matters here is whether we will be obedient despite who we are and have been from before the foundation of the world when we face the challenges and struggles of mortality. And those challenges He may give us include imperfect bodies. People are blind, deaf, handicapped, and imperfect in a myriad of ways. So as a transwoman, I've always been female, but my mortal body is part of the challenge of will I be obedient in these circumstances? Will I put the kingdom first? Will I keep the commandments? Receive all the ordinances? And have a family? Nothing is awry. It's all part of my plan He has for me.

LISA KNAPP (MOTHER OF GAY SON)

As members of the Church, we are taught about and hopefully understand the importance of personal revelation.

The Lord has born witness to me, through the Spirit, that my son is exactly as his Heavenly Parents created him to be. This includes his loyalty, his innate talent for music, his sexuality (gay), his compassion, his ability to be a wonderful friend, and so much more. He is not inherently broken or flawed (other than the normal effects of the Fall), like any other person.

HEATHER ROBERTSON (MOTHER OF GAY DAUGHTER)

The sheer number of families with LGBTQ children disproves the notion that this could be a mistake. Isn't it clear that God is trying to teach us something? As difficult as this journey is, as a parent of a gay child, nothing in my life has ever pulled me closer to God and taught me to look at things another way like this has. I thank Him for that every day.

KATE SHERMAN (MOTHER OF GAY SON)

My bishop told me this week that my son accepted his gayness in the premortal life and said, "Sure, I can handle that assignment! I'll deal with the prejudice, injustice, loneliness, depression, etc."

KIM CRUMP (MOTHER OF GAY SON)

Heavenly Father has not stopped this from happening. If you believe being gay [happens because of] a mistake . . . in the womb, then that is your choice, but Heavenly Father is letting this happen for a purpose. His ways are not our ways nor His thoughts our thoughts (see Isaiah 55:8).

MONICA PHILLIPS (MOTHER OF TRANSGENDER SON)

When someone says to me that "God doesn't make mistakes," I simply reply, "You're absolutely right!" God creates each of us exactly as we were meant to be. We come to this earth to learn and grow and return to Him. He allows us to have experiences and struggles and trials and successes and joys. All of this helps us to become the person Heavenly Father intended us to be. Absolutely no mistakes.

ANNE ELIASON (MOTHER OF TRANSGENDER CHILD)

When my teenager came tiptoeing into my room in the middle of the night, shaking like an earthquake, she whispered, "Mom, I need to tell you something. Please don't be mad." The Spirit was so strong in that moment—maybe the strongest I've ever felt it. The Spirit told me in no uncertain terms that my job right [then] was to believe my child and to love her fiercely. And that our Heavenly Father loves her, totally and completely. As I hugged her tight and told her that nothing she said would change the way I love her, she came out as transgender. The Spirit never left us that night, and through the days ahead we have seen our Savior's profound love for her and for our family in so many ways, both huge and subtle. She is not a mistake. Our Father's perfect plan includes her. She is a living example of God's love.

COLLEEN HARRIS (MOTHER OF GAY SON)

Is the only purpose for us to come on earth, get married, and then have kids? There are just so many variants that are out there. What about those who are infertile? What about those with disabilities? Or those who just never get married or have kids for one reason or another? Are those of a different race second-class citizens? Are they all just a huge mistake? I believe God created diversity so we can learn to embrace and work out our differences and create understanding and unity. I believe Heavenly Father wants us to learn how to love all His children and learn to minister and love all.

False Statement 7:

People are LGBTQ because of the Fall of Adam and Eve from the Garden of Eden, or the "natural man."

Our restored gospel has beautiful insights into the doctrines of the Fall of Adam and Eve and of the "natural man" that provide greater understanding of our mortal experience as part of the plan of happiness. But connecting the Fall and the "natural man" to being LGBTQ in an effort to explain their existence as an unfortunate outcome of a mortal world is hurtful and dismisses the importance of LGBTQ people in our lives, in the Church, and as part of society.

Some of our LGBTQ Latter-day Saints do link sexual orientation to the Fall of Adam and Eve. For these individuals, being LGBTQ may be a result of living in a fallen world, and that means that being LGBTQ is not a choice. But they feel their existence should be considered on equal footing with cishet Latter-day Saints, who also did not choose their gender or sexual identity. Further, LGBTQ individuals are not somehow "less than" other people. They are a part of the planned and needed diversity of the mortal world. They have gifts and contributions that are equal to those of cishet people. And they should not feel shame for how they were created. Further, as shared in some of the stories below, LGBTQ people usually find it problematic to have their sexual orientation or gender identity compared to a birth defect like congenital blindness[28] because they do not feel any defect occurred and therefore nothing needs to be healed in the next life.

King Benjamin in the Book of Mormon taught about the "natural man," which is generally understood to be the base, selfish parts of humanity. He said the "natural man is an enemy to God . . . unless he yields to the enticings of the Holy Spirit, and putteth off the natural man and becometh a saint through the atonement of Christ the Lord, and becometh as a child, submissive, meek, humble, patient, full of love, willing to submit to all things which the Lord seeth fit to inflict upon him, even as a child doth submit to his father" (Mosiah 3:19). Yes, the temptations and weaknesses of the natural man are real. But it is unfair to assume that the doctrine of the natural man somehow applies more to LGBTQ people than it does to other people. Moreover, I know many LGBTQ Latter-day Saints who have all these childlike attributes King Benjamin described.

We also should not suggest that people are LGBTQ because they yielded to the natural man. Everyone, including LGBTQ Latter-day Saints, can acquire, through the Atonement of Jesus Christ, all of the attributes listed in Mosiah 3:19 that are used to overcome the natural man. Developing meekness, humility, submissiveness, and so on are actions within our control. However, being or not being LGBTQ is not something within our control. Suggesting that anyone is LGBTQ because of the natural man incorrectly puts everything on their shoulders—that somehow they did something to cause themselves to be LGBTQ and therefore they can do something to undo this and become cishet. This may cause LGBTQ people to feel shame and see themselves as second-class citizens, unworthy of God's love and perhaps conclude they are unwelcome in our congregations—whether they are already members or if they are investigating the Church.

ANN PACK (TRANSGENDER WOMAN)

I'm only going to speak from my perspective and not for any other LGBTQ person. I don't speak for any other trans person or the trans community either.

For me, I equate being transgender as a direct result of being born into a fallen world. God does not make mistakes. But nature makes mistakes all the time as a result of the Fall. I don't understand how some people believe that so many things can and do go awry during pregnancy and birth because of the Fall but that gender would be the one thing that God would not allow to be affected by the Fall.

As for the "natural man," I don't connect it to being transgender. No one would suggest that someone who is born with poor eyesight should "put off the natural man" and not wear corrective lenses or get surgery to fix their eyesight. This is how I view being transgender.

DAVID DOYLE (GAY MAN)

Adam and Eve lacked the ability to reproduce while in the Garden. The command to "be fruitful, and multiply, and replenish the earth" (Genesis 1:28) could only be fulfilled after the Fall. It seems heterosexuality, as we think of it, was introduced into the world because of the Fall. If that's when sexuality came into the world, then I think it's fair to say homosexuality was introduced at the same time. Both are variants of sexuality that occur throughout nature.

BLAIRE OSTLER (BISEXUAL WOMAN)

In the Garden of Eden, God commanded, "Of every tree of the garden thou mayest freely eat, but of the tree of the knowledge of good and evil, thou shalt not eat of it, nevertheless, thou mayest choose for thyself, for it is given unto thee; but remember that I forbid it, for in the day thou eatest thereof thou shalt surely die" (Moses 3:16–17). Because Adam and Eve transgressed and partook of the fruit, they were cast out from the presence of the Lord (D&C 29:40–41). In other words, they experienced spiritual death. They also became mortal—subject to physical death. This spiritual and physical death is called "the Fall."

As descendants of Adam and Eve, we inherit a fallen condition during mortality (Alma 42:5–9, 14). We are separated from the presence of God and subject to physical death. We are also placed in a state of opposition, in which we are tested by the difficulties of life and the temptations of the adversary (2 Nephi 2:11–14; D&C 29:39; Moses 6:48–49).

In this fallen condition, we have a conflict within us. We are spirit children of God, with the potential to be "partakers of the divine nature" (2 Peter 1:4). However, "we are unworthy before [God]; because of the fall our natures have become evil continually" (Ether 3:2). We need to strive continually to overcome unrighteous passions and desires.

The solution to the Fall is not to criticize queer genders and/or sexuality. The solution to the Fall is to "partake of our divine nature" and overcome our fallen state. Again, our fallen state is spiritual and physical death. To overcome physical death, we must be resurrected. To overcome spiritual death, we must dwell in God's presence. To do that we must dwell in love. The scriptures say, if we dwelleth in love, we dwelleth in God (John 4:16), and if we do not know love, we do not know God (John 4:7–8). Quite literally, we overcome our fallen state when love wins.

JILLYAN ADAMS (CISGENDER LESBIAN WOMAN)

As far as [the] natural man goes, I think the most dangerous of [the] "natural" tendencies is that of hatred, of judgment, of blaming, of focusing on the faults of others rather than on their virtues, on their sins rather than on their holiness as [children] of God, purified every moment by the infinite Atonement of Christ.

JOHN J. TRAU (GAY MAN)

Yes, we *all* live in a fallen state and are subject to it, to mortality and all its diversities. I strongly feel (through the Spirit) that there is divine purpose in all of it, in all of us, all conditions, all sexualities. I think the Lord is testing us. Will we learn to love one another despite these differences? Will we be Christlike? Will we love people where they are? Will we love them into the gospel and help build the kingdom with LGBTQ people in it? Or will we let Satan win and divide us from our precious families and faith?

JOHN GUSTAV-WRATHALL (GAY MAN)

This idea is something I've thought a lot about and questioned and sought understanding of in relation to my sexual orientation. First of all, there are things it seems pretty clear to me that I would call "physical evil" that are a consequence of the Fall. Death and everything related to death—disease, deformity, pain, [and] natural disasters that cause untimely death and destruction. Some have put homosexuality in this category as a kind of unfortunate defect, assuming that in a perfect world, there would be no homosexuality.

Unlike most things we put in this category, however, homosexuality does not in itself cause unhappiness or suffering. Actually, quite the opposite. It's people's hateful/hurtful reactions to homosexuality—homophobia—that causes unhappiness or suffering. So if anything is a consequence of the Fall, it's homophobia. Not homosexuality.

If homosexuality were a birth defect, then you would expect people to be compassionate toward homosexuals. But unfortunately most people who have this opinion of homosexuality are not. And it seems that birth defects are something we work to prevent before birth or fix after birth, while we can't change someone's sexual orientation or gender identity.

False Statement 8:

More people are LGBTQ now because of increased cultural acceptance, being around LGBTQ people, or conversations and clubs at school.

Since most of us are seeing an increase in young people who identify as LGBTQ, it could seem a logical conclusion that an outside influence, such as school, is causing people to become LGBTQ.

This idea of outside influences has increased in circulation as more schools have begun including LGBTQ issues in their curriculum, and offering clubs and programs to support LGBTQ students. Many, particularly parents, are worried that if their children associate with LGBTQ individuals, those friendships could influence their children to become LGBTQ. However, I believe that discussing LGBTQ issues does not cause people to become LGBTQ.

On my podcast I interviewed Dr. Aaron Wilson, a junior high school principal in Salt Lake City. He spoke about the school's role as a safe place for all students and its role in providing accurate education about LGBTQ and other topics.[29] Aaron, an active Latter-day Saint, hosts his own podcast called *America's Principal* and has released several episodes discussing LGBTQ issues in public schools, such as supporting LGBTQ youth, addressing LGBTQ bullying, and rights of LGBTQ students.[30]

The Church has weighed in on this issue. The following instruction is from an LDS Family Services training meeting I attended: "Help members understand that being around those who experience same-sex attraction does not mean they will also experience same-sex attraction."[31]

This false statement—that one can become LGBTQ by association—is deeply concerning because it creates and perpetuates fear: fear of being near LGBTQ friends and family (those who presumably need us the most) as well as fear that being LGBTQ is an undesirable outcome. By combating this myth, we can start to overcome our fear and become more accepting. Both of these steps are necessary in learning to communicate and minister with love and compassion.

DEBRA OAKS COE (MOTHER OF GAY SON)

Dr. Alli Martin, who wrote her doctoral thesis on this topic, shared with me that researchers have found that schools with active gay-straight-alliance clubs (GSAs) have overall better climates than those without GSAs. Schools with GSAs also have decreased risk of suicidality and suicide attempts, dropping out, and drug and alcohol abuse. One common finding in this body of research is that these outcomes benefit all students, not just LGBTQ students.[32]

GSAs have also been found to have protective effects. Youth who are receiving social services, such as those in foster care or homeless shelters, are especially at risk for the aforementioned negative consequences. However, in a study of LGBTQ students receiving social services, Walls et al. (2008) found that those who went to schools that had GSAs were significantly less likely both to experience suicidality and to report suicide attempts. Students at schools with GSAs were only two-thirds as likely as students at non-GSA schools to report suicidality, and about one-third as likely to report an attempt.[33]

This finding illustrates the relationship between having a GSA in a school and improved school climate, regardless of whether a student is a member of the club. While these clubs improve the climate for all youth at a school, they are of particular importance for multi-marginalized youth.[34]

STACEY NERDIN (MOTHER OF PANSEXUAL DAUGHTER)

Some worry that learning about sexual orientation and gender identity in schools would influence them—plant seeds of confusion and maybe convince a child to choose those paths.

All of the stories I've heard are [that] this (being gay) is something they already know about themselves and was often something they initially hated about themselves, would change, and maybe have tried to change by throwing themselves into prayer, Church service, a mission, even marriage to the opposite gender. It isn't a whim; it isn't something they were encouraged or influenced into.

EMILY EARL NELSON (MOTHER OF GAY SON)

This is simply not true. If sexual orientation "rubbed off" or was contagious, it would follow that gay kids would be turned straight since the vast majority of people they associate with are heterosexual. My gay son (17) had many friends through adolescence and not a single one was "turned gay" through their association.

KIM PEARSON (FATHER OF GAY SON)

Does talking about crime make our children criminals? Does talking about drugs make them addicts? Does talking about dancers make them all want to be dancers? No. Part of education is talking about things that exist in the world around us. LGBTQ people exist and are very much a part of the world around us.

CAROL M. COLVIN (MOTHER OF GAY SON AND BISEXUAL DAUGHTER)

I have two LGBTQ adult children, a boy and a girl. Neither of them chose to be gay or thought it was cool. In fact, they both hated themselves and tried as hard as they could not to be gay for as long as they could. I don't believe anyone, even if they did think being gay was cool, would or could choose to change their orientation. There is still far too much risk of alienation, physical harm, verbal assault, religious and spiritual trauma, family loss, etc.

Also, if school clubs could influence orientation, my son would be straight. Every kid he knew in every club was straight. And my son was into sports—he played baseball, soccer, and basketball with a lot of very straight boys. It didn't change his orientation no matter how hard he tried or how much he wanted it to. He even joined the Air Force to try to become straight.

My daughter just came out last fall. She is twenty-nine and only realized she was bisexual in the last couple years. She ended a long relationship with a man because she couldn't overcome the depression and anxiety she was feeling the closer they got to the wedding date. And she lives [in a major US city], where it's very easy to be gay and to fit in with the "in crowd." I think this myth that kids will choose to be gay because of school or a school club is one of the most harmful myths out there. Fear of these clubs is keeping our LGBTQ kids from feeling good about themselves during those vulnerable teen years, and they carry that self-loathing with them for years after high school.

MONICA PHILLIPS (MOTHER OF TRANSGENDER SON)

My son had never met another trans person until he attended a North Star[35] conference, and oh, how nice it was to know he wasn't alone. Since he's been out, I don't know anybody who became trans from knowing him. When you look at a transgender person's life and the struggles they encounter, nobody looks at them and says, "Hey, this looks fun! I think I'll be transgender so I can go through all this pain and suffering!"

PAM KEENY (MOTHER OF GAY SON)

My son knew in third to fourth grade that he was somehow different from the boys around him, but he didn't have the vocabulary to discuss it. When he did start being able to identify that he was gay, his only resources were condemning and led to confusion. He spent years trying to figure out where he went "wrong" to have ended up this way. He also had no idea where to go to seek answers and had no friends to even discuss his dilemma. As an adult, those same friends he has known his whole life are still there. They hang out when he comes home from college. This last weekend they played games and interacted with him and his boyfriend. While all of these other friends are still single and looking, not one of them has decided to "experiment and see what the other side" looks like. In fact, of the three boys that have come out around his age in our ward, none of them have been "best friends." These are isolated events, not some form of contagion. Whenever I hear stories about avoiding these programs [e.g., LGBTQ school clubs] to discuss this issue at a young age (including my previous reaction), I know it stems from fear. We are all afraid as moms. We want to protect our kids. We want them to be safe and learn healthy lifestyles. When we feel that fear, we have to look at the source. There are certainly ways to discuss these issues in an age-appropriate manner and with respect.'

AMANDA SMITH (MOTHER OF BISEXUAL DAUGHTER)

A few years ago when I took my daughter to her junior high open house for the beginning of her seventh-grade year, the first thing I noticed when I walked in the door was a poster for an LGBTQ club. Not having that be part of my reality yet, I felt a pit in my stomach that my kid would have to go to a school that had this kind of influence. I couldn't believe that teachers would have rainbow flags on their door to encourage this kind of behavior. I had thought myself loving towards those in the LGBTQ community but had a fear that if this was present in schools, my children would be influenced to be LGBTQ (which at that time I couldn't think of anything that could be worse for my kid).

Fast forward to the middle of the year when I noticed a huge change in my daughter's personality. Our once goofy, witty, interactive relationship had taken a 180 and felt like it had completely dried up. She was struggling with friends and figuring out how and where she fit in. There were some subtle signs that gave me some inklings that she was somehow involved with the LGBTQ crowd. I wasn't sure how to react or respond. Things just seemed to keep going downhill and [becoming] darker in her life. I remember one sleepless night sitting in my bathroom just crying, praying, and pleading for my daughter. I knew things weren't okay, but I couldn't put my finger definitively on anything. The next day through a series of events, I found out that my daughter had a girlfriend and had gone on a date with her. My world was rocked . . . flipped upside down.

For the next few weeks I was so lost and confused. I didn't know what to do or what direction to take. My husband and I had many prayerful discussions on how we thought best to handle this. We had discussions with our daughter, who told us she was bisexual. We let her know that we love her. We let her know that we didn't doubt her feelings of attraction. In one conversation with my daughter, she told me that she and some of her other LGBTQ friends had made a pact that if someone's parents kicked them out, the others would take them in. This broke my heart. Knowing that my daughter and some of her peers had this fear was a catalyst in helping me understand the need for more discussions in our schools with regard to our LGBTQ community. I went from feelings of fear and detest towards these LGBTQ clubs and teachers to strong feelings of gratitude and love.

JOY SOUTHERN (MOTHER OF TRANSGENDER SON AND BISEXUAL SON)

Being LGBTQ is not a contagious disease. It's who they are. I'm left-handed, and if I talk to someone who is right-handed, that isn't going to change or influence me so that I can now write and do other things with my right hand.

Human beings have an innate need to feel loved, accepted, and . . . like they belong. Many groups are created to help foster that sense of belonging and to provide a support system to the members of that group. LGBTQ groups can provide a similar support and are especially vital because there are still many of these kids who are rejected by their own families. They need safe places where they can know that they are not broken but [that] they are beautiful just the way they are.

MATT ROBERTSON (FATHER OF GAY DAUGHTER)

I promise kids are talking about this [LGBTQ subjects] already. A lot. And we need to let it sink in that people are LGBTQ+ because that's who they are, not because they heard about it somewhere. School is one of several places where these topics can and should be addressed responsibly and in a way that helps promote healthy choices. If adults don't get involved in the conversation, our kids end up hearing, at best, a mix of helpful and harmful information with huge doses of falsehood and surrounded by the sense that the whole thing is shameful. And shame itself is what most often leads to risky choices. As adults we don't get to avoid the responsibility of providing children with accurate information just because the topic makes us uncomfortable.

False Statement 9:

More people are LGBTQ now than before because we are in the Last Days and Satan is increasing his attacks.

I've heard this statement several times. After spending a lot of time thinking about, praying about, and pondering this assertion, I'm listing it as a false statement because I have come to believe that is exactly what it is. There are good reasons to believe that there are not more LGBTQ people today than there were in the past. There is documented homosexuality throughout all eras of history. The perception that more people are LGBTQ could simply be a result of sampling bias—in the past, people may not have known many *openly* LGBTQ people since LGBTQ people felt unsafe coming out. But as society has slowly started to accept LGBTQ individuals, more and more people have stopped hiding their sexuality or gender identity. Today LGBTQ issues are frequently the subject of news stories and civil rights efforts. The reality could simply be that we are more aware of LGBTQ individuals since our culture has made it safer to share this aspect of their lives.

Yes, Satan is real and wants to destroy us, but I don't feel God gave Satan the power to make someone LGBTQ, just like I don't feel God gave Satan the power to change someone's green eyes, red hair, or left-handedness. I believe differences in sexuality and gender identity are all part of God's plan, which includes needed diversity. No one should feel that how they are created is a mistake or a result of Satan.

PAM KEENY (MOTHER OF GAY SON)

Let me . . . say that God created these wonderful individuals and knows who they are by name. They are not a threat to families or society as a whole. Remember that what God creates and loves, Satan will try to warp and manipulate and induce fear. It's not the LGBTQ that are evil or should be condemned. Prophets have seen these last days and have set standards and blessings to keep us safe and healthy. But make no doubt that God wants these children of His to be safe and healthy as well. They are not meant to be "changed" or "fixed." They are meant to be loved and to teach and to thrive.

STACEY NERDIN (MOTHER OF PANSEXUAL DAUGHTER)

I'm not sure we have more gay people now; maybe we just have a language for describing what people are experiencing.

And if there really ARE more gay people now, could that be an accident? We talk all the time in the Church about Heavenly Father sending us to the time and place we're meant to be. What if Heavenly Father has purposely sent more of these spirits to earth at this time? If that's the case, maybe He's giving us an opportunity to show just how Christian we are.

Some may feel LGBTQ people [are] "celebrated" in this world and mention pride flags and parades, etc. Think about that and acknowledge the limited times and places where those things occur or are seen, and then think about the in-and-out, everyday lives of gay people—do we really think they walk through their lives feeling celebrated?

HEATHER ROBERTSON (MOTHER OF GAY DAUGHTER)

I know I'm not the only parent to say that my gay child is intensely spiritual and has always had a connection to Heavenly Father in ways that astound me. So yeah, maybe it [the number of LGBTQ people] is a sign of the last days. Heavenly Father saved His most valiant spirits for this time—spirits who have come to teach us what it means to have Christlike love.

AMANDA SMITH (MOTHER OF BISEXUAL DAUGHTER)

As I have grown to know and love my LGBTQ friends and family, I have felt a closer connection with my Heavenly Father and Savior. I have felt greater love in my life. I have felt peace. I don't believe those are feelings I would feel if I was facing something that was responsible for the destruction of the world.

LIZ MACDONALD (MOTHER OF GAY SON)

I don't think there is any way to quantify past percentages versus current percentages of LGBTQ people. I do think it is probably just about the same. Today, it may seem like there is a higher percentage—but this is likely because people can speak more freely, and it is accepted more.

Watching shows like the *Lavender Scare* and reading up more on LGBTQ history show that it was not acceptable to be gay in society—you would lose your job, your family, your ability to worship. . . . In the case of Alan Turing (World War II enigma code cracker), he was stripped of his job; he was convicted of the crime of gross indecency for having a relationship; and he was required to be chemically castrated. He ended his life a few years later [through suicide]. Certainly, stories like this demonstrate that, in the past, it was not a safe time to be gay.

CHER PETERSON MCCOY (MOTHER OF GAY SON)

I believe in my heart that the LGBTQ souls that are coming down are the true warriors coming down to teach us about Christ's love. I believe [that] as a family in the preexistence, we made choices and discussed it as a family. Knowing my gay son as I do, he stepped up and said, "I'll do this." He takes on the hardest tasks and has been my most spiritual child. These are the children that we are so incredibly blessed to have in all of our lives. So is this a manifestation of the last days? Yes, and we better get ready because a lot of people may fail this test in showing love. When people state that being gay is chosen, my answer is yes—in the preexistence the most righteous answered the call.

EMILY EARL NELSON (MOTHER OF GAY SON)

We don't actually know if there are more LGBTQ people or not. It's likely that there are not more and it only seems like there are more because more are coming out of the closet as society becomes more accepting. LGBTQ people are feeling more comfortable revealing their true selves to the world.

If, in fact, there are more LGBTQ people, I think we can safely assume that it is by divine design for a divine purpose. God created LGBTQ people. He is in charge, and He knows what He is doing.

CAROL M. COLVIN (MOTHER OF GAY SON AND BISEXUAL DAUGHTER)

First, there is no way of knowing if there are more LGBTQ people now. Not so long ago, it was dangerous to admit being LGBTQ. When my son was in high school, one boy came out and was beaten so badly, he was in a coma for six months. Last year at the same school, our gay exchange student was one of the most popular kids on campus. There may be more LGBTQ people now, but it may just be that it's safer to admit it. Also, if there are more LGBTQ people now, it's a good thing, because they are teaching the world how to love better. They are helping to prepare the rest of us to be in the presence of Jesus Christ in all His glory. We can't "see Him as He is" (Moroni 7:48) unless we are filled with light (love). I am eternally grateful (in a big here-and-now, bursting-with-love way) for my two rainbow kids—gay son and bisexual daughter—and what they have done for our family.

MONICA PHILLIPS (MOTHER OF TRANSGENDER SON)

We don't need to count the LGBTQ population to know we are in the last days. There is evil around us for sure, and Satan is having a heyday. I don't believe his work has been to deceive people into being LGBTQ. Instead, he takes these precious children of God and tells them they are worthless. He tells them that there is no place for them in God's plan. He tells them God no longer loves them. He resides in their shame. He also resides in our fears, knowing that our fears will hinder our ability to truly love. His goal is to tear apart families and drive people away from the gospel of Jesus Christ. He is succeeding, but not because this group has been deceived and are now gay or trans. He is succeeding because he is keeping us from coming together as the body of Christ and loving with pure Christlike love. We could do better to help heal those members who are hurting and feel they have no place with us. Every member is vital—without them we cannot function as a Church to our fullest potential. The answer to overcoming Satan, strengthening family, and bringing people to Christ is LOVE.

MATTHEW AYDELOTTE (QUEER MAN)

First of all, of course there are going to be more; there is a bigger population, so there are going to be more queer people. We also aren't being killed as often or dying from conversion therapy and being kicked out and exposed to things like homelessness (as often). Basically, we aren't being killed or forced into hiding as often as we used to be.

KARL MALCHUT (GAY MAN)

I don't think the numbers are different from in the past. LGBTQAI people have always existed, it is nothing new.[36]

JEFF CASE (GAY MAN)

The "wickedness" of which they refer is actually the false imprisonments, murders, social castigations, and pathologizing that are finally coming to an end, allowing for safer visibility. We've always been here.

BRIANT CARTER (GAY MAN)

Back in the sixties, this topic was rather taboo, and when it came up, it was dismissed quickly. That was one of the reasons I never brought it up back then, even though I was gay. I think more people are feeling comfortable with sharing these feelings with others; however, there are still friends of mine who choose not to be so public. We've always been here; and the current openness is not breeding more "converts."

JONATHAN MUIRHEAD (GAY MAN)

Haven't we also been taught that the most valiant souls of God's children have been saved for the last days? Perhaps the "increase" in LGBTQ people and valiant souls are connected somehow.

DAVID DOYLE (GAY MAN)

In the past, LGBT people would conform because the social and economic costs of not conforming were high. As the danger faced for being "out" has decreased, more and more LGBTQ individuals are willing to take the risk of coming out and being known. But there's still risk involved, especially for trans women—just look at the number of them who are still killed each year.[37]

Another thing that helps is more people are aware of gender identity language and sexual orientation language to describe what's always been there. When a person learns the word *asexual* or *nonbinary*, they may recognize themselves in the description.

We should all be happy that things are better now than when people hid or killed themselves. That was wickedness and Satan's influence.

ENDNOTES

1. "Becky's Story," The Church of Jesus Christ of Latter-day Saints, accessed February 19, 2019, churchofjesuschrist.org/topics/gay/videos/the-mackintoshs-story. For more on the Mackintosh story, please read Becky Mackintosh's book, *Love Boldly: Embracing Your LGBTQ Loved Ones and Your Faith* (Springville, UT: Cedar Fort, 2019).
2. "Interview with Elder Dallin H. Oaks and Elder Lance B. Wickman: Same-Gender Attraction," 2006, Newsroom, The Church of Jesus Christ of Latter-day Saints, newsroom.churchofjesuschrist.org/article/interview-oaks-wickman-same-gender-attraction.
3. M. Russell Ballard, "The Lord Needs You Now!", *Ensign*, September 2015, churchofjesuschrist.org/study/ensign/2015/09/the-lord-needs-you-now.
4. "Sexual Orientation Is Not a Choice," Resources, *Listen, Learn, & Love*, January 2018, listenlearnandlove.org/articles. The website listenlearnandlove.org is a Latter-day Saint LGBTQ resource center. It is not an official Church-sponsored website or organization. Its mission is to support the Church and our LGBTQ members.

5. Schilaty, "What I Wish People Understood," benschilaty.blogspot.com/2018/04/what-i-wish-people-understood.html.
6. Ballard, "Questions and Answers."
7. See listenlearnandlove.org/solving-porn-drug-abuse-podcasts for episodes focused on pornography.
8. Episode 104 of the *Listen, Love & Learn* podcast.
9. *God Loveth His Children* (Salt Lake City: The Church of Jesus Christ of Latter-day Saints, 2007), churchofjesuschrist.org/manual/god-loveth-his-children/god-loveth-his-children, emphasis added.
10. Henri J. M. Nouwen, *The Wounded Healer: Ministry in Contemporary Society* (New York: Doubleday, 1972).
11. Jeffrey R. Holland, "Like a Broken Vessel," (general conference address, Salt Lake City, October 2013), churchofjesuschrist.org/study/general-conference/2013/10/like-a-broken-vessel.
12. See A. L. Roberts, M. M. Glymour, and K. C. Koenen, "Does Maltreatment in Childhood Affect Sexual Orientation in Adulthood?" *Archives of Sexual Behavior 42*, no. 2 (2013): 161–71, available at National Center for Biotechnology Information, ncbi.nlm.nih.gov/pmc/articles/PMC3535560/.
13. Christofferson, *That We May Be One,* 17.
14. See American Psychological Association, "Report of the American Psychological Association Task Force on Appropriate Therapeutic Responses to Sexual Orientation" (2009), 73, apa.org/pi/lgbt/resources/therapeutic-response.pdf.
15. "Interview with Elder Dallin H. Oaks and Elder Lance B. Wickman: Same-Gender Attraction," 2006.
16. Jeffrey R. Holland, "Helping Those Who Struggle with Same-Gender Attraction," *Ensign*, October 2007, churchofjesuschrist.org/study/ensign/2007/10/helping-those-who-struggle-with-same-gender-attraction.
17. See American Psychological Association, "Report of the American Psychological Association Task Force on Appropriate Therapeutic Responses to Sexual Orientation" (2009), 73, apa.org/pi/lgbt/resources/therapeutic-response.pdf.
18. See Stephan O. Murray, *Homosexualities* (Chicago: University of Chicago Press, 2000); and Bruce Bagemihl, *Biological Exuberance: Animal Homosexuality and Natural Diversity* (New York: St. Martin's Press, 1999).
19. American Academy of Child and Adolescent Psychiatry, "Children with Lesbian, Gay, Bisexual and Transgender Parents," Facts for Families, no. 92 (August 2013), aacap.org/App_Themes/AACAP/docs/facts_for_families/92_children_with_lesbian_gay_bisexual_transgender_parents.pdf.
20. Please check out the short film created by Bryan Fugal at longhaulfilm.com/.
21. Jenny Mathews in episode 94 also talks about her love and support for her gay father and the difficult road he walks. Episodes with children talking

about their LGBTQ parents can be found atlistenlearnandlove.org/straight-kids-and-lgbtq-parents.

22. Evan and Cheryl Smith have created www.gayldscrossroads.org to host a navigable e-book that "shares the personal story of [Evan] learning through his calling [as bishop] why he should try to be an LGBTQ ally and how that helped his teenage son finally feel comfortable opening up to him about being gay. [The book] uses numerous resources to examine church teachings about gay sexual orientation and explores a scripture-based path to a more hopeful doctrine."
23. American Academy of Child and Adolescent Psychiatry, "Children with Lesbian, Gay, Bisexual and Transgender Parents," *Facts for Families*, no. 92 (August 2013), aacap.org/App_Themes/AACAP/docs/facts_for_families/92_children_with_lesbian_gay_bisexual_transgender_parents.pdf.
24. Dr. Qazi Rahman, "'Gay genes': science is on the right track, we're born this way. Let's deal with it," *The Guardian*, July 24, 2015, theguardian.com/science/blog/2015/jul/24/gay-genes-science-is-on-the-right-track-were-born-this-way-lets-deal-with-it. Pam Belluck, "Many Genes Influence Same-Sex Sexuality, Not a Single 'Gay Gene'," New York Times, August 29, 2019, nytimes.com/2019/08/29/science/gay-gene-sex.html.
25. Michael Balter, "Homosexuality may be caused by chemical modifications to DNA," *Science Magazine*, October 8, 2015, sciencemag.org/news/2015/10/homosexuality-may-be-caused-chemical-modifications-dna.
26. Howard W. Hunter, "All Are Alike unto God," *Ensign*, June 1979, churchofjesuschrist.org/study/ensign/1979/06/all-are-alike-unto-god?lang=eng.
27. Dieter F. Uchtdorf, "Four Titles" (general conference address, Salt Lake City, April 2013), churchofjesuschrist.org/study/general-conference/2013/04/four-titles, emphasis added.
28. Some of my friends have what I consider a disability or birth defect, but they do not see themselves this way. Like our LGBT friends, they too feel that there is nothing to be healed in the next life. However, others do want to be healed. We should listen to each person about their hopes for the next life.
29. See episode 218 of *Listen, Learn & Love* podcast.
30. See episodes 7, 15 and 26 of *America's Principal*, americasprincipal.org/podcast-episodes.html.
31. "Same-Sex Attraction," *Counseling Resources*, The Church of Jesus Christ of Latter-day Saints, providentliving.churchofjesuschrist.org/leader/ministering-resources (only accessible to members of ward and stake councils).
32. See Salvatore Ioverno, Alexander B. Belser, Roberto Baiocco, Arnold H. Grossman, and Stephen T. Russell, "The Protective Role of Gay-Straight Alliances for Lesbian, Gay, Bisexual, and Questioning

Students: A Prospective Analysis," *Psychology of Sexual Orientation and Gender Diversity 3*, no. 4 (December 2016): 397–406, available at National Center for Biotechnology Information, ncbi.nlm.nih.gov/pmc/articles/PMC5193472/.

33. Walls NE, Freedenthal S, and Wisneski H, "Suicidal Ideation and Attempts among Sexual Minority Youths Receiving Social Services," *Social Work 53*, no. 1 (2008): 21–29.
34. Rose Eveleth, "Simply Having a Gay Straight Alliance Reduces Suicide Risk for All Students," Smithsonian, January 23, 2014, smithsonianmag.com/smart-news/simply-having-gay-straight-alliance-reduces-suicide-risk-all-students-180949462/?fbclid=IwAR2wcPRQeEuNGCrqwi1EWg-uxwaReFF5J5Cyti562HmS9Oh-YWNSPtiHJdM.
35. See northstarlds.org/.
36. See Sarah Prager, "Queer and Trans People Have Always Existed," *Advocate*, October 22, 2018, advocate.com/commentary/2015/10/02/lgbt-history-da-vinci-degeneres.
37. "A National Epidemic: Fatal Anti-Transgender Violence in the United States in 2019," Human Rights Campaign, hrc.org/resources/a-national-epidemic-fatal-anti-trans-violence-in-the-united-states-in-2019

CHAPTER 4

FALSE STATEMENTS ABOUT LGBTQ PEOPLE

False Statement 1:

Youth and young adults are too young to know if they are LGBTQ.

A consistent theme on the *Listen, Learn & Love* podcast is that LGBTQ individuals are generally aware of their sexuality and gender identity at a young age. They may not have vocabulary to describe how they are feeling or why they know they are different, and they often need to come out to themselves before they can come out to others. After meeting with and hearing stories from hundreds of our LGBTQ members, I believe this statement is false. Tom Christofferson, for example, wrote, "I guess I have always known [I was gay] too, or at least from about age five, when I didn't have language to describe it. What I did have was a profound sense that I was different from my four older brothers in an important but not-to-be-talked-about way. In junior high school, I looked up the word homosexuality in the library dictionary, my heart pounding in my ears, afraid someone would look over my shoulder and learn what had just been confirmed to me."[1]

We should honor what children are feeling and saying, even though that may bring us unsettled feelings about their future. Yes, there is a lot of fear for the future of an LGBTQ child, but the earlier an LGBTQ child is out to their parents, the better the family can come together to support their child, receive personal revelation, and access and use needed resources.

CALEB JONES (FATHER OF GAY SON)

We ought to trust an LGBTQ person's understanding of their sexual orientation just as much as we would a heterosexual person's understanding of their sexual orientation. There is no evidence that LGBTQ people have any less or delayed ability to understand their own sexual orientation.

WHITNEY FRANK (MOTHER OF GAY SON)

The younger the better! As a parent, I am so grateful that my fourteen-year-old told me he was gay. I wish that he had felt safe enough to tell me when he first knew—at age twelve. I want to be the person who helps him process his emotions and feelings about ALL significant aspects of his reality.

KAREN PENMAN (MOTHER OF TRANSGENDER SON)

I knew that I liked boys at a very young age. I don't think that it's so unrealistic that LGB people would know that they like a person of the same gender. As far as transgender goes, my son exhibited feelings and behavior to us as young as three that he was a boy, instead of a girl. He did not get to do anything about it really except for dressing [like a boy] until he was a teenager.

MATT ROBERTSON (FATHER OF GAY DAUGHTER)

LGBTQ children experience the beginnings of attraction and a sense of gender identity around the same age as everyone else. But there is a huge difference in the feedback they receive when they express that awareness. For example, straight kids are never told they should hold off on putting a label on themselves. This is part of how the shame, the awareness of being "broken" or "wrong" begins. Yes, they know they are LGBTQ at a young age. These precious young children also carry, to varying degrees, the burden of hiding that identity.

MICHELLE PERRY (MOTHER OF TRANSGENDER SON)

Recently a ward member contacted me privately to ask me some questions because her three-year-old was showing signs of dysphoria (refuses to wear dresses and is adamant that she is a boy). I love that this family was willing to take the time to learn and prepare themselves and work at creating an environment in their home where their daughter won't be shamed. I think being open to the idea that a child just might know these things early on, will give the parents a chance to learn and grow together while their child makes these discoveries about themself.

PAM KEENY (MOTHER OF GAY SON)

I can only go by what my child told me. He knew he didn't feel or think the same way as his friends. It wasn't sexual at all, but the jokes and the crushes just didn't feel right to him. It was in junior high it started to really come together that he was gay, but he tried to deny it for years. His earliest notion of "differentness" came when he was only eight.

MARISSA HARDY (MOTHER OF TWO GAY DAUGHTERS AND TRANSGENDER SON)

In kindergarten my oldest sat around with other classmates talking about who they were going to marry. When she picked a girl, everyone laughed, and she started to hide that aspect and felt shame about it, which had negative effects on her self-esteem. (I only learned about the kindergarten incident after she came out.) In contrast, when one of [my other daughters] was in kindergarten, she asked me if a girl could marry another girl. I told her, "in some states" (which was the situation then). She told me she would move there to marry her best friend. I said okay and moved on. We didn't label it then. She's now in high school and loves to tell her friends she came out at six. She doesn't have the shame about it her older sister did.

LORI BOLLAND EMBREE (MOTHER OF TWO LGBTQ+ CHILDREN)

They are not too young to know they are children of God.

BECKY EDWARDS (MOTHER OF GAY SON)

I had a crush on a boy in the second grade, passing notes and exchanging gifts at school, just like many other children our age. If straight people can have crushes that young, why would it be any different for gay children? Many of them don't have words to label what they're feeling, but they know they don't fit the norm. Many of them don't enjoy the same activities [other] kids of their gender enjoy—like boys enjoying playing with Barbies rather than sports. And many of them have crushes on other kids of the same gender, just as many young straight kids have crushes on kids of the opposite gender.

DREW ARMSTRONG (FATHER OF TRANSGENDER SON)

[Our son] came out to us as transgender at age three. I feel blessed that this was the case as I have never thought he was choosing this. He did not figure out he liked girls till he was about thirteen. Just wasn't specifically interested.

JAKE SHEPHERD (GAY MAN)

I knew at eleven.

KARL MALCHUT (GAY MAN)

I knew around middle school.

SAM SKIDMORE (GAY MAN)

Is there a magical number when somebody is suddenly ready to know their sexuality? If a child at the age of eight knows enough to choose to dedicate their entire lives to following Jesus, then I think they would also be old enough to understand if they prefer one sex over the other (or both/neither sex).

JONATHAN MUIRHEAD (GAY MAN)

If they are old enough to learn about and see heterosexuality and being male/female, then they are old enough to learn about the diversity that exists for both sexuality and gender.

False Statement 2:

Being LGBTQ is just a phase.

Closely aligned with the "they are too young to know" is the idea that "it's just a phase." I'd like to address two versions of the idea:

Version one is the belief that someone who is cishet will go through a phase of believing they are LGBTQ and eventually return to being cishet. While this could be true in some short-term situations, based on my experience, the vast majority of LGBTQ people truly are LGBTQ. Further, I'm not sure that if a person "tried being LGBTQ," it would change that person's orientation.[2] We have learned that conversion therapy has not been successful in making LGBTQ people cishet, so I don't believe the reverse is possible. Yes, there may be some exceptions, but we shouldn't apply those stories to others and demand the same outcome. As discussed in earlier sections, being LGBTQ can be a difficult road, and it seems unlikely that someone would choose this path.

Some who believe this false statement point to LG members who have ended same-sex relationships and returned to full Church fellowship. In my experience, these members are still LG. One stake president, at the baptism of a gay man, was asked if this brother would still be gay now that he was a member of the Church. The stake president answered yes—baptism doesn't change a person's orientation.

Dennis Schleicher, a gay convert and author of *Is He Nuts? Why a Gay Man Would Become a Member of the Church of Jesus Christ*, tells his story of being gay before and after joining the Church.[3] Dennis and two other gay converts, Patrick Patterson and Jerry Chong, have been on my podcast to share their stories. All three report being gay before their baptisms and after.[4] These good men are helping other LGBTQ people consider joining our church without suggesting a person's sexuality or gender will change as a result.

Version two of this myth is the idea that someone within the LGBTQ spectrum moves to another identity within the LGBTQ spectrum. I have seen this happen at times and feel at peace that this is an honest reflection of people's feelings. When I see this happen, I accept their reality. It doesn't cost me anything, and they don't need to clear some hurdle before I accept them. I don't roll my eyes and think, "Here we go again."

Perhaps the most common shift is from bisexual to LG. Since being gay is often looked down upon, one may first identify as bisexual because it feels safer. Or perhaps they are still in the process of fully understanding their orientation. However, when someone comes out as bisexual, we shouldn't conclude they are LG. There are many people who are indeed bisexual. Several have been on my podcast.

When one identifies as LGBTQ we should honor and validate how they feel. Their feelings may change based on time, personal revelation, and increased self-understanding. It is their road to walk, and our role is to walk alongside them as a trusted friend, parent, or local leader. Sometimes there are additional "coming outs" as they grow to better understand their sexual orientation or gender identity.

CALEB JONES (FATHER OF GAY SON)

In what could be the highest stakes [legal case for] the whole industry of conversion therapy (Ferguson v. JONAH), and during an extended period of evidence and witness review, JONAH could not produce a single witness who testified that their sexual orientation was changed.[5]

However, and this is important, sexual attraction is more than just heterosexual or homosexual. There's bisexuality or pansexuality (to name just two), which could appear from the outside as "phases" when, in fact, they are different types of sexual attraction altogether. A bisexual or pansexual person does not become heterosexual just because they are with someone of the opposite gender and vice versa; they do not become homosexual just because they are with someone of the same gender.

I'd also add that grace needs to be extended to people (especially youth). Sexuality may develop over time (it's not necessarily an instantaneous all or nothing).

These facts underscore that families/friends of LGBTQ youth should see their role as being supportive and accepting, not prescriptive and condemning:

1. LGB youth who come from highly rejecting families are 8.4 times as likely to have attempted suicide as LGB peers who reported no or low levels of family rejection, 5.9 times more likely to report high levels of depression, 3.4 times more likely to use illegal drugs, and 3.4 times more likely to report having engaged in unprotected sex.[6]
2. LGBTQ youth who have undergone conversion therapy are more than twice as likely to attempt suicide as those who did not.[7]
3. Families who accept LGBT family members reduce suicide rates of those LGBT family members by 50 percent.[8]
4. An LGBT youth who has just one accepting adult in their life reduces suicide rates by 40 percent for the LGBT youth.[9]

Whatever we might think about root causes or fluidity/phases, it seems clear that rejection and denial leads to destructive outcomes.

WHITNEY FRANK (MOTHER OF GAY SON)

I understand why people feel this way because my son desperately hoped that being gay was a phase. He begged God in prayer every night for two years for it to pass. Finally, feeling completely defeated, desperate, and devastated, he accepted that it was not going away, and he came out to me. It was then my turn to hope it was a phase.

Certainly, there are many phases that we experience—jobs are gained/jobs are lost, babies are born/conception is difficult, health is good/health is poor, children are young/children grow older, family dynamics are peaceful/family dynamics are difficult, prosperity occurs/finances are tight. If someone I know is dealing with a challenge, how could I possibly know if it is a phase or not? How could I possibly know more about a situation than the person who is actually dealing with it?

Hoping that this is a phase is a defense mechanism, like denial is part of the grief process. By hoping something is not true, we can buffer the impact of difficult emotions and situations. I had to find the strength to face my complicated, painful, paradigm-shifting emotions because my son needed my help in working through his devastation. Being gay was not a phase that passed, but thankfully devastation and desperation were.

KIM CRUMP (MOTHER OF GAY SON)

I was just talking to a member of my ward, and he confided in me that it's hard to think it's not a choice when you see celebrities or teens claiming they are bi or gay and then change their minds or flip flop. I know this happens once in a while, but [not believing what someone says about their sexuality] does the LGBTQ population such a disservice.

Trust is also another issue. People are telling the truth about their sexuality, and we need to take people for their word on this. That's what I tried to explain to my friend.

MONICA PHILLIPS (MOTHER OF TRANSGENDER SON)

It's not up to us to decide if it is a phase or not. It's up to us to provide a loving family unit so that our children can figure this out in a safe, Christ-centered environment. I never realized the impact that our family relationships had on our kids until I found myself prepping for a talk on eternal families. I decided to ask my older kids what being a part of a family meant to them, and the response from my trans son blew me away. He shared his thoughts with me through a letter that he wrote while on his mission. At this time, we knew about the gender dysphoria, but he was not out publicly. Here is what he had to say.

"My family has given me a setting where I can learn and grow. It's a safe zone for expressing, discussing, and applying what I learn. It's a place to make mistakes. It's a place to forgive and to be forgiven. It's a place where we learn to share, learn to be humble, and learn to serve. It's the only place where we can really, truly learn the doctrine of Christ because it is the only place where we experience even the tiniest bit of His unconditional love. Having a family helps me to feel that love and learn how to have that same love for others and grow to be more and more like my Savior. I feel like we live in a world built of temporary things. Everything is breakable, everything can be bought in a bigger and better version, and everything can be thrown away. The family is built out of eternal things. It is built on the foundation of Christ, and it can't be thrown away or upgraded. It is only by work, love, and service that we progress together to eternal life, and those kinds of lessons and that kind of joy cannot be found in very many other places."

His thoughts made me realize how vitally important my role as a parent is and how families can provide the space we each need to learn and grow. I didn't know if the dysphoria "was a phase" (trust me, I hoped and prayed it was!), but I allowed him room to figure this out for himself and his words describe perfectly what our focus should be. These words have become personal family scripture for me! The best we can do for our loved ones is to create a "safe zone" for them to work all this out.

MATT ROBERTSON (FATHER OF GAY DAUGHTER)

There does not appear to be any "correct" speed, timing, or length of process in coming to an understanding of one's sexual orientation. My job as a parent is to create an environment where my child will know she is loved and supported and that I will believe her and walk with her while she figures herself out. Whatever she says, [I] believe her, show love, and show trust. [I] help her think things through and guide her towards healthy choices. But there is no way to attempt to control another's sexual orientation or gender identity without exercising unrighteous dominion.

LORI BOLLAND EMBREE (MOTHER OF TWO LGBTQ+ CHILDREN)

Well, dang it. A person could argue that everything is just a phase. Teenage life is about phases. It's where we try on the things that are out there to see if they fit. Our job as parents and adults is to simply love and accept our kids through all of them. You know—so they can be good, healthy adults, which is also a "phase," I suppose . . . Maybe being straight is a phase too—and that particular phase has more social support than any other social phase ever. So imagine the phases that go against social conventions. That takes some bravery. A lot of people have some pretty amazing kids going through those "phases."

JOSEPH ELDREDGE (GAY MAN)

It's definitely not a phase. Children may be figuring out their sexuality at an earlier age simply because LGBTQ+ topics are much more accessible through technology. They gain the vocabulary of sexuality much faster than their parents ever did. The parents, who did not have the vocabulary or access to queer culture like their children do, understandably believe that "they're too young to know" because they were too young to know at their age. Different times call for a different approach.

DAVID DOYLE (GAY MAN)

Saying "it's just a phase" indicates that this is a temporary condition, one they will outgrow or they will choose to no longer engage in.

For most straight people, their sexual orientation and their labels don't change.

People use labels to describe how they understand themselves. As their understanding changes, or as they become aware of another label that seems to fit better, they should be able to change the label they use. This may appear to others as people going through a phase, but that's not what is going on.

For example, a boy who was socialized to be straight with expectations he'll date and marry a girl, may at some point realize he likes boys. At that time he might choose the label of "bisexual" to indicate that in addition to girls, he has figured out he also likes boys. But as time goes on, he understands that he's not actually attracted to girls in a romantic or sexual way, and so then he may change his label to "gay."

For the majority of people, sexual orientation is stable and unlikely to change. Research shows that some people do experience a change. It's important to understand that the person doesn't choose to have their orientation or gender identity shift. Some people want to change their sexual orientation and will seek treatment and therapy, but research shows that people can't force a change to happen. Sexual fluidity is not something a person chooses.

Whether a person finds a label that better fits how they understand themselves or if the individual has experienced a shift in their orientation, to call it a "phase" can sound condescending. Calling it a "phase" sounds dismissive, that their label and identity are not being taken seriously.

False Statement 3:

If an LGBTQ person is out of the closet, that means they are sexually active.

We need to learn to dispel this false statement. Sexual orientation and sexual behavior are different. When someone comes out of the closet, we should not assume the person is sexually active.

What do we think about when we see a coming-out post or see one of our LGBTQ members walk into church? Do we first think, "Are they keeping the commandments?" "Are they going to leave the Church?" Do we assume they no longer are or want to live the law of chastity? Do we feel a need to remind them of the Church's teachings? In my experience, our LGBTQ members understand the teachings of the Church. Many have read every word ever said by our leaders on this subject. Some are walking encyclopedias.

When we see a single straight member walk into church, we don't wonder to ourselves, "Is he or she acting on 'it'?" We can extend the same courtesy to our LGBTQ members. There should be no double standard.

Let's train our minds to hear LGBTQ voices and not think or talk about behavior. Let's give everyone the benefit of the doubt and not think about sexual activity. We can leave judgment to Heavenly Father and local bishops. As we do this, we free up our mental energy for lifting their burdens and helping them feel welcome in our families and congregations.

KATE CARPENTER (MOTHER OF GAY SON)

No. No more than any straight person is always sexually active.

STACEY NERDIN (MOTHER OF PANSEXUAL DAUGHTER)

One of the first things I almost always say to people about LGBTQ folks is that when someone is talking to you about their sexual orientation, they are not talking to you about their sexual activity. But that's where so many minds go first—sex, sex, sex. Do people look at my husband and I and think about what happens behind closed doors? Gosh, I don't *think* so. So I am constantly trying to instruct people to extract the idea of "sex" from orientation and instead look at LGBTQ folks as people.

KAREN PENMAN (MOTHER OF TRANSGENDER SON)

I would say that most heterosexual people, and mainly men, equate LGBT experience with sex. But when you are a young person and you realize that you have a crush on somebody, it's not about sex. It's about infatuation and butterflies in your stomach. It's not a sexual thing. I think one of the big problems with the way that people are classifying the LGBT experience is that they are thinking automatically of sex. But it's more about liking someone and innocence. That's the way that my attractions began for men. I had a crush on a boy, so I showed him that I liked him.

PAM KEENY (MOTHER OF GAY SON)

This one makes me angry. My son came home from his mission anxious and depressed. We had no idea at the time that he was gay. When we finally found out, it was like a huge weight had been lifted from his shoulders. He continued to go to the temple, and we went together to the temple. He held callings and started dating. He just needed validation that 1) he wasn't crazy, a sinner, or unlovable and 2) that he had support from his family and from his God. Being attracted to other men is one issue. Dating and becoming sexually active is a completely different issue. We don't assume that our other children are sexually active just because they are dating or even seeing someone seriously. The same should go for our LGBTQ children. It's validation, not promiscuity.

CONNIE HICKEN (MOTHER OF GAY SON)

It's about attraction—not sexual activity. Straight people know who they are attracted to without participating in sexual behaviors with them. If we can draw more on our personal experiences, like when we first realized members of the opposite sex were attractive to us, understanding our LGBT friends would be a lot easier. For some reason we like to assume that the differences between us are greater than they really are.

MARION MCCLELLAN (MOTHER OF GAY SON)

When your second grader tells you that they love "so and so," do you assume they are sexually active? When your sixteen-year-old asks a kid to a dance, do you assume they are sexually active? Those are both examples of how people "come out," whether gay or straight.

LYNETTE BRADDOCK (MOTHER OF TRANSGENDER DAUGHTER)

The following instruction is from a resource for ward and stake councils: "Feeling same-sex attraction or choosing to use a sexual identity label (such as gay, lesbian, or bisexual) is not a sin and does not violate Church policy or doctrine. Words like gay and lesbian mean different things to different people.

Identifying as gay may mean a member experiences same-sex attraction but chooses not to act on these feelings. This label may also describe how they express themselves emotionally, physically, romantically, sexually, or politically. Do not assume a member is breaking the law of chastity because they use a sexual identity label."[10]

EVAN SMITH (FATHER OF GAY SON)

That definitely wasn't the case for our son. He came out publicly as part of coming home early from his mission. He hadn't even kissed a boy at that point. I don't think it's unusual for young people today to come out before they have been sexually active at all.

JULIE WOOLLEY (MOTHER OF GAY SON)

I came out as straight when I was fourteen. I was not sexually active till I was twenty and married. But seriously, I think people are sexually active when they are ready, whether they are gay or straight. Being gay doesn't mean being sexually active any more than being straight does.

MONICA PHILLIPS (MOTHER OF TRANSGENDER SON)

I used to think that if someone came out as gay, it implied they were sexually active. On the other hand, if someone told me they were heterosexual, I never just assumed they were sexually active. This is such an unfair assumption. This is why I think many Church members prefer to use the term "same-sex attracted" instead of the label of "gay." For some reason, many still feel that the "gay" label applies only to those who are acting on their attractions.

BECKY EDWARDS (MOTHER OF GAY SON)

When my son came out publicly at seventeen, his mental health improved. He had always wondered if his friends would still be nice to him if they knew who he really was. The hiding can feel so heavy, even suffocating. He needed to breathe. He is not sexually active. He's moral, pure, and virtuous. At Thanksgiving dinner, as we were sharing what we're grateful for, he shared being grateful that not one family member disowned him when he came out as gay. Sadly, he knows LGBTQ kids who aren't that blessed.

JOY SOUTHERN (MOTHER OF TRANSGENDER SON AND BISEXUAL SON)

Definitely not the case for either of my kids! They've had challenges with just finding people to date, especially my transgender son. He's very up front and honest about who he is, and it's been challenging for him to find girls who are still interested in him after he discloses that. It makes me sad that it sometimes changes the way that they see him, but I also have to respect that they have their own individual attractions as well. I would rather have him find someone who adores him fully as he is and doesn't want him to be someone that he is not.

False Statement 4:

LGBTQ people are pedophiles.

Another dangerous myth is that LGBTQ people are, or are more likely to be, pedophiles. This false statement can be extremely hurtful. After people come out, they are often vulnerable, and to be treated as someone who is untrustworthy or guilty of heinous crimes that they did not commit can do an immense amount of damage. They already feel different, and this myth intensifies that ostracization.

The Church teaches this is false with this statement: "Help members understand that being around those who experience same-sex attraction does not mean they will also experience same-sex attraction, nor does the experience of same-sex attraction increase the risk of pedophilia."[11]

Ben Schilaty, a committed member of the Church, wrote on his blog in April 2018:

> I wish more Latter-day Saints could see the hearts of their LGBT brothers and sisters instead of condemning them. My experiences with being open about my sexuality have been overwhelmingly positive. However, there was that active woman who emphatically accused me of being addicted to pornography because that was the only way someone would develop such deviant thoughts as same-sex attractions. There was the bishop's wife who compared me to a pedophile multiple times. The church has some amazing resources, but not nearly enough people know about them. It's easier for them to cling to things [from the past] than to open their minds to the further light and knowledge that has been received and will continue to be received.[12]

The pain Ben felt due to these hurtful statements prevented him from feeling "the balm of Gilead" at church. His experience is an example of how the myth that those who are gay are pedophiles adds to the burdens of our LGBTQ members.

According to the American Psychological Association, children are not more likely to be molested by LGBT parents or their LGBT friends or acquaintances. Gregory Herek, a professor at the University of California–Davis and one of the nation's leading researchers on prejudice against sexual minorities, reviewed a series of studies and found no evidence that gay men molest children at higher rates than heterosexual men.[13]

I hope the following responses are helpful in dispelling this myth, which causes LGBTQ members to feel unwelcome in our congregations or families. Yes, there are examples of LG adults molesting young boys and girls. But there are also examples of straight adults molesting young boys and girls. To pin pedophilia on our LGBTQ members is unfair and adds to the cross they already carry.

HEATHER ROBERTSON (MOTHER OF GAY DAUGHTER)

This statement is based on fear. It keeps someone or a group who we may not know or understand as far away as possible. It justifies this behavior and helps the accuser feel safe but has no basis in reality.

TEMBER HARWARD (GAY MAN MARRIED TO A WOMAN)

I am sexually attracted to adult men, not children. Simple as that. Just because I'm homosexual doesn't mean I have a greater propensity to be pedophilic. The vast majority of pedophiles are heterosexual anyway.[14]

AUSTIN HODGES (GAY MAN)

When I first came out to my parents, they changed very noticeably towards me. I have five younger brothers, and they [my parents] didn't want me watching them alone anymore, didn't want me to take them out, and I was worried it was because they thought I was all of a sudden a pedophile. It hurt a lot.

This line of thinking is what I feel causes the bigotry, fear, hatred, and pain. It's people thinking being gay isn't from God [and] therefore is from the devil. And if it isn't from God, then you aren't "born that way"; therefore something had to have caused it. And the only thing that can cause something so "evil" is something else so evil, so it must have been because you were molested by a pedophile.

If people can see us LGBT as whole, as full of love, as goodness, as designed by God, as healthy, as complete, as perfect, as human—then all of these ideas and fears go away. Pain is changed to healing; fear [is] overcome by love; hate, anger, and bigotry are erased and replaced with understanding, acceptance, and connection.

If people could just see us as whole, all of this would go away.

DAVID DOYLE (GAY MAN)

First, the idea that gay people are pedophiles is a myth. This accusation has traditionally been aimed at gay men. Medical and scientific studies have proven it false. There is no evidence that gay men molest children at higher rates than straight men.[15]

Queer people have the same instincts to be protective of children as everybody else. Being gay does not excuse, explain, or justify the abuse of children.

It's a very damaging perception. Fear that queer people will hurt children has been used to justify discrimination and even fuel violence. This fear has kept queer people from being able to fully participate in society. This falsehood causes many people to be uncomfortable having queer people around children. I have a sister-in-law who never allows me to be alone with my nephews, even for brief moments.

ANNIE HOLLIS (BISEXUAL WOMAN)

This is one of those questions I find very interesting, because while I have most definitely heard this in regard to gay men, I have never heard it in regard to gay women. It's something for me to think about next time I hear it and point out the double standard.

KHRISTIAN TOELUPE (TRANSGENDER WOMAN)

The definition of pedophilia is "sexual feelings directed toward children."

The definition of homosexuality is "sexual attraction towards the same sex."

The definition of bisexuality is "sexual attraction towards both sexes."

The definition of pansexuality is "sexual attraction towards all genders."

There are some who accuse transgender people of being pedophiles. The definition of *transgender* is "denoting or relating to a person whose sense of personal identity and gender does not correspond with their birth sex."[16] As someone who is transgender and is uncomfortable with using public restrooms, I can fully testify that I am not a pedophile.

LGBTQ has no relation to pedophilia.

KURT NIELSEN (GAY MAN)

My bishop had an impression a year before I actually came out to him that I was gay. I was the deacon's quorum adviser at the time when my bishop had this impression. He told me because of his own ignorance, his first thought was he needed to immediately release me from my calling. He related to me that after he had that thought that, in one of the most powerful directions he had ever had in his life, by the Spirit he was told not to release me and that God had me exactly where he wanted me to be. I was grateful for a leader that could be taught by the Spirit.

KYLE ASHWORTH (GAY MAN)

I served as the Young Men's president for four years prior to coming out. After I was released and the ward eventually found out that I was gay, many of the mothers sat down with their sons to ask if they had been molested or coerced by me. I hadn't even considered the idea that my own ward family would think that of me.

False Statement 5:

After we are resurrected, everyone will be cishet.

In December 2015, I instructed the young single adults in my ward about the Church's teachings on eternal marriage, a beautiful doctrine that I sustain and support. During the lesson, I mentioned that in the Resurrection, our LGB members would become straight. That subject was not a central focus of the lesson, and I didn't think much about it until several LGB members told me later that this statement can be hurtful.

Some of our leaders have commented on this subject. In 2006, Elder Lance B. Wickman said:

> One question that might be asked by somebody who is struggling with same-gender attraction is, "Is this something I'm stuck with forever? What bearing does this have on eternal life? If I can somehow make it through this life, when I appear on the other side, what will I be like?"
>
> Gratefully, the answer is that same-gender attraction did not exist in the pre-earth life and neither will it exist in the next life. It is a cir-

> cumstance that for whatever reason or reasons seems to apply right now in mortality, in this nano-second of our eternal existence.[17]

Yes, this statement indicated that everyone will be cishet in the next life, but in 2019 President Oaks stated that there is much we don't know: "What do we really know about conditions in the spirit world? I believe a BYU religion professor's article on this subject had it right—'When we ask ourselves what we know about the spirit world from the standard works, the answer is 'not as much as we often think.'"[18]

The idea that everyone will be cishet in the next life provides hope for many of our LGBTQ members who want to be cishet. However, as part of my responsibility not to add to the burdens of others, I've learned to not make this blanket statement for all LGBTQ members. Though it may be meant to provide hope, it often doesn't make the challenges of daily living any easier for LGBTQ Latter-day Saints. For some, it makes things more difficult.

As I asked LGBTQ members about their feelings on the Resurrection, I was surprised with the range of responses. Some want to be cishet in the next life. Being LGBTQ and a Church member can be a brutal road to travel on, and they would welcome the relief. However, others (including many who are active in the Church) do not view their sexual orientation or gender identity as a weakness, limitation, or liability and therefore not something they feel needs to be fixed in the Resurrection.

For some of our LGBTQ members, suggesting that sexual orientation or gender identity will change in the Resurrection can lead to increased thoughts of suicide as the final option to be cishet. One day on Twitter (where 1,000+ LGBTQ Latter-day Saints are available for me to learn from), I (@Papa_Ostler) asked, "If you are LGBTQ, what are your hopes of the Resurrection to change or not change your sexual orientation or gender identity in the next life?" Vance Bryce (@vancebryce), a gay Latter-day Saint, answered: "If a person teaches your wrong orientation will change to the correct orientation when you die, you should expect they will want to die. Even if someone rules out suicide, living is hard when you exist wrongly."

Ben Schilaty shared his experience with this topic in his April 2018 blog post:[19]

> I wish that people wouldn't try to comfort me by pointing to the next life. I have been told many times that my feelings of same-sex

> attraction are just an affliction of this life that I won't experience in the next life. I can see how some people might think this belief is helpful, but to me it wasn't. I hated my same-sex attractions so much that I yearned to be dead. Death felt like the answer to my problems. During this time, I would have welcomed being diagnosed with cancer because it would have meant the end of my suffering. I would have rather been dead and straight than alive and gay. I have seen how teaching people that they won't experience same-sex attractions in the next life can lead to thoughts of suicide.[20]

Many whom I've met with have expressed feelings of suicide because they are not cishet. Since they are taught they will be "fixed" in the next life, they look to suicide as their final solution. We can all agree we don't want to do or say anything that increases the chance someone will die by suicide.

Often in my visits with LGBTQ Latter-day Saints, we talk about an imaginary big red button on the table labeled "make me cishet." I ask my friends if they would press the button. Many say "yes" with tears in their eyes. They would love to be cishet if it meant they would better fit in at church and in society. It is often isolating and hard to be different. Many, however, especially those who have been walking this road for a while, tell me they would not press the button. They don't see being LGBTQ as a weakness or as something that needs to be changed. They bristle and find it very problematic when someone compares being LGBTQ with having a physical weakness or disability (such as missing a limb), which our church teaches will be corrected in the Resurrection. They do not view their sexuality and gender identity with this lens—they are not disabilities but rather inherent traits.

These individuals see being LGBTQ as one part of their whole essence, which also includes their Christlike attributes, gifts, abilities and talents, and contributions to society. They view these traits along with their sexual orientation and gender identity as all parts of their complete identity as children of Heavenly Parents. So, they would not push the button. I think having that perspective is a great place to be emotionally. Living without shame and having a positive foundation allows people to make more thoughtful decisions moving forward.

Many report having a better relationship with their Heavenly Parents because they don't see themselves as a mistake but as Their children who were created just as our loving Heavenly Parents intended. Believing that they were created intentionally also means believing that there is a purpose for their sexual orientation and gender identity. When people feel a sense of purpose, life begins to have meaning and they are able to better face their challenges.

As you read the following comments from LGBTQ members, you will recognize a variety of viewpoints, including some that do not fit neatly into what we generally believe about the next life. Though it may be challenging at times, I've learned to simultaneously support the Church's teachings and honor the individual personal revelation of LGBTQ Church members, even if they seem to be at odds.

Some may conclude that those who believe they will be LGBTQ in the next life are on the road to leaving the Church and living outside its doctrine. I caution against that conclusion. I don't feel it is required that Church members have the exact same feelings about the next life, and no temple recommend question asks about next-life beliefs. While much is known about the afterlife, there is much we don't know. Many of the following responses are from active Church members who hold temple recommends and have spent hundreds of hours in thought and prayer on this topic. It would be unfair to dismiss their insights. One of the main tenets of the gospel is that each person can receive personal revelation. We should honor the answers these individuals have received, just as we would want others to respect our beliefs and choices that were made based on our own personal revelation. Principles of ministering include listening to others and respecting their feelings, even if we don't feel the same way they do.

If I were teaching that December 2015 YSA lesson again, I would continue to teach the doctrine of eternal marriage, and include insights from LGBTQ members about the next life. They have thought and prayed about this more than I have. I would express the importance of hearing a variety of perspectives and not locking into a position that might inadvertently cause someone to feel that suicide is a good option. I would extend a reminder of how much we do *not* know about the circumstances of the next life.

LANDON LARSEN (GAY MAN)

I believe that I was gay in the premortal existence and that I will be gay after this life and that right now we just don't know all that we will know in the future about how this fits into the plan.

We are taught that after death our spirits will have the same attitudes, appetites, and desires we had at the time of our physical death on earth—"that same spirit which doth possess your bodies at the time that ye go out of this life, that same spirit will have power to possess your body in that eternal world" (Alma 34:34). I have no desire to be married to a woman now. That would not make me happy—it would make me miserable. (I tried and am so grateful that I didn't go through with it). So if I'm being told that I will have the desire to be with a woman after this life (homosexuality would disappear, and I would be heterosexual), then I believe that would make this quoted scripture false.

AUSTIN HODGES (GAY MAN)

When I was growing up and really hating myself, if I had been given a button that would make me straight, I would have pressed it in a heartbeat. I would have given anything for that button. I hated who I am, I thought God hated who I am, and I would have done anything to get rid of it.

The older I've grown and the more I've learned to love me and the more I've come to know how much my Father in Heaven loves me exactly for me, I've come to know that God made me as a gift. Now if I was given a "button," I wouldn't even consider it for a moment. I am exactly who and how I am meant to be, and I truly know it is by divine design.

The more I learn to love myself and the more I learn to listen to God, the harder it is for me to imagine God just taking away this beauty from any of His LGBT children. My orientation doesn't define me, but it is an integral part of who I am. If I became straight all of a sudden in the next life, a huge chunk of me would be missing—a part of my heart would be empty.

I see the way I loved playing the piano growing up. When I started playing the piano, I sounded awful. I hated practice. I hated playing in front of people. I didn't want to play. The more I practiced, the more I learned what a blessing and talent music was to me, the more I began to love piano, and the more I began to use it to bless other people's lives. I started to sound better and better and feel more comfortable being a pianist. What huge blessings music and piano are in my life now. I can't imagine God telling me that my piano was just an experience of mortality and all of a sudden taking a beautiful part of my life away from me because "it's not needed anymore." I see being gay the same way. It is a part of me. It is a beauty that is mine. It has taught me and others so much and has built me into a stronger person.

Ultimately God knows best, and there may be so much more beyond our belief in the worlds to come. Our mortal eyes and hearts cannot comprehend what God has in store, but, being here, experiencing the love and power I have now, I can picture God only magnifying all of his children's beauty and gifts—one of which I fervently believe is the experience of his LGBTQ children.

ANN PACK (TRANSGENDER WOMAN)

I believe that gender is eternal and that my spirit is female. So for me personally, I believe that my gender dysphoria is only temporary, during this life. I know there are others that experience gender dysphoria who believe differently. I'm in no position to tell others what they should believe about their gender dysphoria. That is between them and God.

BRIANT CARTER (GAY MAN)

Being gay is such a central part of my identity that it's difficult to imagine myself otherwise. I take comfort in a God who knows me better than I do, so I'm not too concerned what, or if there will be, changes in this part of my person. I believe there will be lots of changes and developments in the eternities and look forward to them.

BLAIRE OSTLER (BISEXUAL WOMAN)

Queer folks don't need to be "fixed" to be worthy of celestial glory. Queer folks need to be embraced as beautiful children of God with the seeds of divinity in us, and our queerness is part of our godly image.

DALLIN STEELE (GAY MAN)

My only expectation of what happens in the next life is I get to have a conversation with my Savior and Heavenly Father. I hope we will be able to talk, sad cry, happy cry, laugh, ask questions, and get answers. I know They have answers for me that nobody on this earth has. I know They have a love greater for me than anyone in the universe. I know They have the answers, and so I want to be ready to be humble enough to listen, learn, and understand as they explain with the purest love. There are so many confusing and frustrating things in our lives, so I try to focus on my relationship with those who matter most. I believe I will get my answers and all will be made right however it needs to be.

MORGAN BURDI (GAY WOMAN)

I attempted to take my life. Thankfully it didn't happen. This topic in my opinion is definitely a factor for those that do take their lives. I guarantee it. Even if I was successful with my suicide attempt, that wouldn't make me straight in the afterlife. I don't want to be straight in the afterlife. My sexuality is a gift from Heavenly Father.

BRIAN SPITTLER (BISEXUAL MAN)

To suggest that an LGBTQ member's identity is temporary and didn't even exist in the preexistence or the hereafter insinuates that . . . something is wrong in the here and now. It is reduced to a mere attraction that can be categorized as a temptation. This feels so futile. I spent so. much. time trying to do everything I could to overcome this "temptation." This is why LGBTQ members are especially vulnerable to conversion or reparative therapy. I deeply grieve that part of my life. It is not a far stretch to see why people choose to end their lives if they are faced with this reality. You feel like a fraud and a failure.

TEMBER HARWARD (GAY MAN MARRIED TO A WOMAN)

I believe SSA [same-sex attraction] or gender dysphoria are strictly mortal experiences. They are gifts given to us by our Heavenly Father to help us develop the Christlike attributes we need to develop for mortality and ultimately to prepare us for the eternal realm. But, upon our deaths and resurrection, SSA and gender dysphoria will no longer be present, as they negate our eternal identity and destiny to become gods/goddesses after the exact marriage model of our Heavenly Parents.

JOEL MCDONALD (GAY MAN)

I often think that as we progress from this life to the next and onward, things that seem so important and all-encompassing now will seem so small the further we progress. The drama of the elementary school playground seems so foreign and small now; but at the time, we were totally immersed in it and it was so critical in our daily lives. I think our sexual orientation and gender identity may have little importance in our post-mortal experience. If somehow I wake up in the Spirit World being attracted to the opposite sex, I think I would feel a tinge of disappointment. Suddenly being straight would minimize a significant aspect of my mortal experience, one that I don't think of as a physical imperfection needing to be corrected, but as a part of my spiritual being. I hope that my understanding at that time will enable me to accept this possibility, but it's not something I dwell on or hold out hope for. I don't believe my sexual orientation is something that needs to be fixed, either in the Spirit World or in the Resurrection. I feel that such expectations or hopes help fuel suicidal ideation.

DAVID DOYLE (GAY MAN)

Resurrection, as I understand it, isn't fundamentally changing the core of who I am—it's a perfecting of it. I work at becoming more Christlike in how I love and interact with others and at helping the marginalized. Denying my core attributes and gifts doesn't help me in that process.

There's a multitude of scriptures that say all people are alike unto God—that all are privileged and none forbidden. In order to erase our queerness, people are ignoring the teachings about the Resurrection, which talk about restoring the spirit with the body. It doesn't say that the spirit and body will be rebuilt with a new foundation and change of character: "That same spirit which doth possess your bodies at the time that ye go out of this life, that same spirit will have power to possess your body in that eternal world" (Alma 34:34). To say that someone will not be queer when they're resurrected fundamentally alters the scriptural understanding of the resurrection.

My orientation shapes the way I view the world and how I understand myself. It colors so many aspects of my world, not just who I find attractive, but how I love, socialize, and many other things. It's intertwined completely with who I am. So much of how I understand me is tied up in that.

I wish straight people could understand that once I was out and being myself, how happy being gay makes me. There's a reason we talk about being "authentic" to describe how we feel when we stop fighting our nature. Maybe people would view it less as a sin or trial and more as a positive thing to be out.

False Statement 6:

Single life within the Church is the same for LG people as it is for single straight people.

I've heard this comparison several times over the years, and it seemed to make sense since both LG and single straight people are asked to live our doctrine, including the law of chastity, and stay in the Church. After listening to my LG friends, however, I see significant differences between these two groups of people. Understanding these differences helps us minister more effectively and compassionately to our LG members who are working to stay in the Church and helps us better understand why some choose to step away.

Ben Schilaty shares a helpful perspective since both he and his straight sister Lindsay are not married:

> I wish that people would stop comparing single gay members to older single women. The first reason is because our situations are so different. My sister is 36 and single, and we've talked about this a bunch. She gets to date and flirt and pray every night that she'll find a man who will take her to the temple. But my biggest fear is that I'll fall in love with a man. It's much easier to be an active gay Latter-day Saint when I have no dating prospects. The second reason this comparison is unfair is because many of the single women are not doing well. I have many older single friends, and I have sat with them as they have cried because they feel no one wants them. I know that many of my single female friends are doing quite well and thriving, but their singleness has brought much sorrow throughout their lives. A few weeks ago I got a call from a single friend in her mid-30s who lives in a different state. When I asked how she was doing, she burst into tears and said, "How do you do it? How are you happy single? I'm so lonely." So being told, "Older single women are happy so you should just be happy single," is dismissive, invalidating, and not entirely true.[21]

Ben makes an often-overlooked point that comparing straight single people with LG members diminishes the pain that many single people feel in the Church. Though Ben faces his own challenges, he has empathy for the single straight women among us. During my YSA assignment, I learned more of the pain that many of these single sisters feel, and I have wept with them as they shared their desires to be married and have children. They are doing everything they know to achieve this dream, but sometimes that dream is outside of their control. They bravely move forward in a Church that, with its focus on family, can increase their feelings of loneliness. They give back to the community in many worthwhile vocations, often with a focus to serve and lift others. They are some of my heroes.

Conflating the experiences of LG and straight single Latter-day Saints also overlook another important difference between the paths of these two groups: *hope*. Hope is still on the table for Lindsay. She can flirt, pray to find a companion, have crushes, go on dates, introduce her boyfriend to her family or ward members, and not feel guilty. Because she is straight, her hopes for marriage and companionship are still intact. Hope is one of my favorite aspects of our restored Church, and though Lindsay may feel pain and loneliness, she still has hope that one day she will have what she desires.

I've given priesthood blessings to and read some of the patriarchal blessings of our single sisters and strongly believe that those who do not marry in this life will be able to do so in the next life, though I know this trust doesn't negate the pain they feel in mortality. I believe they will have an eternal companion and children with all the accompanying joy. They face a difficult road, but there is hope.

Conversely, Ben and other LG Latter-day Saints choosing to be celibate lack this same kind of hope. Ben lives in a defensive mode, trying *not* to have crushes, look twice at a person he's attracted to, pray to find a companion, or flirt—all things our single straight members are encouraged to do. LG Latter-day Saints may feel shame and self-loathing every time they see someone they are attracted to, something our single straight members don't feel. Instead of feeling hope that their desires for marriage or companionship will be fulfilled, LG Church members often try to shut their feelings down and try to keep themselves from falling in love.

In an *Ensign* article titled "Bearing One Another's Burdens," Elder Holland talks about the lack of hope for a family our LG members face. He quotes these words from a Latter-day Saint with same-sex attraction:

> I face a lifetime of lonely nights and dreary mornings. I attend my YSA ward faithfully and each week leave church knowing that I can never really fit in. I will never teach my son to ride a bike. I will never feel my baby girl hold my finger as she learns to walk. I will never have grandchildren.
>
> I will come home to an empty house, day after day, month after month, decade after decade, anchored only by my hope in Christ. Sometimes I wonder why He would do this to me and ask me to make such an impossible sacrifice. I cry at night when nobody can see. I have not told anybody, not even my parents. They and my friends . . . would reject me if they knew, just as they all have rejected those who have walked this path in front of me. I will live life at the margins. I have the option of either being harassed and avoided for being single, or pitied and ignored for telling the reason. Life looms long before me. Is there no balm in Gilead?[22]

We might be tempted to say that what Ben and other LG Latter-day Saints go through is simply one of life's challenges, similar to ones we all face. But as we follow Elder Holland's example and take a closer look, we can better understand the uniqueness of the road that LG Latter-day Saints must walk. I sometimes try to imagine what the life of an LG Latter-day Saint is like. When I was dating, I was filled with hope that I would find my wife and start a family. That hope was a major focus of my prayers, spiritual growth, temple attendance, mental energy, and family conversations. The hope of a future family provided motivation for academic success. That hope became reality as I met my future wife during my last year at BYU. What if that hope was taken off the table? What would it be like to be an LG Latter-day Saint pursuing career goals without the hope of finding a companion? What if I had to spend emotional capital suppressing same-sex feelings to stay within the teachings of the Church? I wonder how that road would impact my motivation for the future and my emotional health.

I once visited with a cishet man who has a wife and children. As we visited, I learned that he stayed single well into his forties. While that was a lonely road, he prepared throughout his single years to be a wonderful husband and father, including reading, praying, learning, and observing others in successful marriages. What about our LG celibate members? They are locked out of these kinds of internal conversations that provide hope and motivation.

In our YSA ward, Sheila and I worked with the leadership to create a culture focused on things the YSAs could control such as coming unto Christ, living the commandments, and receiving temple ordinances—and less on things they couldn't fully control, such as getting married. This approach, we felt, was not only in line with the gospel but also benefited both our cishet and LG members. Our goal was not to try to get everyone married—a goal that often diminishes single people's sense of worth. We figured that marriage was already high on their radar, and we wanted the young single adults to feel that they were whole now and not that they had to wait until some future event like marriage, graduation, or financial stability to feel that way.

The number of available role models is another significant difference between LG Latter-day Saints and straight single women in the Church. Several single female role models serve in significant callings and professional assignments in the Church. For example, Sharon Eubank serves as the first counselor in the Relief Society General Presidency, and Sheri Dew is currently president and CEO of Deseret Book.[23] Further, at the stake and ward level, single women often serve in significant callings. These wonderful women are making great contributions to the Church, and their skills are mostly valued and appreciated; these women help give vision to our younger single women and set an example for the type of life they can lead. I hope the voices and roles of women within the Church only continue to increase.

However, can you think of any similar role models for our LGBTQ members in the Church? Up until a few years ago, I didn't know any. In recent years, a few have bravely come forward, such as Tom Christofferson, author of *That We May Be One*.[24] Tom is a celibate, gay Latter-day Saint, and many other LGBTQ, active Latter-day Saints have been guests on my podcast. They have my love, admiration, and respect. These members are committed to the gospel, but even they report having to travel a difficult road. I hope we will someday have more role models for our LGBTQ members at all levels of the Church. Having LGBTQ individuals serve in meaningful and visible ways will help give our younger LGBTQ members a clearer road map and a more positive vision of what their lives could be like in the Church.

False Statement 7:

LGBTQ people are not good parents.

This statement can be hurtful to LGBTQ Latter-day Saints, including those who know that they will likely never have children. Implied in this statement is the message that LGBTQ people are somehow unable to nurture or care for others, which is not true. Being LGBTQ does not diminish a person's ability to love and support other people, including children. Like many of the other false statements discussed in this chapter, this message may cause our LGBTQ Church members to believe that they are, by nature, defective and inferior individuals instead of important and valued children of Heavenly Parents.

This may also assume that LGBTQ people could or would do harm to children. We have already mentioned the damaging myth that LGBTQ people are more likely than others to abuse children. In his book *My Dad's a Muslim, My Mom's a Lesbian, and I'm a Latter-day Saint*, Mike Ramsey (an active Latter-day Saint and father of four) talks about his journey being raised by a lesbian mother and her partner.[25] Some people have mistakenly assumed that gay parents cause their children to be gay, but this is not the case.[26] Mike is not gay even though he had a gay mother, and in my experience, many LGBTQ parents actually hope their children are not LGBTQ because they know firsthand how difficult being LGBTQ can be in today's world. Yes, there were some difficult times for Mike and his parents, but all families face challenges. Mike also writes about the beautiful relationship he currently has with his mother and her active role in the lives of his children.[27]

I'm sure some LGBTQ people are not good parents, just as some cishet people are not good parents. But when we hear of LGBTQ people who have children, let's assume the children are being raised by parents who are doing their best and deeply love their children. Let's hope and do what we can to help these families succeed. The quality of people's parenting has much more to do with their ability to develop traits such as patience, love, and understanding than it does with their sexuality or gender identity.

False Statement 8:

Latter-day Saints should lose their temple recommends if they support or associate with LGBTQ individuals.

I decided to include this topic since it has become near and dear to my heart as I've met with and read stories of active, committed Latter-day Saints who have lost (or fear they will lose) temple privileges because they support their LGBTQ friends and family members. I've prayed for guidance to create more understanding and find common ground by drawing on gospel principles and leaders' statements. My hope is that Latter-day Saints who want to participate in temple ordinances will not lose, or fear they will lose, temple privileges because of their feelings or beliefs regarding their LGBTQ friends. I think we can all agree that everyone wins when we lift the burdens of Latter-day Saint LGBTQ members and when more temple ordinances are completed.

BEHAVIOR QUESTIONS AND BELIEF QUESTIONS

I believe in and support all of the temple recommend questions. They can be divided into two categories: questions about behavior and questions about belief. Behavior questions include paying tithing, living the law of chastity, and obeying the Word of Wisdom. Belief questions are about having faith in God and a testimony of the Atonement of Jesus Christ and of the Restoration.

When I conducted temple recommend interviews with young single adults, some could answer positively to all the behavior questions but struggled with some of the belief questions, though they had a "desire to believe" (Alma 32:27) and wanted to attend the temple. We learn in Doctrine and Covenants 46:13-4 that we have different spiritual gifts: "to some it is given to know . . . to others it is given to believe." Elder Uchtdorf similarly teaches: "The Church of Jesus Christ of Latter-day Saints is a place for people with all kinds of testimonies. There are some members of the Church whose testimony is sure and burns brightly within them. Others are still striving to know for themselves. The Church is a home for all to come together, regardless of the depth or the height of our testimony. I know of no sign on the doors of our meetinghouses that says, 'Your testimony must be this tall to enter.'"[28]

Elder Uchtdorf and these scriptures indicate that we should extend latitude or grace to these members doing their best to believe so they can attend the temple. I also felt that temple attendance can help belief grow as taught in Alma 32.

TEMPLE RECOMMEND QUESTION 7 OVERVIEW

Before October 2019, temple recommend question 7 had both a behavior component and a belief component: "Do you support, affiliate with, or agree with any group or individual whose teachings or practices are contrary to or oppose those accepted by The Church of Jesus Christ of Latter-day Saints?" The "affiliate with" phrase marks the behavior component, and the rest of the statement is about belief. Some Latter-day Saints have told me that they asked the leader (or in some cases, the leader expounded on a question, which is against instructions) to interpret the "affiliate with" portion of the question, and in response, the leader said that a person could not associate with an LGBTQ friend or family member who was not living the standards established by the Church. That interpretation has caused a great deal of unsettledness, as family members feel torn between the Church and their loved ones, and LGBTQ individuals feel ostracized by their Latter-day Saint friends and family.

In October 2019, however, question 7 was updated to focus only on belief: "Do you support or promote any teachings, practices, or doctrine contrary to those of The Church of Jesus Christ of Latter-day Saints?"[29]

The revised question no longer has the "affiliate with" wording (the behavior component), helping to eliminate a perceived line in the sand between Latter-day Saints and our LGBTQ friends.

This change in wording better matches the behavior demonstrated by Christ in His ministry (as shared in chapter 2). Christ first went to those whom society had declared were "unworthy" or "unclean" and associated with them, dined with them, loved them, and often healed them. Think of the woman taken in adultery; the man at the pool of Bethesda; the woman with a certain blood issue who touched Christ's garment; Zacchaeus the tax collector, whom Christ invited to dinner; and the Canaanite woman whom the disciples tried to keep from Jesus. Jesus was criticized for associating with these people: "And the Pharisees and scribes murmured, saying, This man receiveth sinners, and eateth with them" (Luke 15:2). By loving and ministering to those who live outside of the Church's teachings, we are following Christ's example. We can create space for different levels of belief regarding question 7 so more committed Latter-day Saints can maintain temple privileges.

HOLDING DIFFERENT POSITIONS ON LEGISLATIVE ISSUES

Can someone be temple worthy and hold a different legislative position from the Church? For example, can Latter-day Saints who support legal gay marriage be considered Church members in good standing as long as they support Church leaders and doctrine and are not advocating for change? Elder D. Todd Christofferson outlined the Church's position on this after being asked, "What about [LDS members] who support same-sex marriage privately among family and friends or publicly by posting entries on Facebook, marching in pride parades or belonging to gay-friendly organizations such as Affirmation or Mormons Building Bridges? Can they do so without the threat of losing their church membership or temple privileges?"

Elder Christofferson responded: "We have individual members in the Church with a variety of different opinions, beliefs and positions on these issues and other issues. . . . In our view, it doesn't really become a problem unless someone is out attacking the Church and its leaders—if that's a deliberate and persistent effort and trying to get others to follow them, trying to draw others away, trying to pull people, if you will, out of the Church or away from its teachings and doctrines." That's very different, he said, than someone who backs an LGBTQ-support group such as Affirmation.[30]

In 2016, 47 percent of Latter-day Saint millennials living in the United States supported legal gay marriage.[31] I don't believe they, or any other Latter-day Saint, should lose temple privileges for supporting legal gay marriage as they continue to sustain Church doctrine.

In other legislative examples, in 2018 some Utah Latter-day Saints supported Utah Proposition 2, which would legalize medical marijuana and which the Church opposed, saying it went "far beyond what we consider the appropriate use of medical cannabis."[32] In 2020, a poll showed that 64 percent of active Utah Latter-day Saints said they would favor Utah ratifying the Equal Rights Amendment, while the Church opposed it.[33]

I hope that for legislative issues, we allow members to have different beliefs and feelings. As long as they support and sustain our leaders, follow Church teachings, and do not campaign for Church doctrine to change, then we should not harbor concerns about their temple worthiness.

HOPING SOMETHING WILL CHANGE IN THE CHURCH

Can someone be temple worthy and hope that certain Church teachings will change, even as they follow those same teachings? For example, is it okay for someone who adheres to the Word of Wisdom to hope (and to share among family or close friends) that coffee or tea consumption will one day be permitted? Can someone hope that women will have more responsibility in the Church or that the Church will someday allow same-sex couples to participate in the Church in some way?

Revisiting Elder Christofferson's words, Latter-day Saints who hope for change should not lose temple privileges as long as they are not "trying to get others to follow them" or "trying to pull people . . . out of the Church or away from its teachings and doctrines." If members open up about their hopes, we should continue to support their temple attendance, avoid criticism, and appreciate the sacrifice and devotion it takes to obey teachings one hopes may change. And perhaps their hopes will be resolved in future adjustments since we know the Restoration is an ongoing process.

I believe we need to create space so Church members can stay in the Church and participate in temple ordinances even if their personal beliefs differ from the majority of Latter-day Saints. Will the Church or temple work really benefit if some of our members doing their best to live the restored gospel leave because they feel they are not welcome? What about new converts who gain a testimony of the restored gospel, are willing to live its teaching and follow our leaders, but hold some views not held by the majority of Latter-day Saints? Patrick Mason, an active Latter-day Saint, talks about creating space for members in his book *Planted*, in which he talks about those who feel "squeezed out":

> Oftentimes our squeezed sisters and brothers fully embrace the basic principles and ordinances of the gospel. But sometimes they feel alienated by things like the dominant political conservatism among the members, or a sense that church membership is an all-or-nothing proposition, or heartfelt questions about whether girls and women have all the opportunities for spiritual growth and recognition in the church that boys and men do, or how the church ministers to our LGBT brothers and sisters. Some people who can bear testimony of all the basic principles of the restored gospel but who disagree with certain aspects of the dominant social, cultural, economic, political or ideological views held by most other members sometimes feel that their presence is unwelcome, or that the things that they feel strongly about are not only dismissed but in some way held in suspicion by fellow members. Feeling isolated, alienated, and sometimes pressured, they sense that there is no place for them in the church in spite of their core commitments. And they leave us.[34]

To me, Patrick Mason's words are consistent with Elder Christofferson's statement. A recent story from Stacy Nerdin, parent of a pansexual daughter, about talking with another active member illustrates the messages of both Elder Christofferson and Patrick Mason:

> She [the other active member] shared her fear as a Church member about where is the "line" between loving and supporting LGBT people and . . . encouraging or condoning. I told her I thought she was making it more complicated than it needed to be. I asked her to think of the covenants she's made—which one would she be breaking by attending a gay wedding? She couldn't point to exactly what covenant or commandment she would be breaking. I reminded her that mercy is a quality that is extended, not taken. We can stand firm in our own commitments and still extend ourselves to people outside of that.
>
> But then she [brought up] the temple question [prior to October 2019] [that] asked, "Do you affiliate with . . . ?" I asked if she's ever asked for any clarification about that. She said she hadn't—she had just

> always assumed it meant getting "too close" to people and situations outside of Church standards. Now, this answer might be different with different leaders, but I told her our stake president clarified that question to me by saying they were most concerned about people who were actively, publicly seeking to dismantle the Church and encouraging others to do the same. He said the question is more about organized efforts and distinct goals opposing the Church—not if you want to go to your gay niece's wedding.

The stake president's answer seems consistent with the principles taught by Elder Christofferson. In Moses 7:18 we read, "And the Lord called his people Zion, because they were of one heart and one mind, and dwelt in righteousness; and there was no poor among them." I've heard some members use the "one heart and one mind" as a call to "get in line" with uniform beliefs. To me "one heart and one mind" means we are all unified in our desire to come unto Christ, follow our leaders, honor our covenants, complete temple ordinances, and serve others. It doesn't mean we all have the same feelings about every church issue.

I hope these thoughts help unite us behind the principles of the temple recommend questions and that fewer Latter-day Saints feel tension wondering if they might lose their temple privileges if they feel different than other Church members or leaders.

As we sustain our leaders, live gospel teachings, and make room for people with different beliefs, our Church is strengthened. More members stay and more converts join, resulting in more temple patrons performing needed ordinances for themselves and for those on the other side waiting for their work to be completed.

False Statement 9:

If we have LGBTQ friends or family in our lives who are not living Church teachings, we are condoning their behavior.

The word *condone* has always been a sticky word for me since it seems to mean different things to different people, especially regarding relationships with our LGBTQ friends. In a 2018 devotional address at Brigham Young University, Professor Eric Huntsman shed some light on this, quoting Tom Christofferson's book: "Accepting others does not mean that we condone, agree with, or conform to their beliefs or choices, but simply that we allow the realities of their lives to be different from our own."[35] The phrase "that we allow the realities of their lives to be different from our own" is an important principle of ministering; we should honor where people are and what they are experiencing, even if it differs from our own experiences. Professor Huntsman further taught, "Whether those different realities mean that [others] look, act, feel, or experience life differently than we do, the unchanging fact is that they are children of loving Heavenly Parents and that the same Jesus suffered and died for them and for us. For not just our LGBTQ+ sisters and brothers but for many people, the choice to love can literally make the difference between life and death."[36]

Professor Huntsman poignantly continued, "We should never fear that we are compromising when we make the choice to love."[37] To love is not to condone behavior that we might disagree with or that we even feel might be harmful to the person we care about; rather, to love others is to be disciples of Christ and to obey one of God's great commandments. By maintaining loving relationships with others in this way is to keep a door of trust and influence open that God may yet use to bless both their lives and ours.

Elder Dale G. Renlund has also provided counsel that should offer comfort to those who worry that loving and associating with others who do not share our beliefs is a form of condoning behavior contrary to gospel teachings: "We may on occasion find ourselves in uncomfortable situations where we differ in doctrine with our acquaintances, friends, and family members. But the doctrine can never be used to justify treating others with anything less than respect and dignity. We can stand firm in our beliefs and have a loving relationship with those who hold differing opinions. It is never an either-or choice. We love and live our doctrine, and we love those who do not live it. We need not create false dichotomies."[38]

Elder Renlund later added:

> We can stand firm in our beliefs and have a loving relationship with those who hold differing opinions. For example, I believe drinking alcohol is a violation of God's law. So what do I do when I am hosting friends who do not believe as I do? My wife and I arrange to go to a restaurant with them where they can order as they choose to. And when they order wine with their meal, I do not get in their faces and call them out as sinners. Similarly, can I be friends with individuals who are living together without the benefit of marriage? Absolutely. And when I am with them, do I stand up in great indignation and call them

to repentance, even though they are presently engaged in behavior I do not agree with? No, of course not. We can stand firm in our beliefs and have a loving relationship with those who hold differing opinions. Let us not forget that the plan of salvation offers the love and mercy of our Savior Jesus Christ to all.[39]

Elder Ronald A. Rasband shares similar thoughts:

> Some of you wrote of the conflict that you've felt in showing #Fairness4All, especially with individuals who see life differently from you. You expressed worry that such friendships might betray your beliefs. I want to reiterate that the Savior is the perfect example of reaching out in love and support. His interest in others was always motivated by a pure love for them. Sometimes we approach relationships with the intent to change the other person. We follow our Savior best when we base our relationships on principles of love. Others posted comments about the struggle they experience in trying to understand and love family members who are gay. I commend you for seeking to follow the Savior's example and pray for His love and understanding. You will be blessed in your efforts to treat your family members with fairness and kindness.[40]

These statements teach it is a false dichotomy that to fully love and follow God we need to stop loving or pull away from His children—even if some of their practices are outside the teachings of our Church.

LAURA STURM (MOTHER OF BISEXUAL SON)

I remember having a discussion a lot of years ago about this topic with my cousin who I'm very close to. Her husband's brother is gay, and he was getting married, and she was initially trying to decide whether to attend the wedding. She basically had a spiritual experience where the Lord told her that she needed to show love to her brother-in-law by attending the wedding.

That got my wheels turning about what the Lord thinks about how we interact with those who believe differently than us. My own son came out as bisexual a couple years after that conversation, and I was blessed to have had many other similar conversations and promptings in preparation for that fact, so I was ready to love and embrace my son in the way the Lord expected of me.

Here are some similar situations that I've thought through or experienced that could be seen as condoning:

Being invited to a baptism or religious ritual of a person in another faith. We believe that infant baptism is an "abomination" in our faith because innocent children have no reason to be baptized, but that did not stop me from celebrating my friend's son's christening. It was a joyous day for their family, and I felt honored to be invited.

Being invited to a dinner to celebrate a new job for a family member's new business that had taken off. This was a real thing that someone near to me had to make a decision on. [The business] was a new manufacturing process for cannabis that has changed the industry and the life of my friend's family member. Did my friend agree with what his sibling's business does? Not even a teeny bit. But did he attend the dinner? Yes. He loves this person and wants them to know that he loves them.

I am highly opposed to abortion, but if someone close to me came to me and confessed they had had one and needed comfort through the healing process, I would take them in my arms and do all that I could to ease their pain.

God's job is to judge; mine is to love.

We believe that a major part of our baptismal covenant is to mourn with those who mourn, but I think it goes the other way too—we should rejoice with those who are rejoicing. True Christlike love dictates meeting people where they are and showing them that we truly care about them by being there for them at the crossroads of their lives—weddings, funerals, and everything in between.

SHAUNA EDWARDS (MOTHER OF LGBTQ CHILD)

The Lord has not asked me to judge other people's decisions about how they live. Each person has the sacred right and responsibility to make their own decisions; I have been commanded to love them. Celebrating life events and milestones with them is loving them. Being happy with them when they are happy is loving them. Loving and accepting people who are important to them is loving them.

HAILEY RUSSELL (MOTHER OF GAY DAUGHTER)

Years ago when I was serving as Young Women president, one of our dear Laurels [sixteen to eighteen years old] became pregnant. She and I had many conversations, and I felt Heavenly Father's love for her deeply. She decided to keep the baby. Her mom rented an event room at a local hotel for a baby shower. Unfortunately, it was planned on a day I was going to be out of town. When I returned, I learned that not one person went to the shower. The whole Relief Society had been invited. Years later this still breaks my heart. Do you think this young woman felt that God still loved her if she didn't feel love from her own ward members? She eventually left the Church, and her whole family went with her.

Attending an important life event has nothing to do with the event. It's about the person. Otherwise, why would we see so many grandparents at a four-year-old's dance recital? It's not about the performance. It's the memory created for that child to see who always shows up—who really loves them.

STACEY NERDIN (MOTHER OF PANSEXUAL DAUGHTER)

It seems like most Church members have managed to work this out in other scenarios, but not gay weddings. For instance, going out to dinner and your friends are having drinks—you're present while they're doing something you don't agree with, but you're able to stand in your values while respecting their agency. . . . Somehow most members are able to understand that nothing about showing up and showing love in these scenarios compromises their covenants or their commitment to the Church. What makes a gay wedding any different? I'm convinced it's because of how it might look to other people. Truly. I've heard it from more than one person: "What would people think?"

When my first daughter came out publicly on Facebook, a friend contacted me privately and sent all her love and support. Then she explained that she couldn't do it on the Facebook post itself because she didn't want anyone else to wonder if her Church values had changed. I was dumbfounded. Ultimately, I feel like the word "condone" is a way we distract ourselves (and others) from getting to the important, uncomfortable work of really loving each other. There's no way that one word should define how we show up for each other (even if it's a gay wedding).

JENNIFER ATKINSON (MOTHER OF GAY SON)

The topic of loving versus condoning was probably the hardest thing for me to sort out in my brain. It took me a long time to grasp the idea that showing support, mostly from a financial perspective, did not mean that I was condoning something. When my son told me he was going to get married to his boyfriend, my immediate feeling was that I did not want to financially support this because it would mean I was condoning his marriage. Just as immediately as I had this thought (and unfortunately verbalized some of it to my son), the Lord let me know that he wanted me to financially support this wedding, by reminding me of the story of the prodigal son and how that father gave his son his fortune, even though he knew he would spend it in a way other than he would choose.

Even after having this reprimand from the Lord, I had to do some research to help me understand whether or not my financial support of a same-sex marriage meant I was still able to answer all of the temple recommend questions in order to qualify to attend the temple. I learned that showing my love and support to my son on one of the most significant days of his life was not the same as supporting groups who are actively trying to tear down the Church. We ended up attending his destination wedding, helping all of his siblings be there, and hosting a dinner celebration after the marriage. It was a day filled with a feeling of unity and love for all of us. I was so happy to have not only my immediate family attend, but also most of my extended family. In hindsight, I can now clearly see the destruction it would have caused to our relationship with our son, had we chosen not to financially support his wedding. I am beyond grateful for the direction and inspiration I received from the Lord, in a very personal way, that loving and supporting people where they are is what matters the most, and that by doing this we are not making a statement about our own beliefs.

CHRISANN RICHINS TOELUPE (MOTHER OF GAY SON AND TRANSGENDER DAUGHTER)

My gay son deserves to be healthy and happy, and if being married and committed to a same-sex partner is part of their journey, of course I will be there to support him. It would be morally wrong for me not to be. I choose love!

ANABEL HITCH (MOTHER OF GAY SON)

A little back story first. My son told us he was going to marry the man he had met and acknowledged that he wanted to be happy. I was torn with the whole thing. Initially it was dealing with the reality that my son was going to choose to live a life of a gay man. He had already told us he was gay, came home from his mission because of it, and had, in his own words, "tried the way the Church wanted him to live," and it made him miserable. I immediately knew I needed to make a choice; I would either push my son away and out of my life or accept this choice. I loved my son, and so there really was no choice. When our stake president attended our ward one Sunday a couple of weeks before the wedding, he sought me out to talk to me. He asked what we had decided about attending the wedding, and I told him I wasn't going to miss it. He grabbed my hand tenderly, looked me in the eye and said, "There is nowhere else you should be!" I was so loved at that moment. Using the official definition of *condone*, I was of course condoning his decision; I chose to accept and allow his wedding to the love of his life. It is not my choice; it is not my life. I had a simple choice, my son or not my son. I am not the one responsible for his choices as he is an adult. It really wasn't about getting my permission (allowing it). As for accepting it, of course I did because I love my son.

DEBRA OAKS COE (MOTHER OF GAY SON)

Our son, a returned missionary and a closeted gay man, decided to come out by announcing his engagement to another man. The engagement took us by surprise. I was honestly very concerned about how this would go in our most conservative Utah ward. I met with our stake president to let him know ahead of time so he would be aware. I didn't know what his reaction would be or what the reaction of our ward would be. We would be the first family in our stake with a same-sex marriage—at least the first that was public about it. As Elder Andersen said, "It is a whirlwind of enormous velocity."[41] We learned that it is a whirlwind of enormous velocity for the whole family.

Our stake presidency understood the need for us to show love and keep our family unified. More important, they understood the need for our ward and stake to show love to our son. The stake president said that going to a wedding is just showing love for the person. It should not be used as a statement of either approval or disapproval. He encouraged us to work at keeping our family unified and our love strong for each other. Just as Elder Cook said, "They need to be part of the family circle . . . let us be at the forefront in terms of expressing love, compassion, and outreach to those and let's not have families exclude or be disrespectful of those who choose a different lifestyle as a result of their feelings about their own gender."[42]

When our son did marry, we received a huge outpouring of love from our ward. Many, including our bishop and stake president, came to the reception to express their love for us and our son. As parents, it drew us closer to our ward family and to Christ's teachings. It was the first I realized just how powerful and healing showing love is, especially in the most difficult circumstances.

KATIE ORMAN (MOTHER OF GAY DAUGHTER)

A few years back, our daughter was dating a girl, and there was an occasional comment between them regarding marriage.

At this point in our journey, we were uncertain about what we would do. We had just paid for a lovely wedding for her sister, who was married in the temple, and we knew that if we weren't willing to pay for her wedding that it would create a huge wedge in our family. Whenever my husband and I would pray regarding situations with our daughter, the answer was always "just love her." Still, my husband had some reservations due to the Church's stance on gay marriage. How would Heavenly Father feel about us paying for a gay wedding? We wanted to come to a clear and united decision before we were faced with the situation so that we didn't say or do something that we would later regret.

At the time, my husband and I were serving in a YSA stake, so we decided to meet with our stake president . . . for some counsel. There were many things that we took away from that meeting, but this really stood out and is applicable to this conversation. He asked us if we would pay for the wedding if our daughter was marrying a man in the temple. Yes, of course. Would we pay for the wedding if our daughter was marrying a man outside of the temple? Again, yes. Then why wouldn't we pay for a wedding if our daughter was marrying a woman outside of the temple? Simple as that!

Our daughter is still unmarried, but when the day comes, not only will we attend, but we will joyfully pay for a lovely wedding, as we did for her brother and sister.

LIZ MACDONALD (MOTHER OF GAY SON)

I bristle each time I hear that someone can or cannot condone anything having to do with an LGBTQ person, whether it is a wedding or their "lifestyle." The definition of *condone* is "to regard or treat something bad or blameworthy as acceptable, forgivable, or harmless." Other synonyms on Merriam-Webster.com are *excuse*, *pardon*, or *forgive*.[43] We are taught by Jesus to love one another: he states that as I have loved you, love one another [see John 13:34]. Further, he teaches us that we are to forgive as he has forgiven us (i.e., that forgiveness is due to his atoning sacrifice, which is much different from my ability to have mercy in forgiving others their mistakes). I do not recall hearing that I am to judge anyone else; in fact, I believe Jesus taught us to avoid judgment of each other because we lack the ability to understand the entirety of their circumstances.

So that condoning comes up regarding a same-sex wedding so often is deeply painful to me. We value the chance in this life to choose and learn from our mistakes and our triumphs.

Of course, when someone is causing physical harm or breaking the law, I believe we are to act; but in the case of a same-sex marriage, I think we can only show our love to someone as we support and celebrate them on a blessed and happy day. Brené Brown states that we are neurologically wired for connection and then goes on to say "I define connection as the energy that exists between people when they feel seen, heard, and valued: when they can give and receive without judgment."[44] I hope that, someday soon, we as a culture can lose the verbiage of "condoning" regarding our LGBTQ brothers and sisters.

SHERINE HARDING SMITH (MOTHER OF GAY SON)

Last night we had a lengthy discussion with our oldest son about just this topic. He was having a hard time picturing himself attending and supporting a future marriage of his brother (who is only sixteen so nothing is happening soon). He loves his brother . . . and has only shown kindness to him but feels like going to the wedding would mean he was supporting something he does not think God supports. I don't think at the Judgment Day God will ever fault us for choosing to love our family. Whatever the "sin" is, whether it be not wearing garments, drinking coffee, I can't ever imagine God saying, "Well, you shouldn't have loved or supported that person because he/she was sinning."

JEFF FOWLER (FATHER OF GAY SON)

This is a sensitive subject near and dear to our hearts. Like others have stated, the terms *condone* versus *accept* seem to position an either-or answer. I don't think an appropriate answer always fits into a nice, tidy box. Our son was married to an incredible man this summer [2019], and we were blessed to experience a day of happiness, tenderness, joy, and there wasn't a dry eye in the audience as these two exchanged vows. . . . We had some family members that chose to not attend, [but] we had a good majority who did attend and spent the day with us. At the end of the day, I think those family members that did attend experienced a wonderful day celebrating the happiness of two people in love and committed to each other and the seriousness of marriage. Those that attended showed love and support; no one questioned beliefs one way or the other. I firmly believe you can accept without condoning when hearts are open.

MATT ROBERTSON (FATHER OF GAY DAUGHTER)

If my teenage daughter someday marries someone who treats her with love and respect; if they lift each other up, make each other better, and share the burdens of life together; if they share a deep and abiding commitment to each other and to doing all the good they can do—if the person she marries is another woman (which at this point seems very likely), then I will be crying tears of joy and shouting the news from the rooftops. I won't condone. I will celebrate.

ENDNOTES

1. Christofferson, *That We May Be One*, 3.
2. Cishet people exploring same-sex physical activity would probably lead to feelings of confusion. I realize there are some voices in society that encourage this type of activity, but I strongly discourage it.
3. Dennis Schleicher, *Is He Nuts? Why a Gay Man Would Become a Member of the Church of Jesus Christ* (Springville, UT: Cedar Fort, 2019).
4. See episodes 39 (Patrick Patterson), 41 (Jerry Chong,) and 108 (Dennis Schleicher) of *Listen, Learn & Love* podcast.
5. "Ferguson v. JONAH," Wikipedia, accessed February 13, 2020, en.wikipedia.org/wiki/Ferguson_v._JONAH.
6. Caitlin Ryan, David Huebner, Rafael M. Diaz, and Jorge Sanchez, "Family Rejection as a Predictor of Negative Health Outcomes in White and Latino Lesbian, Gay, and Bisexual Young Adults," *Pediatrics* 123, no. 1 (January 2009): 346–52, doi.org/10.1542/peds.2007-3524.
7. The Trevor Project, National Survey on LGBTQ Youth Mental Health (2019), thetrevorproject.org/wp-content/uploads/2019/06/The-Trevor-Project-National-Survey-Results-2019.pdf.
8. Caitlin Ryan, Stephen T. Russell, David Huebner, Rafael Diaz, and Jorge Sanchez, "Family Acceptance in Adolescence and the Health of LGBT Young Adults," *Journal of Child and Adolescent Psychiatric Nursing 23*, no. 4 (November 2010): 205–13, doi.org/10.1111/j.1744-6171.2010.00246.x.
9. The Trevor Project, "The Trevor Project Research Brief: Accepting Adults Reduce Suicide Attempts Among LGBTQ Youth," June 2019, thetrevorproject.org/wp-content/uploads/2019/06/Trevor-Project-Accepting-Adult-Research-Brief_June-2019.pdf.
10. "Same-Sex Attraction," *Counseling Resources*, The Church of Jesus Christ of Latter-day Saints, providentliving.churchofjesuschrist.org/leader/ministering-resources (only accessible to members of ward and stake councils).

11. "Same-Sex Attraction," *Counseling Resources*, The Church of Jesus Christ of Latter-day Saints, providentliving.churchofjesuschrist.org/leader/ministering-resources (only accessible to members of ward and stake councils).
12. Ben Schilaty, "What I Wish People Understood," *Ben There, Done That* (blog), April 12, 2018, benschilaty.blogspot.com/2018/04/. This quote was also referenced in chapter 3.
13. "Sexual Orientation, Parents, & Children," *Council Policy Manual*, American Psychological Association, July 28 and 30, 2004, apa.org/about/policy/parenting; Gregory M. Herek, "Facts about Homosexuality and Child Molestation," accessed November 20, 2019, psychology.ucdavis.edu/rainbow/html/facts_molestation.html; Evelyn Schlatter and Robert Steinback, "10 Anti-Gay Myths Debunked," Intelligence Report, Southern Poverty Law Center, February 27, 2011, splcenter.org/fighting-hate/intelligence-report/2011/10-anti-gay-myths-debunked.
14. See Gregory M. Herek, "Facts About Homosexuality and Child Molestation" Psychology, UC Davis, accessed February 12, 2020, psychology.ucdavis.edu/rainbow/html/facts_molestation.html. According to Herek, "The empirical research does not show that gay or bisexual men are any more likely than heterosexual men to molest children. This is not to argue that homosexual and bisexual men never molest children. But there is no scientific basis for asserting that they are more likely than heterosexual men to do so. And . . . many child molesters cannot be characterized as having an adult sexual orientation at all; they are fixated on children."
15. See Herek, "Facts About Homosexuality and Child Molestation."
16. See "LGBTQ+ Basic Terms and Definitions," Office of Diversity, Inclusion, Equity & Access, South Dakota State University, accessed February 12, 2020, sdstate.edu/office-diversity-inclusion-equity-access/lgbtq-basic-terms-and-definitions.
17. "Interview with Elder Dallin H. Oaks and Elder Lance B. Wickman: Same-Gender Attraction," 2006, Newsroom, The Church of Jesus Christ of Latter-day Saints, newsroom.churchofjesuschrist.org/article/interview-oaks-wickman-same-gender-attraction.
18. Dallin H. Oaks, "Trust in the Lord" (general conference address, Salt Lake City, October 2019), churchofjesuschrist.org/study/general-conference/2019/10/17oaks?lang=eng.
19. Ben writes about his experiences as a gay member in the Church on his blog *Ben There, Done That*. Through his own experiences and his work reaching out to other LGBTQ Latter-day Saints, he has shared several valuable insights, which I quote frequently throughout this chapter.
20. Schilaty, "What I Wish People Understood."
21. Ibid.
22. Jeffrey R. Holland, "Bearing One Another's Burdens," *Ensign*, June 2018, churchofjesuschrist.org/study/ensign/2018/06/bearing-one-anothers-burdens.

23. Sheri Dew's talk on grace is one of my all-time favorite talks and was one of the most frequently handed-out articles to my YSAs. See Sheri Dew, "Sweet above All That Is Sweet," *BYU Magazine*, Fall 2014, magazine.byu.edu/article/sheri-dew-sweet-above-all-that-is-sweet/.
24. Tom Christofferson, *That We May Be One: A Gay Mormon's Perspective on Faith and Family* (Salt Lake City: Deseret Book, 2017).
25. Mike Ramsey, *My Dad's a Muslim, My Mom's a Lesbian, and I'm a Latter-day Saint* (Springville, UT: Cedar Fort, 2019).
26. American Academy of Child and Adolescent Psychiatry, "Children with Lesbian, Gay, Bisexual and Transgender Parents," *Facts for Families*, no. 92 (August 2013), aacap.org/App_Themes/AACAP/docs/facts_for_families/92_children_with_lesbian_gay_bisexual_transgender_parents.pdf.
27. For Mike's interview and other interviews with children of LGBTQ parents, please see listenlearnandlove.org/straight-kids-and-lgbtq-parents.
28. Dieter F. Uchtdorf, "Receiving a Testimony of Light and Truth" (general conference address, Salt Lake City, October 2014), churchofjesuschrist.org/study/general-conference/2014/10/receiving-a-testimony-of-light-and-truth?lang=eng.
29. "Church Updates Temple Recommend Interview Questions," Newsroom, The Church of Jesus Christ of Latter-day Saints, October 6, 2019, newsroom.churchofjesuschrist.org/article/october-2019-general-conference-temple-recommend.
30. Dallin H. Oaks and D. Todd Christofferson, interview by Jennifer Napier Pearce, *Trib Talk*, Salt Lake Tribune, January 29, 2015, YouTube video, 8:00, youtube.com/watch?v=UIJ6gL_xc-M&t=619s.
31. Jana Riess, *The Next Mormons: How Millennials Are Changing the LDS Church* (New York: Oxford University Press, 2019), 145.
32. Jason Swensen, "Church Says Yes to Regulated Medical Marijuana but No to Utah Initiative," *Church News*, The Church of Jesus Christ of Latter-day Saints, September 20, 2018, churchofjesuschrist.org/church/news/church-says-yes-to-regulated-medical-marijuana-but-no-to-utah-initiative.
33. Bryan Schott, "Poll Shows Broad Support among Utahns for Ratifying the Equal Rights Amendment," UtahPolicy.com, January 7, 2020, utahpolicy.com/index.php/features/today-at-utah-policy/22596-poll-shows-broad-support-among-utahns-for-ratifying-the-equal-rights-amendment; Becky Jacobs, "LDS Church Announces It Still Opposes Equal Rights Amendment as Supporters Rally at Capitol," Salt Lake Tribune, updated December 4, 2019, sltrib.com/news/2019/12/03/lds-church-announces-it/.
34. Patrick Q. Mason, *Planted: Belief and Belonging in an Age of Doubt* (Salt Lake City: Deseret Book, 2015), 3.
35. Christofferson, *That We May Be One,* 60.

36. Eric D. Huntsman, "Hard Sayings and Safe Spaces: Making Room for Struggle as Well as Faith" (devotional address, Provo, UT, August 7, 2018), speeches.byu.edu/talks/eric-d-huntsman/hard-sayings-and-safe-spaces-making-room-for-both-struggle-and-faith/.
37. Huntsman, "Hard Sayings and Safe Spaces."
38. Dale G. Renlund, "This past Sunday, I participated in a satellite broadcast," Facebook, February 17, 2016, facebook.com/DaleGRenlund/posts/1680589855551190.
39. Dale G. Renlund, "We can stand firm in our beliefs" Facebook, March 28, 2016, facebook.com/DaleGRenlund/posts/1697666753843500.
40. Ronald A. Rasband, "I enjoyed the opportunity to speak at the BYU devotional," Facebook, September 29, 2015, facebook.com/RonaldA-Rasband/posts/458781240991085.
41. Neil L. Andersen, "Spiritual Whirlwinds" (general conference address, Salt Lake City, April 2014), churchofjesuschrist.org/study/general-conference/2014/04/spiritual-whirlwinds.
42. "Let Us Be at the Forefront," The Church of Jesus Christ of Latter-day Saints, video, accessed February 19, 2020, (churchofjesuschrist.org/topics/gay/videos/let-us-be-at-the-forefront).
43. *Merriam-Webster*, s.v. "condone," accessed November 22, 2019, merriam-webster.com/dictionary/condone.
44. Brené Brown, *The Gifts of Imperfection* (Center City, MN: Hazelden Publishing, 2010), oprah.com/own-super-soul-sunday/excerpt-the-gifts-of-imperfection-by-dr-brene-brown/

CHAPTER 5

FALSE STATEMENTS ON WHAT LGBTQ PEOPLE SHOULD DO

False Statement 1:

You should not label yourself as LGBTQ.

The official position of the Church is that people may identify themselves with the labels *gay*, *same-sex attraction, lesbian*, or *bisexual*: "The Church distinguishes between same-sex attraction and homosexual behavior. People who experience same-sex attraction or identify as gay, lesbian, or bisexual can make and keep covenants with God and fully and worthily participate in the Church. Identifying as gay, lesbian, or bisexual or experiencing same-sex attraction is not a sin and does not prohibit one from participating in the Church, holding callings, or attending the temple."[1]

Some Church members, however, have argued that LGBTQ individuals should not take on a label regarding their gender identity or sexuality. They may have the best of intentions. Perhaps they have sincere concern that if someone takes on a label such as *gay*, they will be more likely to leave the Church. Others may feel that taking on such a label reduces the many components of a person's identity down to just one thing. People are, after all, more than just their sexuality or gender identity. Before I heard our LGBTQ members' feelings on this subject, I felt much the same way. However, I now feel differently.

The covenants I made at baptism teach me to show respect as I mourn with others, help bear their burdens, and offer comfort. Part of showing respect to a group of people includes acknowledging that they, as a people, exist. President Ballard did this when he said, "I want anyone who is a member of the Church who is gay or lesbian to know I believe you have a place in the kingdom and recognize that sometimes it may be difficult for you to see where you fit in the Lord's Church, but you do."[2] In this statement, President Ballard uses the terms *gay* and *lesbian* to acknowledge that LGBTQ Latter-day Saints exist and have a place in our Church. President Russell M. Nelson also used these labels (and added *transgender* and *bisexual*) in an address given at Brigham Young University in September 2019.[3] I'm grateful to the examples of Presidents Ballard and Nelson. Using the labels that others use to describe themselves validates their identities and the unique positions they are in—both in our society and in the Church. We can't minister, support, and help our LGBTQ members if we don't first acknowledge that they exist.

Of course, our primary label and identity is that of beloved children of Heavenly Parents. This identity is central to our restored doctrine. However, we often take on additional labels to create a sense of community with others who are in some way similar to us. Belonging to such a community can provide opportunities for us to create authentic connections, share experiences with those who are in a comparable situation, cope with difficult things, and find healing. As I have listened to others and visualized their paths, I have come to understand the need for people to use the labels they choose for themselves. If they feel denied a part of their essence, we may be adding to the shame that they have already been made to feel about who they are.

Letting groups or individuals decide what they want to be called also humanizes them. Some have criticized concerns about using the "correct" label for different races, religions, ethnicities, and sexualities, arguing that people are too easily offended and too worried about "political correctness." But labels are really a matter of respect and humanization. For example, I've learned that the term *illegal alien* dehumanizes a group of people—that is, it erases the positive qualities that make them humans and casts them as negative objects—while *undocumented worker* is a more thoughtful and respectful term. Dehumanizing a group of people makes it easier to say and do unkind things to them.[4]

As we know, Jesus humanized and valued everyone. He set the example by associating with (and teaching about) those who society said He shouldn't be with, such as the woman at the well and the good

Samaritan. Further, Jesus teaches, "Thou shalt love they neighbor as thyself" (Matthew 22:39). I've reflected on why Jesus added "as thyself" to this commandment. It teaches us how to live this commandment: we treat others the same way we want to be treated. We use terms that show respect to an individual, just like we would want to be respected.

Respect means giving individuals the right to be called by their preferred name. For example, Saul changed his name to Paul (see Acts 13:9) to help with his missionary efforts—others didn't choose the name for him. During my college days, I was once introduced to a woman named Kimberley. I then introduced her as Kim to someone else, and she gently and appropriately said her name was Kimberley. I learned an important lesson that day.

Latter-day Saints have been called *Mormons* for more than a century. Sometimes that term has been used without bad intentions, but sometimes it was used by the Church's opponents to mock the Latter-day Saints. In 2018, President Nelson asked both Church members and those not of our religion to stop using that label. Even though *Mormon* may have been okay in the past, today we prefer *Latter-day Saint*, and when people outside our faith use the label we have chosen, we feel respected.

During my YSA service, I met Lee Liston. Lee is a dear friend doing great things with his life, and he was a wonderful member of our ward. Lee is three feet and eleven inches tall. How should I refer to Lee? Well, one day I asked him, and he told me the best term is *little person*. Without asking, I might have used a term offensive to Lee and other little people (such as *midget*, which Lee describes as "one of the harshest terms"). I show respect to Lee by asking what term I should use. Now, I rarely use this term when I see or talk about Lee. I see him first and foremost as a child of God and a fellow human being. But on occasion when we discuss this attribute of Lee's beautiful existence, I try to use language that is respectful to him. Lee may also find community with other little persons with whom he can discuss, share, and draw strength. It wouldn't be fair for someone who is not a little person to ask Lee and his friends to not take on a label or not form a community with one another.

I hope we can see how these examples parallel the issue of labels for LGBTQ Latter-day Saints. Like everyone else, they want to feel respect. Each has the right to decide what label (or no label at all) works for them. Some call themselves *gay*, some use *same-sex attraction*, and some prefer *same-gender attraction*. I don't dictate how they should describe themselves.

Personal names and pronouns often indicate gender, and so many transgender Latter-day Saints use a new first name that reflects their gender identity. I show respect by using their desired first name and the appropriate pronouns (he/she/they). I don't require them to somehow prove their gender before I extend this courtesy. It costs me nothing to call them by their preferred name, but it means everything to them. Yes, understanding our transgender Church members may take us outside of our comfort zone, but showing respect to others is a Christlike behavior that we should all strive for (see chapter 8 for more on transgender Latter-day Saints).

I love the powerful and instructive words of Ben Schilaty:

> I wish I could label myself as I please. I have been told many times by church leaders to not label myself as gay and I obeyed that counsel during my 20s. I didn't want to be gay. I didn't want to be attracted to men. And I hated myself for having those feelings. The times when I didn't identify as gay were the hardest, darkest times in my life. Choosing to identify as gay has been wonderful and freeing. I'm no longer trying to change something about myself that I can't change, but I'm acknowledging the unique circumstances of my life and choosing to live in them. My beliefs and commitment to the restored gospel have not changed since I started labeling myself as gay. I live church standards as much as I always have. But what has changed is that I don't hate myself anymore. I wish church leaders would honor our agency and grant us the freedom to choose how to define ourselves.[5]

Some Church members may feel that by using LGBTQ members' desired labels they will somehow be endorsing all they say and do. But that isn't true. We don't use that same logic for other groups of people. I reflect on Elder Patrick Kearon's powerful general conference talk about refugees.[6] He boldly acknowledged that there was a group of people who needed help, a group he described with the label of *refugees*. I will never forget the image of Elder Uchtdorf, a refugee, who had tears in his eyes as he introduced the next part of the program. Many in our Church have answered our leaders' charge to minister to refugees. Our local Salt Lake City high school is blessed to have more than 250 refugees (as of 2018). My dear wife, Sheila, served over a decade in our public schools, and many others offer services and programs for this group. Before serving them, do we put on our "are they keeping the commandments" glasses? No! We just see them as a group of people who Jesus wants us to help.

And using the *refugee* label better helps us better understand and meet their needs. We can extend the same courtesy to our LGBTQ members.

False Statement 2:

You should not come out.

On Friday, April 26, 2019, BYU student Matt Easton came out as gay during his valedictorian speech at the convocation for the College of Family, Home, and Social Sciences. In the expansive Marriott Center, he declared, "I stand before my family, friends and graduating class today to say that I am proud to be a gay son of God."[7]

Matt's speech was interrupted by applause. The speech, which was approved by the appropriate faculty at BYU, garnered widespread attention from local, national, and international media.[8] Matt did not anticipate the amount of attention he would receive for his speech—it was not meant to be a publicity stunt. During his freshman year, a gay BYU student, Harry Fisher,[9] had died by suicide, which caused Matt to worry about his future and that of his fellow LGBTQ Church members. As a graduating senior, Matt wanted to give hope to other LGBTQ Latter-day Saints. The speech was covered by Church-affiliated media outlets, such as the *Deseret News*, KSL, and *LDS Living*.

Others connected to BYU have recently come out. In late 2018, Stacey Harkey, an actor in BYUtv's series *Studio C*, came out as gay.[10] In February 2019, Charlie Bird, a former Cosmo the Cougar, came out as gay in a *Deseret News* opinion piece.[11] Alongside the online articles covering Matt, Stacey, and Charlie, many comments were posted by readers. Some comments were supportive and others asked questions akin to "Why does he need to come out?'" or "I don't need to tell everyone I'm straight. Why does he need to tell everyone he's gay?" or "A commencement speech was not the right place to come out."

Implicit in "Why do they need to come out?" is an assumption that LGBTQ individuals are not that different or special and their experiences are not significant enough to be discussed publicly. Suggesting that an LGBTQ person shouldn't come out because cishet people don't feel the need to declare their sexual orientation or gender identity ignores the fact that many LGBTQ Church members have unique and difficult challenges that cishet people do not endure. Because of these challenges, the process of learning to accept one's self, like Matt, as a "proud . . . gay son of God," can be a hard journey and is one that deserves to be appreciated and supported.

Suggesting that an LGBTQ person should not come out may be a way to stay emotionally safe. I too have been guilty of not fully considering the experiences of LGBTQ members or my responsibility to lighten their load. The concept of feeling "emotionally safe" is captured by Berta Marquez, an LGBTQ Latter-day Saint who died by suicide on June 25, 2018. These beautiful words from Berta's November 2015 Facebook post were included in her obituary:

> I know it is important to try to protect our hearts—to explain the suffering of others to keep our own hearts from hurting or being confronted with dissonance. I do this sometimes too I think. But please, if you can, try not to explain away our suffering in order to feel emotionally or spiritually comforted and comfortable. We are taught to have a ready answer in all things. If you can, mourn with us, for we are mourning. I know that to many we are the unwashed, the Samaritan, we are other. But we are not. We are yours. If you can, walk with us, talk with us, hear our stories. The resplendent gift of listening is a balm of Gilead.[12]

Berta's formula is not complex. It doesn't require formal academic training. To honor Berta and lighten the burden of our LGBTQ members, let's be better listeners. (Please see chapter 7 for more on listening.)

Elder Christofferson offered the following counsel for how we should respond when someone comes out:

> Initial reactions are critical. And the inclination, the temptation that people have often is anger or rejection. Sometimes it's simply denial, on both sides of the question, whatever it may be. And it's important to have enough self-control to lay all that aside and to have a little patience, and to begin to talk and begin to listen and begin to try to understand better. We lose nothing by spending time together, by trying to understand, even where there's not agreement on a course to follow at the moment or how to respond or how to react. We don't have to do everything today. We don't have to resolve everything in a month or a week or a year. These things are questions of resolution over time and accommodation over time and seeking the will of the Lord over time and guided by Him over time. So, I hope we will give ourselves the time and have the patience to listen and understand and not insist on everything being resolved within a certain framework of time.[13]

On September 15, 2018, I asked the following question on Twitter: "What are good answers for someone who says, 'Why do LGBTQ people need to come out? I don't need to tell everyone I'm straight or cisgender.'" Vance Bryce answered: "The closet can be an isolating place. It was for me. I need my family, friends and ward members to know who I am. If you take Elder Ballard's call to listen to us seriously, you're going to need to know who we are. Straight people do come out. They talk about their crushes, celebrate dating, get married, and wear rings.[14] Having a crush makes me feel unworthy, dating feels deviant, getting married would get me thrown off the good ship Zion. Coming out helped me make sense of the pain."

Another respondent stated, "If people knew [LGBTQ individuals were around], maybe the mean jokes and hurtful words [would] stop. People are more likely to say mean things when they don't think any LGBT people are around."

Ben Schilaty writes:

> When I was 30 I posted my coming out post on my blog. A few days later I was teaching Elders Quorum in my singles ward. When I began the lesson, I had no intention of telling my quorum that I was gay, but I felt prompted to say something, so I did. I awkwardly blurted out, "I'm gay" towards the end of the lesson without much build up. The unexpected way those words came out must've been jarring for some people in the room. I shared a few stories, ended the lesson, and sat down. I remember feeling the comforting presence of the Holy Ghost as I bore my testimony at the end of the lesson and contemplated what had just happened as I sat in my chair. I was recently talking to one of the bishopric members who was present at that lesson. He said that what he remembered most was watching me sit down. He said, "You looked lighter and more relaxed. You looked so relieved. It was evident in your body language that you felt a burden had been taken off your shoulders." He is exactly right. That's how I felt. I had been lying to people and hiding an important part of my life story from my Quorum and it was such a relief to just be honest and not have to hide anymore.[15]

Several LGBTQ YSA friends have told me how relieved they felt after coming out in their wards. Before coming out, people would ask them who they were dating and when they would be getting married. Instead of church being a balm of Gilead, Sunday could be the most difficult day of the week because of triggering comments. Even the days leading up to Sunday could be difficult because of the anxiety they felt about comments they might hear at church. For some, going to church became a better experience after they came out. After coming out and feeling the support of those around them, many LGBTQ people reported a significant relief of stress, anxiety, and, in some cases, suicidal ideation.

Some assume that coming out is associated with leaving the Church and its teachings. Hearing someone call themselves *gay, lesbian, bisexual, transgender,* or *queer* should not cause us to think that they are guilty of some kind of sin or that they no longer believe in or support Church teachings. Occasionally I have seen a "coming out" post on Facebook from one of our LGBTQ Church members. Most of the comments to the post express love and support for the individual. But there are usually a few comments reminding the person of the Church's doctrine on marriage. Our LGBTQ members are well aware of the doctrine of our church. When they post about something as personal as coming out, they make themselves vulnerable. Their intent is usually to let people know this aspect of their lives so they can live more honestly, without fear or shame. Their prayer is that the people whom they love will continue to love them. A reminder about the doctrine on marriage can come across as insensitive. Perhaps a person making that comment feels they are standing up for the Church, but the most helpful thing they can do to minister to that LGBTQ individual is to reassure them of their love and compassion.

One of the stories I've found most helpful to this point is that of my friend Brian Spittler, a bisexual Latter-day Saint married to a woman. I had previously assumed that being bisexual wasn't a big deal; that a bisexual man could easily marry a woman and raise a family the same as a straight man. On my podcast, Brian bravely shared some of his journey.[16] In their marriage, Brian and his wife were open about everything—everything except the fact that Brian was bisexual. It was painful for Brian to not share this aspect of his life with his wife when she shared everything about her life with him. Brian wasn't withholding this information from his wife because he wanted to have a relationship with someone else. He was just worried about how his wife would respond. After some time and with great courage, Brian shared that he was bisexual with his wife, and though it took some time for his wife to process this information, his coming out ultimately made their marriage stronger. Brian is just as committed to his marriage and family as he was before, but now he feels on equal footing with his wife, and their marriage is based on sharing and honesty—pillars of a successful marriage.

Another reason LGBTQ people come out is to feel a greater sense of belonging. Brené Brown explains the powerful difference between belonging and simply fitting in: "Fitting in is about assessing a situation and becoming who you need to be in order to be accepted. Belonging, on the other hand, doesn't require us to change who we are; it requires us to be who we are."[17] Our LGBTQ members report how exhausting it can be to fit into our heteronormative world. Imagine a wooden square peg being hammered into a round hole; under the pressure of trying to fit in, the corners of the square peg splinter. Similarly, when our LGBTQ Latter-day Saints try to change themselves to fit in, they experience emotional pain. The harder the peg is pounded, the more it splinters. Instead of trying to force an LGBTQ person to become a round peg, inflicting pain and hurt along the way, we can help them feel true belonging in our Church by accepting them as who they are—as how our loving Heavenly Parents created them.

In the past, our Church (along with society) taught that someone's sexual orientation could change. As a result, the responsibility to fit in—to become round pegs—was on the shoulders of LGBTQ Latter-day Saints. But now that we know otherwise, the responsibility is on us to create a feeling of belonging by accepting our LGBTQ members just as they are.

There are probably closeted LGBTQ members who do not feel a desire or need to come out, and I do not see those individuals as weak or inauthentic. I believe they are working with their Heavenly Parents to find the best road for them. There should be no universal requirement for our LGBTQ members to come out. We should, however, work to create an environment so that those who do wish to come out can do so with confidence that they will be met with love and support. Reading the perspectives of those who have come out can help us better understand how to help them feel a greater sense of belonging.

BLAKE FISHER (GAY MAN)

I always appreciate when people ask me sincere questions about LGBTQ+ and SSA (same-sex attraction) topics. I'm often asked the following question by straight people who are trying to understand better: "Why do LGBTQ+ people feel like they have to label themselves, 'come out,' or talk about their experience with sexuality? I mean I don't go around talking about my sexuality all the time."

There are many ways to respond to this question, but sometimes I use the following metaphor (let's just say I'm sharing this metaphor with a straight man):

Okay, imagine that you wanted to get away . . . just take a vacation by yourself. You decide to go on a ten-day cruise. You forget to read the fine print, and you discover shortly after leaving port that you are, in fact, on a gay cruise. Wonderful married gay couples, dating couples, and single gay people are everywhere, and they're having a great time.

Many of these people see that you're by yourself and come and talk with you, and yes, most of the time they assume you're gay. They ask you if you're interested in finding a nice guy on the cruise. They ask you about your "type." They even make assumptions about how you live your life, your interests, goals, political views, and religious beliefs. The group will make jokes about shared experiences. "We've all been there," they'll say laughing (even though you've definitely not been there).

Single gay men keep approaching you and striking up innocent flirtatious conversations; some of them even ask you on dates. The married gay couples around you encourage you to go on these dates because they want you to be as happy as they are. You try to decline without hurting anyone's feelings, or "outing yourself" [as straight]. You join these wonderful people in all their activities and have a lot of fun with them, but in the back of your mind is the question, "Would my new friends still like me if 'they knew?' How would that fact [that I'm straight] change the relationships?"

You realize how stressful it is when everyone's assumptions about you, your life, your goals, and your perspective don't match your actual experience. It would be so nice if they just actually had a full picture of your experience and who you are. You don't define your whole life by your sexuality, but you begin to realize that it actually informs more of your choices and conversations than you previously thought. All the people around you talk about sexuality more than they probably realize, but being in the majority, they probably don't realize it.

What do you do?

Perhaps you could say you're simply not interested in dating right now, but that doesn't really address all the other assumptions made about your lifestyle, goals, perspective, religious views, etc. Then you realize that the simplest thing to do would probably be to tell them you're straight (you worry about which label to use).

"Whoa, whoa, whoa . . . don't throw your sexuality in our face!" they'll say. "What you do in your bedroom is your business; the world doesn't need to know your personal stuff." You're a little surprised and even offended when they assume your talking about your sexuality, goals, and experience is automatically connected to an agenda. "You're just wanting attention." What if the married gay couples even assume that you being "out" as a straight man will actually [cause] their children to [become] straight (which would be the worst)? They say that they don't go broadcasting their sexuality all the time and you think, "Well, yeah . . . you don't have to. Everyone assumes you are gay; this whole cruise is designed with the assumption that you're gay." Some will even say, "You only think you're straight, you haven't even really tried being gay . . . you'll see."

Some of the gay people would say, "Oh, we 'still' love you; this doesn't change anything." And then they proceed to talk about gay things, rarely taking time to ask you about your experience. The lesbians on board find out you're a straight man, and they assume you're attracted to all of them, you know, because they're women.

And, of course, there would be many . . . gay people who would be great about you coming out as straight (or *opposite-sex attracted* . . . your choice). They'd apologize about some of the assumptions they made, and they would be excited to learn more about your life, your perspective, and your goals. They would ask if there was anything they could do to make your cruise more comfortable. You don't talk exclusively about sexuality with them, but when it seems pertinent, you feel comfortable talking about it. Awesome.

Once in a while you get a little tired of navigating false assumptions or explaining your sexuality to people, so you think it could be nice to find some other straight people on the cruise to connect with. The "whoa, whoa, whoa-ers" are pretty critical of this decision. They assume you are just looking for other straight people so that you can have sex and showcase your relationship. When you're with your straight friends, the gay majority on the boat can't help but notice, observe, and even comment. Part of you wonders if there are other straight people around you who are keeping quiet, feeling a little lonely. You talk about your sexuality a little more, just in case it could help a "closeted" straight person feel less alone and know where they could find some empathy.

You wonder if it would have been easier just to continue to pretend you're gay. But you remember how frustrating it was to have so many false assumptions made about you, to be set up on dates, to be hit on, and to feel like the people around you didn't see the whole picture of your life (including sexuality) . . . it can be really lonely. Thank heaven for the cool gay people on the cruise who are okay with you being straight (and talking about it).

The End.

This metaphor is clearly imperfect and has a lot of holes, but hopefully it was a little thought provoking, and maybe it gives a little insight about why some people come out. So why do LGBTQ+ and SSA individuals feel like they want to talk about their experience or come out?

There are many reasons (many not addressed in my analogy), but sometimes straight people can understand a little better when they try to imagine if everything was switched. There are also many reasons someone may choose not to talk about their sexuality, and that's fine too. I have generally noticed that people become a lot healthier when they can talk to people about their complete experience.

TEMBER HARWARD (GAY MAN MARRIED TO A WOMAN)

[Coming out is] a way for me to be comfortable with myself and not feel shameful of or hate myself. It's a way for me to let my brothers and sisters know what I'm dealing with or experiencing, so they can support and help me along my path.

DALLIN STEELE (GAY MAN)

As a teenager I wish that I'd had someone out and open, so I would know that I wasn't alone. Being out not only helps me feel free and open about who I am, but I also know it gives me more opportunities to answer doubts and questions that everyone might have.

DAVID DOYLE (GAY MAN)

In my congregation or my neighborhood, I'm taking a risk by disclosing that I'm gay. They could withdraw from me, shun me, not let their children be near me, feel sorry for me. I may have someone decide to lecture me, ask inappropriately invasive questions, like am I "acting on it?," or tell me I'm evil or worse. By sharing my orientation, I'm showing trust in you and am hoping you respect that trust.

JERRY CHONG (GAY MAN)

Coming out is an ongoing process that will continue throughout your life. It does get easier the more you choose to come out. Trust those who support you, and know you make a difference.

We come out because we love you. We come out because we trust you. We come out so that we can truly be ourselves with you.

Both the individual and the parent should come out when they feel comfortable and safe to do so. It will surprise you how many people in your life will support you. It is the fear of rejection and exclusion that keeps people in the closet. You never hear people say, "I wish I had stayed in the closet longer." I have been coming out for thirty-six years now, and I still take a deep breath before I open up to someone new. Sometimes I feel more nervous for them than for myself.

Coming out is a matter of learning to be comfortable in your own skin. For some, this is a long, difficult process. Come out when you feel safe to do so.

BLAIRE OSTLER (BISEXUAL WOMAN)

During pride month, I hear comments from straight folks expressing their frustration. Most commonly I hear, "Can't they just keep that stuff private?"

We listen to heteronormative music where a boy and girl fall in love, get married, and have kids. Ads display heteronormative relationships where a boy proposes to a girl. Movies depict heterosexual love, intimacy, affection, and praise. Heterosexual couples hold hands, cuddle, and kiss in public. Even children's shows depict a princess falling in love with a prince or boys and girls getting crushes on each other at school. We take our children to weddings filled with heterosexual displays of affection.

There's a misconception that heterosexuality is a private affair, while queerness is a publicized affair. Historically and presently, the opposite is true.

VANCE BRYCE (GAY MAN)

I felt isolated and afraid before I came out as gay. I have a wonderful family and many friends. Most of them made fun of gay people and blamed LGBTQ folks for the breakdown of family values and for bringing sorrow to the whole world. I internalized this blame and shame. I prayed every day for over a decade to stop feeling attracted to men. I prayed to die, rather than to frustrate our Heavenly Parents' plan of salvation. I didn't want to be a rebel. I didn't want any attention. I didn't want to be the enemy. The last thing I wanted was to ruin family happiness for eternity.[18] I felt like if I could hollow myself out and remove that whole set of mannerisms, characteristics, emotions, and thoughts that make me gay by myself, I would be worthy to be friends with the righteous kids, a worthy member of my family, and worthy to be called a child of God.

My family and friends had no idea I was carrying this weight. They didn't know I wanted to die. I came out because I needed their support in order to live. I needed connection to my family, friends, and ward. I needed people to help me find the Savior. I needed ministering. It was only by coming out as gay that I was able to get the support I needed to fully accept the Atonement of Jesus Christ. When I came out, I realized that the Savior loved and accepted me. Asking me not to talk about being gay is asking me to isolate myself, to reject ministering, and to deny the blessings of the holy sacrifice of the Son of God. I only came out to God after coming out to friends who didn't reject me. When I came out to God, I learned I was holy.

LAUREN DAILY (GAY WOMAN)

People are presumed [to be] straight. Being in the closet is a lot of different things to a lot of different people. But to me, being in the closet felt like lying. To my family. To my friends. To myself. If people assumed that you, a Latter-day Saint, were actually atheist or something else, wouldn't you feel weird going about your life not getting to show people how proud you are to be you, a proud Latter-day Saint?

JEFF CASE (GAY MAN)

I read/heard this somewhere: I'm not coming out, I'm inviting you in. To further elaborate on that thought, I'm inviting [others] into my world, my intimate space, to know how I love. It's an honor to be invited in. But I do not force anyone to come or to stay. I believe that the way I see the world is unique and that this adds variety to the world. I have something different to contribute. To learn what that is, I invite you in.

DAWN MICHELLE (TRANSGENDER WOMAN)

I feel that when we declare that we are coming out of the closet to reveal to others something about ourselves, that it is simply a way of being genuine and truthful about who we are. Not living a lie and telling others is part of feeling that liberation of being honest with ourselves to others.

BRIAN SPITTLER (BISEXUAL MAN)

I come out because I deserve to be known for who I am and correct all the incorrect assumptions people make about me. Unlike cishet people, queer people have the burden of educating [others] about their experience, and that educating can [make us] so incredibly vulnerable. When people come out, they are putting all of themselves on the line and risk rejection by those whom we love the very most. But we do it. That should tell you how important and valuable it is for human beings to be seen as they really are. I come out because orientation means so much more than who I want to sleep with. It's the lens through which I see the world. I come out because I have hard earned my perspective and it matters and I want to share it with people. I want to be close to people, and I want to feel genuine relationships. I come out because being closeted is hell. I come out because of all the work and effort and exhaustion it took to stay in the closet. People don't understand the effort and hyperawareness queer people go through in order not to tip people off. I look back and think about how . . . all that energy could have gone to creativity, love, education, or any other productive activity, and it feels like a loss. I come out because I decided to make that shift, and I do feel more productive, loving, and educated.

SARAH KEMP (GAY WOMAN)

Why do I need to come out? Because everyone in the Church needs more LGBTQ examples and role models to look to. Because LGBTQ suicide is devastatingly high. I need to come out because as a youth sitting in church, the only stories I heard of members who were gay were either that they left the Church and were overwhelmingly spiteful or that they killed themselves. Those were the only two narratives I saw as a youth, when I was just starting to recognize who I was. After I came out, I felt so much more freedom. I was so much more authentically myself and so much more at peace with myself. Feeling like you have to hide who you are out of fear is exhausting.

I don't go around actively coming out to everyone at church. But because I don't hide it anymore, I no longer pretend that I'm not dating a guy because I'm too busy with school. I no longer make up reasons not to go to that YSA activity. I no longer make up reasons why I don't go to a YSA ward at all. I'm free. "And ye shall know the truth, and the truth shall make you free" (John 8:32).

STANLEY ALVEY (GAY MAN)

There are many reasons that I came out. When I was sixteen years old, I was stuck between a rock and a really hard spot. I was living in a tiny, ultraconservative county, largely filled with members of The Church of Jesus Christ of Latter-day Saints. I figured I had two choices: either I could take my own life to escape the pain of hiding, or I could get on the nearest train and move away from everyone to live a life somewhere else where I wouldn't be shamed for being me. I didn't want to lose my family though.

One Sunday as I sat alone in a pew during sacrament meeting, I prayed for guidance. I prayed one last time for some clarity. And for some odd reason I had taken my patriarchal blessing to church in my scripture bag. I felt like I needed to read it, so I pulled it out, and part of it said, "You should counsel with your parents in all major decisions throughout your life." And the Spirit said, "Just talk to them about this. It's time to tell them." So I texted my mom and dad to meet me at home, and I told them that I had "same-sex attraction" but still wanted to marry a girl. I think this gave them the cushioning to do some learning and growing by my side to prepare them for my future that may include having a husband. It created the ability for me to explore my beliefs and gave us the time to get information and resources. Since I have come out to my family, my friends, and the world, I have become the person God always intended me to be. I have grown closer and come to love each individual more for who they are. My family and friends have grown. Coming out is about saying, "This is who God made me, and I will not be shamed into thinking I am a mistake." It's liberating and can save so many lives.

CHAD CURTIS (GAY MAN IN A MIXED-ORIENTATION MARRIAGE)

Strangely enough, I find quite a bit of overlap in the experience of being a member of the Church and the experience of being queer. I often have nonmember friends or coworkers who ask why I don't drink, smoke, or participate in certain activities on Sunday. When I tell these people about my Church, they understand why some of my actions might be different from theirs. What was once a misunderstanding becomes suddenly clear when I am willing to "come out" as a member of the Church.

I find that coming out as LGBTQ helps resolve questions and misunderstandings others (and particularly other members of the Church) may have about my experience, including marriage and family life. It is a way of letting people know that because of my sexuality, my story may not look like theirs.

SPENCER MICKELSON (GAY MAN)

I think if you state it inversely, it becomes more apparent. "Why do they have to come out?" could just as easily be stated as "Why can't they stay hidden?" It is not psychologically, emotionally, or developmentally healthy for anyone of any gender or sexuality to hide their feelings regarding their gender or sexuality. It is socially acceptable for straight/cis people to make those expressions. Less so for queer people. We come out of hiding to widen the social landscape until being queer is considered normal enough that coming out will be unnecessary. To the individual who feels uncomfortable with someone coming out, that discomfort is why it must be done. Enough people must come out until it is a nonevent and the discomfort of others regarding an LGBTQ person's gender identity or sexuality is negligible or nonexistent.

False Statement 3:

After you come out as LGBTQ, you should stop talking about it.

Not talking about one's sexuality or gender identity with trusted friends and family adds to the burdens of our LGBTQ members. It makes the LGBTQ person feel the family is embarrassed they have an LGBTQ child, which creates shame—one of Satan's greatest tools to feel one is unworthy of Heavenly Father's love. Latter-day Saint parents of LGBTQ children responded to this statement.

STACEY NERDIN (MOTHER OF PANSEXUAL DAUGHTER)

Personally, this [statement] drives me nuts, especially coming from [Church] members (and I hear it a lot). I will often then ask someone how it would feel if a friend said, "Okay, I know you're LDS, but could you please never talk about it or allude to it or act like it?" I have a feeling most members would not respond well to that (and would feel persecuted for it even being suggested). I have also said to others about this: "I'm not sure it's fair or right to ask someone else to act a certain way just so we can feel more comfortable." Because, in my opinion, that's really what it's about.

CAROL M. COLVIN (MOTHER OF GAY SON AND BISEXUAL DAUGHTER)

Coming out is the beginning of living honestly, with full integrity. It would be awful to have to keep quiet again after being brave enough to reveal who you are. People only want LGBTQ people to be quiet about being gay because they are uncomfortable.

LIZ MACDONALD (MOTHER OF GAY SON)

That statement is full of shame and is so damaging. It reminds me of Satan's advice to Adam and Eve to run and hide.

KIM CRUMP (MOTHER OF GAY SON)

How would you like it if we never wanted to hear about your dates you went on, how you love your spouse, that you are so glad you married them. We don't want to see you kiss or hold hands in public ever. Don't even put your arm around them as you sit on the bench at church. It's disgusting, and you are just pushing your relationship in others' faces.

No selfies with your loved one on Facebook and please don't talk about how great they are on Instagram. We don't need to see pictures of you two having fun and living your lives together.

That would be absurd and very unfair and cruel to ask you to do this.

We forget our heterosexual privilege. It is a very real thing.

MARGARET SUTTER (MOTHER OF GAY SON)

My son is dating a great young man. He has mentioned to me that it hurts him that his grandparents don't ask him about his boyfriend and how they're doing. Yet they ask their other grandkids about their dating lives. This is just a small thing, but the small things make up the big things. It is healthy for everyone to be able to talk about different aspects of, and experiences in their lives. We all have an inner desire to be heard and to feel like people are interested in us, as we are.

CONNIE HICKEN (MOTHER OF GAY SON)

I can't think of any other subject in which we expect people to remain quiet. Can you imagine telling your children or anyone you know: "Once you get into graduate school, no one wants to hear about it." Or once you get pregnant, or if you get a haircut, or anything about gaining a testimony . . . It doesn't make relational sense. In healthy, living relationships, everything is on the table for discussion.

Knowing we don't need to censor our humanity is the core of belonging. One element of trust building is knowing that whatever we bring to another individual will be received with curiosity and compassion. That is what radical inclusion looks like. We should not need to make ourselves smaller so that our loved ones are comfortable with us. We make it clear that in our families, there are no black sheep. We all are welcome in each other's lives for the rest of our lives. Don't shrink, don't censor. Be seen, be loved, and belong.

JOY SOUTHERN (MOTHER OF TRANSGENDER SON AND BISEXUAL SON)

My transgender son feels so much more whole by being out and openly talking to people about his authentic self. He tells people that he meets that he is very open to answering questions about himself because he strongly believes that by having open, honest dialogue, we can bridge the understandings of one another's experiences. This is especially important to him as he meets other transgender people who are early in the process of self-discovery. It can be incredibly helpful for them to have someone to talk to who can relate to their experience and educate them on available support resources.

PAULA NICHOLSON EDMUNDS (MOTHER OF TRANSGENDER CHILD)

My child got a mohawk shortly after confiding to me and their close friends that they were transgender.[19] Some felt it was inappropriate—that they were screaming their gender identity and that people don't want to hear that you are different.

But I felt that they had been hiding a part of them for so long that they finally felt free enough to be themself. They could really explore and express themself in a way they never could before. In a sense they were finding themself. After being buried for so many years, that process can seem extreme. But when a part of you is buried, how can you know who you really are? And until you know who you are, you will never know you are a child of God.

False Statement 4:

You can't identify as LGBTQ and still be an active Latter-day Saint.

As mentioned earlier, the Church dispels this myth with these statements:

> The Church distinguishes between same-sex attraction and homosexual behavior. People who experience same-sex attraction or identify as gay, lesbian, or bisexual can make and keep covenants with God and fully and worthily participate in the Church. Identifying as gay, lesbian, or bisexual or experiencing same-sex attraction is not a sin and does not prohibit one from participating in the Church, holding callings, or attending the temple.[20]

> Attraction is not identity. People can make their own choices about how to identify. There are active, temple recommend–holding Church members who comply with the law of chastity and identify themselves as gay, lesbian, or bisexual. There are active Church members who experience same-sex attraction and never choose to identify themselves using a label. Our primary identity will always be as a child of God.[21]

These statements are clear. You can identify as gay, lesbian, or bisexual and be in good standing with the Church. While this statement doesn't talk about transgender Latter-day Saints, I know of many Latter-day Saints who identify as transgender who are in good standing with the Church.

ANN PACK (TRANSGENDER WOMAN)

Watch me.

JEFF CASE (GAY MAN)

By defining myself as gay and a Latter-day Saint, I take power in my identity. It's me on my terms. I define what each of those means to me and do not allow myself to be labeled by others. Also, my label gives me a seat at the table of discussions regarding where LGBTQ individuals belong.

DALLIN STEELE (GAY MAN)

I've already been doing it so just call me the new myth buster.

DENNIS SCHLEICHER (GAY MAN)

I have been often questioned as a convert; why don't you identify as same-sex attracted? Easy, I've been 100 percent gay my entire life. If being baptized into the Church didn't change that, nothing will. Therefore, I identify as 100 percent gay and an active member of the Church.

KYLE FRIANT (GAY MAN)

I do it publicly partially because I want to stop my congregation from "othering." Once they know that someone from the group they consistently refer to as influenced by Satan is in their ward, they are left to confront reality. We are real people and not the negative myth that they have made us into. However, I am aware that for most of those who choose to actively pursue same-gender relationships, they are not welcomed in the same fellowship and understanding at church. In my opinion, that is a big loss for the body of Christ.

JERRY CHONG (GAY MAN)

My stake president has recently asked if he could refer to me as his gay friend who is in leadership in the stake. I told him, by all means, use the term *gay*. I do not have anything to hide. I told him that he could also use the term *queer*. He was taken aback. I told him as long as I and others take ownership of the word, it no longer is offensive. He was surprised in a good way. He kept asking me if I was sure. I told him yes.

DAVID DOYLE (GAY MAN)

I think this myth is from comments that leaders have said, that we should "identify" as children of God. But the thing is, we all have multiple labels we use to describe different aspects of us. Being a member of the Church is one such label. Being LGBTQ+ is another label.

It's ironic members of this Church would say to reject labels when our iconic look is missionaries wearing a label.

MATTHEW AYDELOTTE (QUEER MAN)

I believe this is similar to saying "there can only be one kind of person in the Church," which takes away any kind of individuality. I totally think you can identify as LGBTQ+ and be a member of the Church. However, I want to continue to be involved with the Church, but I also want a family, and unfortunately, I can't have a family and be a full member of the Church. I hope for that to change someday.

ALEX CHRISTOPHERSON (GAY MAN)

Membership and activity in the Church and being gay are not mutually exclusive. My fiancé (a man) and I go to our ward each week. We are friends with our bishop, and he has helped us feel so welcome. We can't participate fully, but we can listen to the talks; we can enjoy Sunday School and feel the Spirit in our chapel. We may disagree with some of the things members of the Church say, but that in no way stops us from going and worshipping with everyone else. For now, this is enough. I love the Church, and I love my fiancé, and I don't feel a need to remove either from my life. I believe I can continue to build my relationship with God best within the Church. I recognize that doesn't work as well for everyone as it does for us (different wards have different tolerance levels, and it's important to feel safe where we worship), but for me, and my fiancé as well, it's working, and we feel it's where we need to be at this point in our lives.

The following individuals identify as LGBTQ and have stepped away from regularly attending church.

SAM SKIDMORE (GAY MAN)

I'm currently working on my thesis project, which is analyzing feelings of belonging in the Latter-day Saint community and in the LGBTQ+ community and how those affect mental health outcomes. From what has already been studied, there are, and likely always will be, a group that does both. I was an active member and openly identified as gay for two years before I decided that I did not want to be part of the Church anymore. I was the ward mission leader and a Sunday School teacher at that time, and all of the members knew that I was gay. It wasn't an issue.

If it helps substantiate my claim, I also didn't leave the Church because of my sexuality. I firmly believe that it is possible to be both; it just depends on the individual's desires and their feeling of belonging in each community.

KATHY CARLSTON (NONBINARY LESBIAN)

To be honest, personally I believe that this myth is not a myth. There are parts of oneself that will be sacrificed on some level for an LGBTQ soul who is touched by [being a Latter-day Saint], whether they choose to be active in the Church, choose to [leave], or choose something in between.

False Statement 5:

You can change your sexual orientation or gender identity.

The Church does not teach that someone who has same-sex attraction can change or eliminate that attraction:

> The intensity of same-sex attraction is not a measure of your faithfulness. Many people pray for years and do all they can to be obedient in an effort to reduce same-sex attraction, yet find they are still attracted to the same sex. Same-sex attraction is experienced along a spectrum of intensity and is not the same for everyone. Some are attracted to both genders, and others are attracted exclusively to the same gender. For some, feelings of same-sex attraction, or at least the intensity of those feelings, may

diminish over time. In any case, a change in attraction should not be expected or demanded as an outcome by parents or leaders.[22]

Elder Holland also dispelled this myth in his October 2015 general conference address titled "Behold Thy Mother." In his talk, he spoke of a missionary with same-sex attraction and his wonderful mother.[23] After describing their challenges, Elder Holland commented, "And, I must say, this son's sexual orientation *did not somehow miraculously change—no one assumed it would.*"[24]

But some may ask, what about the power of the Atonement of Jesus Christ? If someone just has enough faith, can't they access that power to change their sexual orientation or gender identity? Aren't we told that through the Atonement, anything is possible? I strongly testify that the Atonement of Jesus Christ can help us overcome sin and remove pain, allowing us to heal. No one, however, has ever told me that they were able to change their sexual orientation or gender identity through the Atonement. Similarly, I don't know anyone who has been able to change their eye color, their natural hair color, or their dominant hand. Since the Atonement of Jesus Christ doesn't change these aspects, my conclusion is that being LGBTQ is a similar biological trait and is part of the needed and beautiful diversity of mortality. But can the Atonement of Jesus Christ help our LGBTQ members? Yes! We will discuss this topic more in chapter 6.

Putting this myth aside is one of the most important goals of this book, and believing that people cannot change their sexuality introduces a paradigm shift; what society earlier believed and taught put responsibility squarely on the shoulders of the LGBTQ person to try to conform to societal norms. As we accept that this belief is a myth, however, the responsibility moves to Latter-day Saints to help our LGBTQ members feel loved, accepted, and a sense of belonging.

So many LGBTQ individuals have told me of their endless deals with God to "make me not LGBTQ." In their efforts to change their sexuality or gender identity, some become over-religious, reconfessing sins or fasting to an extreme degree, or even develop hyper-religiosity, which manifests as religious beliefs that are so intense, they interfere with living a normal life. When becoming cishet is not attainable, some become suicidal.

Tom Christofferson explained the unchangeability of sexuality in his book *That We May Be One: A Gay Mormon's Perspective on Faith and*

Family. His brother Greg wrote of visiting with the head of the Church's social services program for Southern California:

> Tom told me that his marriage had ended and was going to be annulled because he was gay. Seeing his obvious distress and knowing his wife and her family well, I thought that it all could be resolved if I could find a way to help Tom get "fixed," to change his sexual orientation from homosexual to heterosexual. A few day later I visited a friend who was at the time head of LDS Social Services for Southern California. I explained my goal to him and asked who he would recommend as a counselor to help Tom "change." He responded, "Greg, of all the homosexual men in the world, what group do you think would want more than any other to change their sexual orientation? LDS gay men, because of our doctrine and emphasis on the family and children. I will tell you that I have counseled with more than 400 gay LDS men, most of whom desperately want to change their sexual orientation, and very, very few have felt they were successful at doing so."

Greg added, "My understanding completely changed in those few minutes with my friend. There was nothing to 'fix' about Tom. This was who he was . . . the same brother I had always loved . . . and he still had the wonderful personality and Christlike attributes that made him who he was."[25] When we learn to accept people how they are, we take a step toward seeing them as God sees them.

Though the vast majority of LGBTQ people describe being unable to change their sexuality or gender identity, there are some who report being able to change to cishet. I honor their stories. If this is your hope as an LGBTQ Latter-day Saint, I don't want to write anything to take hope out of your life. Hope is my favorite gospel word. However, I feel this hope should come from an LGBTQ individual's personal revelation and not imposed upon them by others. This is consistent with the Church's guideline: "A change in attraction should not be expected or demanded as an outcome by parents or leaders."

Let's remove this damaging idea of changing sexuality or gender from our LGBTQ members. I am grateful that, based on my observation, more and more Latter-day Saints seem to be putting this aside. I saw this first-hand in a California stake conference in which the stake president boldly declared that there would be no more "pray the gay away" in their stake.

I hope we can end the harmful bargaining with God that some LGBTQ members have engaged in, and focus on the Atonement of Jesus

Christ to heal hearts and make better decisions about their future. Doing so helps our LGBTQ members to remove shame and self-loathing, and build a better relationship with God based on love and hope.

STANLEY ALVEY (GAY MAN)

I was set on the idea that I would be "fixed" if I was the perfect Latter-day Saint. I promised God I would serve a full-time mission, and I started to devote myself to the Church. It wasn't until I was on my mission that I finally heard the Spirit screaming that God would not change my sexuality.

MATTHEW AYDELOTTE (QUEER MAN)

I fasted so often, prayed, and cried, asking God to make me straight. I made all kinds of little deals that never worked, but the biggest one was serving a mission. I thought for sure I just hadn't really shown God that I actually wanted to change or that I hadn't sacrificed enough. I was so angry and sad and sick when I got home and realized that I still wasn't "cured" because there was no sacrifice I could give God that could be bigger than the time and effort I poured into my mission. I spent a long time thinking that maybe punishment from a priesthood leader was what I needed in order to be cured, so I turned into one of those "chronic confessors," turning myself in for ridiculous, little things that I never got punished for. Realizing within the last year that God loves me for who I am and doesn't want me to try and change my sexuality—it's been a very literal life saver.

BEN SCHILATY (GAY MAN)

I don't recall ever making a deal with God. I didn't pray and say, "Heavenly Father, if I go on a mission you need to fix me," because I just assumed that's what happened. Being gay wasn't an option so obviously doing what I was supposed to do would naturally make things right. I never made a deal with God because I didn't have to. That's just the way things worked. You live the gospel, and he blesses you with a family. No deal necessary. Of course, the way I thought things worked was not the way they actually work.

SUNNY ERNST SMART (GAY WOMAN)

I felt deeply that God knew about this most shameful and disgusting part of me and that He hated me for it. I didn't dare bring it up in prayer for fear my instincts about His feelings for me would be confirmed. I just tried to pretend it wasn't there and hoped the good I did would somehow cover this broken part until death made me better.

Coming to accept and then love my sexuality as an adult came in the wake of beginning to feel and understand God's complete love for me as I am. The love I felt and feel from God has made it much easier to have love for myself and feel gratitude for my sexuality and the unique experiences I have because of it.

KURT NIELSEN (GAY MAN)

I don't think I ever made a deal [with God]. There was just this understanding from what I read and heard in church that if I stayed active and kept the commandments, my "gayness" would go away. I thought of this as a covenant between me and God. When my orientation didn't change, I always believed I was the one who wasn't keeping up my end of the bargain. I would become very discouraged and deeply critical of myself. This also led to a lot of bouts with depression. If someone was to be blamed, it must be me. It took me many years to realize I was operating under a false dichotomy. I was grateful when the Church began to teach [that being gay] wasn't a choice but also realized I had suffered needlessly through many years. The changes have been made so quietly that many in the Church still believe being gay is a choice. I would guess that the majority of members still have no idea the Church has a website devoted to the subject.

AUSTIN HODGES (GAY MAN)

In preparation for serving a mission, I prayed and fasted day and night for months, with all the faith that I had, trying to convey to God my sincerity and desperation. I begged and pleaded that if I went on a mission and served as hard as I could, if I put everything on the "altar of sacrifice," and if I returned home honorably, in return God would "cure me." Every night, often tearfully, I would repeat this mantra of a deal that I thought God would accept.

The verse from Moroni 7 echoed in my mind all the time: "Whatsoever thing ye shall ask the Father in my name, which is good, in faith believing that ye shall receive, behold, it shall be done unto you" (verse 26). I had always been taught and believed that if you ask God for something, and it was good, He'll give it to you. I believed with all my heart that turning straight and having a family and marrying in the temple was the most righteous desire possible, and I was so positive that God would make me straight—after all, the scriptures promised it to me.

I served with all my might and worked as hard as I could on my mission every day, believing the harder I worked, the more I could show God this was the desire of my heart—to be straight. I told my mission president of my deal and how I needed to be given the most difficult tasks or areas so I could show God how much I wanted to be straight.

I started having medical difficulties and hid my doctor visits from the mission president and my family because I could not go home early. There was too much on the line. I served harder and played down the medical problems. Eventually I got major bills I couldn't afford by myself, and my savings had run dry. I reached out to my mission president but made him promise not to send me home.

Despite my efforts, I was sent home early and felt like my heart had been ripped out and put through a grinder. I blamed myself for not finishing my mission. I figured I hadn't been righteous enough, sinned too much, or was just too lazy, and this was God's way of punishing me for not working hard enough and holding up my end of the deal. I beat myself up for months because I came home and was still gay. I wanted to go back out, to prove to God I could do it, [and I felt] that it was my duty to show God I really wanted to be straight.

ANN PACK (TRANSGENDER WOMAN)

I never really tried to make deals with God to be made cisgender (in my mind that meant "healed"). However, I did try to be as righteous and faithful as I could and believed that one day He would heal me.

AUSTIN HARTLEY (GAY MAN)

I told God that I'd be willing to lose all my limbs just to be straight. I was also willing to go deaf or blind. I remember some nights I even said that if He promised to make me straight, I'd cut off my own arm. I look back at that now and feel both terrible that I fell that low . . . [and] sad that I rationalized my worth through physical ailments. All of God's children are beautiful, whether or not they have a physical handicap or are queer or anything else. Your value is not dependent on anything [like that].

CRAIG NEWSOME (GAY MAN)

I was raised Jehovah's Witness and hoped that if I went door knocking full time at the ripe old age of seventeen, Jehovah would make me straight. Two years later I got kicked out [of the faith] for being gay.

From age twenty-two to thirty, I joined the Pentecostals. I was in "ex gays for Christ," did a twelve-step program and Christian counseling to get rid of my gay "addiction." I prayed in tongues and fasted sooooo much and begged the Lord on my knees to heal me. I went and saw pastors to have deliverance ministry to cast the gay demons out of me. All to no avail. By thirty I was done!! Twenty-five years later I converted to the Church, and I'm so grateful for the restored gospel. I'm just fine with just being me!

VANCE BRYCE (GAY MAN)

I had a consistent prayer: "Heavenly Father, please make me good." The bad part of me was gay. I couldn't admit it for a long time: I knew I was bad because I was gay. Not just mischievous bad, but full on capital "B" Bad. The worst kind.

I made countless deals with Heavenly Father. I was very sober and serious. I kept rules that didn't even exist. I attributed worthiness to a clean house, good grades, physical fitness, etc., etc., etc.

I fasted. After coming home early from my mission, my therapist encouraged me to fast away the gay. 12, 24, 48, 72 hours of fasting. There were times when I was so weak from fasting that guys weren't attractive [to me]. I would cry in gratitude, because being so numb from hunger and self-hate meant that I was becoming good. During the worst of it, I couldn't hold down food. I lost a lot of weight, and my skin took on a gray hue.

No matter how many times I was "cured" by fasting and prayer, no matter how much I punished myself, I couldn't stop myself from falling in love with one of my best friends. He was too kind, too gentle, too empathetic, and he was gorgeous.

I searched the internet for pills to take it away. I researched castration. I attempted suicide—twice. I wanted to be good. I would have done anything to be good.

I had an army of support. My family, friends, professors, Church leaders, community members, strangers on social networks—they all encouraged me to keep on trying to be good. None of them acknowledged that I could be good and gay.

The first time someone told me I was good and gay, I rebuked them for lying to me and accused them of trying to get me to kiss them. But the seed was planted. It took a few more years of fits and starts, but my prayers changed. I started to feel like the question that I was asking forced God into a box. By asking for Him to make me good, I was defining myself before He could even start to work with me. By asking God why He hated me, I had already answered the question by refusing His love for me, by not giving Him the chance to identify me as a holy son of God.

Then I started asking, "Heavenly Father, do you love me?" And then I held still and listened. I received an undeniable wave of warmth and comfort and security, so I took it a few steps further. "Heavenly Father. I'm gay. Do you love me?"

What I learned was that there is no child of God beyond the limits of His love. I had been told this by countless people, but there always seemed to be a caveat attached. There is no condition of life that separates us from the love of God. We are all holy. We are all sacred. We are God's children. We always will be.

DALLIN STEELE (GAY MAN)

I never made a deal with God, but I asked him to make me attracted to girls . . . I begged to be free of the pain and confusion I dealt with. It never worked out. Then I tried to find women who I could emotionally connect with, but [relationships with them] always ended up not working out due to them liking someone else or me having too much anxiety and ending any possible relationship.

When Heavenly Father told me He wanted me to come out, it healed a lot of pain and confusion I'd held onto unknowingly even though I knew He loved me, gay and all. I finally felt that He fully accepted me, and [being gay] was something I did not need to change.

BOB VERSTEGE (GAY MAN)

I never made a deal with Heavenly Father. I prayed [for Him] to take the bitter cup (being gay) away from me. But He said, "My beloved, why would I do that? I didn't do it for my Only Begotten." Then I knew I would have to endure it, but when I said that to myself, an impression from the Spirit said, "No, embrace it." So I did, and my life has been blessed ever since.

LANDON LARSEN (GAY MAN)

I never made deals with God. I believed that being gay was just some horrible thing that I had to hide from everyone and never let anyone know about it. I was planning on never telling a soul, marrying a woman, and just suffering in silence my whole life. I thought that my life was going to be miserable, yet I felt like suicide was never an option because I was so afraid to die and meet God with this "sin," yet I felt like it was a sin that I couldn't repent of because I recognized that it wasn't going away.

False Statement 6:

You should marry someone of the opposite sex to become straight.

President Oaks has said, "We definitely *do not recommend* [heterosexual] marriage as a solution to same gender feelings. . . . In times past, decades ago, there were some practices to that effect. We have eradicated them in the Church now."[26] Both the Church and society have learned that getting married doesn't change one's sexual orientation, a finding that has been confirmed in my own visits with many couples in mixed-orientation marriages (a marriage in which one or both are not cishet).

Though the Church doesn't recommend this path, I have found that mixed-orientation marriages can and do work for some people. These marriages are valid, strong, and beautiful love stories. They are not fake. If two people willingly choose to enter into a mixed-orientation marriage, we should hope that they will succeed. We should not, of course, encourage people to take this path as a solution to change their sexuality or even as a path that would somehow put them in a better standing with God. And yes, some mixed-orientation marriages fail. But we shouldn't conclude that since some fail, all are doomed to fail. For the stories and experiences of individuals in mixed-orientation marriages, including the importance of sharing being LGBTQ in the dating process, see chapter 9.

Above all, we should respect others' choices, even if we happen to disagree with them. Everyone is worthy of our love, and we should let each LGBTQ member find their own path through personal revelation and staying close to God. We shouldn't take someone else's story and prescribe it to one of our LGBTQ members, saying, "This is what you should do."

False Statement 7:

You are struggling with being LGBTQ.

In the past, I've often heard and even used the phrase "struggling with same-sex attraction." It may seem innocuous at first. Recognizing the unique challenges LGBTQ people face, many well-intentioned Church members imagine that their lives must be very difficult, and thus they say that LGBTQ people "struggle" with their gender identity or sexuality. Or perhaps some view being LGBTQ as a temptation that can be overcome; like someone who "struggles" with an addiction to drugs, an

LGBTQ person must "struggle" with "overcoming" their gender identity or sexual orientation.

Some individuals are fine with this phrase, since they do feel that much of what they go through as a result of being LGBTQ is, in fact, a struggle. For some LGBTQ people, however, this phrase is not helpful. I didn't realize this until I heard from LGBTQ Latter-day Saints who told me that this statement can add to their burdens and make them feel broken, because the word struggling implies that being LGBTQ is a burden or an affliction. In reality, sometimes the main burden is caused by how LGBTQ Latter-day Saints are treated by others, particularly their family and fellow Church members. Even as many of our LGBTQ members do their best to live as committed Latter-day Saints, hurtful comments can make them feel unwelcome and diminished.

BLAIRE OSTLER (BISEXUAL WOMAN)

To be completely honest being queer isn't nearly as much as a struggle as dealing with the insecurities, ignorance, and misconceptions folks have about me being queer. But there never seems to be a polite way of saying, "Look, the problem isn't me. It's your inability to greet me as I am instead of how you want me to be."

When people suggest my queerness is a struggle or a "challenge of the flesh," it hurts because they are attempting to turn one of the most beautiful and godly aspects of my being, the way I love, into something perverse, devious, pitiful, or ugly. The struggle is getting people to understand I like being queer and there is nothing wrong with it.

TEMBER HARWARD (GAY MAN MARRIED TO A WOMAN)

I don't think there's anything wrong with using that word [i.e., *struggle*]. It's become popular to omit that word from our vocabulary when referencing LGBT issues, but many of us *are* really struggling to find our place and path. In fact, I would say most of us are, at least in my spheres of influence. I feel that it is healthy to come to the realization that SSA [same-sex attraction] is an *experience* and not a *struggle*, but it takes a lot of inner work and practice to have that perspective.

DAVID DOYLE (GAY MAN)

Words like "struggle" and "suffer" are the way we talk about diseases, temptations, and addictions: "I struggle with depression" or "He suffers from cancer." Homosexuality is not like being a smoker.

There is a struggle that people go through until they can accept themselves, until they're comfortable with the idea that these feelings are a part of them, and they have to learn to live with them. But that's not how it's meant when someone says, "They struggle with gender identity" or "They struggle with same-sex attraction."

The real struggle and suffering are from being treated differently. From guilt and shame and stigma. From not being accepted by friends and family. From having opportunities limited.

KARSON PHIPPEN (GAY MAN)

For me [the problem is] the negative connotation. LGBT is an identifier, not a condition. It's like saying [someone is] struggling with being Hispanic. The real struggle is being accepted or judged by people who don't understand. You can be attracted to the same sex, be moral, and seek out healthy relationships and righteous things, but people often associate [being gay] with a struggle with the law of chastity or sexual deviancy.

ANN PACK (TRANSGENDER WOMAN)

Speaking only from my experiences, my answer would be different depending on different times in my life. Earlier in my life, if someone had said I struggled with gender confusion or gender identity, I would've agreed with them. But if someone said that today, it would be hurtful. I think I would correct them—that I don't struggle; it is they who have the struggle with me.

JERRY CHONG (GAY MAN)

The phrase "struggling with same-sex attraction" adds to a person's burden because you assume that being LGBTQ is a problem. It indicates that you feel these people are confused and that in time they will "be straight," as the Church community has taught for decades.

TAYLOR WINGET (GAY MAN)

[This statement] implies that the struggle is being LGBTQ, but for LGBTQ Latter-day Saints, the struggle is actually trying to figure out how to reconcile our faith and the Church's teachings with our sexual identity. Saying that I struggle with being gay implies that there is something wrong or that it is something that can be "healed" over time. I don't struggle with being gay; it is a struggle being gay and LDS.

JAKE SHEPHERD (GAY MAN)

Once I accepted it and came out, the struggle lessened. I can see finding your place can be challenging, but once you're passed that, the suffering stops. At least in my opinion. People telling me I am suffering is just insensitive. I end up feeling frustrated, and that is probably the only suffering I receive.

KHRISTIAN TOELUPE (TRANSGENDER WOMAN)

"Struggling" makes me feel like I'm "losing a battle I'm currently fighting"—as my grandpa put it to me when I came out to him the first time as a gay man (I was in denial of my gender identity back then). This word makes me feel like my feelings are of Satan, which makes me feel dirty, unworthy—makes me [want to] hide. I know, however, that's not true. I am a child of God. He is my creator. I don't know why I came to earth in a male body and feel female. I don't. However, I know I am His creation and my only struggle is how to navigate life with my unique circumstances as a trans woman of color.

JEFF CASE (GAY MAN)

I'm okay with the word *struggle*, as that is a ubiquitous part of life. What is burdensome is the notion that simply being gay is a struggle. That's not the struggle. The struggle is against internalized homophobia, societal homophobia, reconciling faith and sexuality, the process to move towards a healthier life and healthier relationships. That's the struggle. And I'm okay with it.

MICHAEL SECRIST (GAY MAN)

When I used to think I was "struggling with same-sex attraction," I was really struggling to find a way to fit the Church's narrative for "the plan." I was struggling to belong in a place I would never fit in. Once I learned that God loves me and made me gay intentionally, I learned to love myself too. Now, there is no struggle.

I don't fit the Church's narrative for the path to exaltation, and many would say I don't belong there anymore. But the great part is this— I belong to God.

False Statement 8:
LGBTQ people should not form community with other LGBTQ people.

Some Church members seem to feel that LGBTQ Latter-day Saints should not form community with one another. A community of people going through similar experiences, however, often provides support as they walk a complicated path. As of this writing (April 2020), there is no official on-campus support group at BYU for its LGBTQ students. There are no official Church-sponsored groups or classes to provide support for LGBTQ Latter-day Saints or their parents. Perhaps there is a concern that forming a community would legitimize or normalize the existence of LGBTQ Latter-day Saints. But I feel our Heavenly Parents already did this when They created some of Their children LGBTQ. Perhaps some worry that if we have Church-sponsored support groups, more Church members will identify as LGBTQ—which we have already suggested is a myth.

I don't sit on the general councils of the Church, so I don't know the discussions around this topic. But my general hope is that, in the future, such groups will be supported by the Church. The benefits of having a network of support in the Church are well illustrated by Ben Schilaty, who helped create a Latter-day Saint LGBTQ network in Tucson, Arizona:

> I wish that we LGBT Latter-day Saints had a place to find each other. We need each other. With the help of my stake president in Tucson, I started a support group for gay Latter-day Saints modeled after the Genesis Group.[27] The Genesis Group is a monthly meeting for Black members of the church that three apostles helped found in the 70s. It was designed to be a place for them to build their faith in Christ together and create a community of saints with similar life experiences. Starting that support group in Tucson was a life-changing experience for me, and it was healing to my soul to spend time with other same-sex attracted Latter-day Saints as we built our faith in Christ together and shared common experiences. I have heard too many stories of gay Latter-day Saints feeling so isolated and alone that they get on a dating app or on Craigslist just to find someone like them that they can talk to. No one should feel that they need to put themselves in those dangerous situations when there are plenty of super rad LGBT members for them to connect with if they only knew how to find them.[28]

I'm grateful to many organizations that have stepped forward to meet the needs of LGBTQ Latter-day Saints such at North Star,[29] Encircle,[30] Affirmation,[31] Mormons Building Bridges,[32] and many others. I've spent significant time with each of these organizations, sat with their wonderful leaders and members, and seen the hope and healing each provide. Some of my most powerful spiritual experiences have occurred listening to LGBTQ members of these organizations share their stories. I believe each of these organizations is saving lives.

As more local leaders see LGBTQ people as members of their congregations (instead of an outside group), they feel stewardship responsibility to meet their spiritual needs. I'm seeing these leaders act on their stewardship by holding LGBTQ educational firesides and creating support-group events (sometime called "LGBTQ FHE" or "Allies Night"). These local leaders experienced what I myself experienced as a bishop, and their perspective has shifted to see LGBTQ people as *our* people.

I'm glad we are learning to create communities within the Church to support our LGBTQ members. We have seen the benefits of these internal connections through the Genesis Group for our Black members, as well as international congregations in the Salt Lake Valley such as a Tongan stake and a Swahili branch.

I've seen individuals do much better emotionally if they can identify and connect with a group of people walking a similar road. We all need support, connection, and understanding from others who are like us.

Because acknowledgment and humanization—the basic elements of respect—have sometimes been denied our LGBTQ members, they have sought ways to create community, connection, and support, including through LGBTQ organizations, social media, and pride parades. As we recognize these core individual needs, we increase our understanding of why these organizations exist, even if some aspects may make us uncomfortable. We can build community for our LGBTQ members at the local level, as we see is already being done in many areas. Our ability to minister will mature as we take even small actions, such as using their preferred labels, that show kindness and respect.

False Statement 9:

You should not use or identify with the pride colors or flag.

The pride flag is a symbol of lesbian, gay, bisexual, transgender, and queer pride and LGBTQ social movements. The most common version consists of six stripes: red, orange, yellow, green, blue, and violet. LGBTQ individuals and allies currently use rainbow flags and many rainbow-themed items and color schemes as an outward symbol of their identity or support. The rainbow flag is also commonly used as a general symbol of social equality and individuality.[33]

Many active Latter-day Saints feel negatively toward the pride flag or rainbow colors. It brings up feelings or memories of activities or events that are not consistent with Church teachings. If you feel this way, your feelings are valid; I've seen the flag used this way.

However, I have noticed a shift among some active Latter-day Saints on how they feel about the pride flag and rainbow colors. LGBTQ members see them as symbols of their identity. Allies see them as symbols of their support for LGBTQ Latter-day Saints and a signal that they are a safe person.

For Latter-day Saints, the word *pride* almost always has a negative connotation. The scriptures and our leaders have taught repeatedly about the negative aspects of pride. The landmark talk by President Ezra Taft Benson in 1989, "Beware of Pride," has an explanation of pride: "The central feature of pride is enmity—enmity toward God and enmity toward our fellowmen."[34] I believe President Benson taught that humility, the opposite of pride, is what connects us with God and our fellow humans. I know that my pride, or enmity toward others, at times keeps me from listening to and having the humility to fully understand, minister to, and connect with marginalized groups such as LGBTQ Latter-day Saints. My pride kept me from being open to learning about their difficult road, bearing their burdens, seeing their contributions, and being their friend.

In his 1988 book, *Pure in Heart*, President Oaks teaches, "Some manifestations of pride are acceptable. There is a kind of pride that is akin to self-respect. It comes from measuring ourselves against an objective standard. There is nothing wrong with a workman who takes pride in his work."[35] I like the pride of self-respect. It is not comparative in nature and doesn't involve enmity toward God or other people. It's about doing our personal best, being honest with ourselves, and measuring ourselves by our own progress. I have felt the inner peace that comes with the pride of self-respect. Perhaps this is the kind of pride that some of our LGBTQ Latter-day Saints feel as they come out and identify with the pride flag or rainbow colors; they feel at their personal best as LGBTQ Latter-day Saints, representing the self-respect that comes with being authentic and honest. For cishet Latter-day Saints the flag may represent a desire to eliminate enmity with LGBTQ Latter-day Saints and better meet their spiritual and emotional needs.

I love this blog post about pride from Ben Schilaty:

> Pride is the opposite of shame. Thesaurus.com lists the first three antonyms of pride as depression, gloom, and melancholy. Further down the list is humility which I was taught in church is the opposite of pride. Not listed as an antonym for pride is the word shame. But if you look up the word shame, there in the list of opposites is the word pride.
>
> I have two rainbow pins displayed on my backpack. Each of them containing a symbol that ties them to BYU. They're rad because they reveal two pieces of me to whomever is standing behind me. I had owned both of them for many weeks before attaching them to my backpack. Each pin was placed on my backpack following an incident that made me feel misunderstood as a gay Latter-day Saint. I put them on my backpack because I felt like gay people like myself needed more visibility.
>
> I distinctly remember walking across BYU campus the day I put the first pin on my backpack, feeling proud to be seen. I walked by the Harold B. Lee library where I had once secretly read a handful of books about how to overcome same-sex attraction. Now, ten years later, I was walking across campus with a small circular object advertising the thing that had brought me so much shame for much of my life.
>
> I also wear a rainbow ring on my right ring finger. My aunt gave it to me for Christmas. At first I thought it was a bit loud, but now I like it. Maybe because I regularly get compliments about it. I always reply, "Thanks! My aunt gave it to me."
>
> I didn't do anything for Pride month. I don't really enjoy parades and festivals aren't really my thing. I just wasn't interested in going to any pride events so I didn't. I didn't hang a rainbow flag, or change my Facebook profile picture, or paint my face. But a lot of people did. I know that Pride makes a lot of people uncomfortable. It might feel "in your face" or flamboyant. While I didn't do anything to celebrate Pride month this June, I can understand why so many people felt the need to celebrate.
>
> I remember times in my 20s when I would've been relieved if I had been diagnosed with terminal cancer. I would've been free of same-sex attraction, my suffering would be over, and I could die a hero. Being dead and straight was a better option than being alive and gay. That's what shame did to me. It made me want to be dead.

Overcoming that shame took years. The antonyms of pride—depression, gloom, melancholy—were often present in my life whenever I thought about dating, marriage, or my future. I don't feel those feelings anymore when I think about my sexuality. The shame is gone. I now accept my sexual orientation as something that I couldn't change. It is a part of me. And I want to live for a very long time. My outlook has completely shifted from wanting to be dead to wanting to live a long, full life. And isn't that something worth celebrating?

My story of growing from shame to acceptance isn't that unique. So many LGBTQ folks have walked a similar path. So when I see a mom hang a rainbow flag from her front porch, I don't think, "c'mon, keep your life to yourself." Instead, I imagine a mom who was once uncomfortable and ashamed to have a gay son who is now saying, "I love my son. All of him." When I see my friends dressed in rainbow colors marching down the street I don't see them as being flamboyant, but I see them celebrating their desire to live. A desire that they may not have always had. And I'm grateful.

I've only been to one pride parade. It was September 2016 in Tucson, AZ. I had been invited to march with Mormons Building Bridges. Those who march with Mormons Building Bridges wear their Sunday best to let the LGBTQ community know that as Latter-day Saints we want to be at the forefront of expressing love and compassion. I was hesitant to go. I decided to go and then decided not to go a few times. I recall discussing whether or not go with my straight friend Josh. He told me that if I decided to go, he would go with me. I even emailed my stake president asking if it was okay for me to march in a pride parade. His simple response was, "I trust you." About an hour and half before the parade started I felt compelled to go. I texted Josh, we both put on our church clothes, and drove over to the parade area.

There were only 14 of us in the Mormons Building Bridges group. One of the women who came was from the Spanish branch I was attending. She didn't speak English and told me that her son had just come out to her and she wanted to walk in the parade so that he knew she loved him. While we were waiting for our turn to march the organizer of the parade greeted us all. She said she had grown up Mormon, but had left the Church in her 20s. She told us how touching it was to see us there.

Josh and I were asked to hold the Mormons Building Bridges banner. As we walked down 4th Avenue, I distinctly felt the presence of the Holy Ghost. Spectators shouted "The Mormons are here!" and we were cheered and cheered. It was a deeply moving experience for me to be in a pride parade dressed as a Latter-day Saint. We could have easily been booed, but instead we were welcomed and praised for our participation. We belonged to the least of any group there and yet we still belonged. And those who saw us were adamant that we belonged and that they were glad we were there. No one was ashamed of our presence. One of the parade officials took a group picture of us after the parade. She said, "Thank you, thank you, thank you for coming." I hope that any LGBTQ person who attends church will feel as welcomed as I felt at that pride parade.

I don't think I'll be hanging a rainbow flag outside my house. I probably won't wear a rainbow tie to church like my dad does. That doesn't really feel like my thing. The way I show my pride is by telling my story. I show my pride by allowing myself to be seen. I show my pride by inviting others to walk in my shoes.

And if the word pride makes you uncomfortable, here are some synonyms that might be easier to relate to—dignity, self-respect, honor. Gay dignity means that I am comfortable being myself around others. Gay self-respect means that I welcome all parts of me as important ingredients to who I am. Gay honor means that I no longer want to die because of my sexuality.

June was a healing, celebratory month for so many people. I hope that we can celebrate our lives and who we are and who we want to become throughout the year. And I hope that every person, especially those who have been previously weighed down by shame, feel an overwhelming sense of dignity, self-respect, and honor.[36]

For Christmas 2018, Allison Dayton, serving as a ward Relief Society president, gave a J. Kirk Richards painting to her gay son Jake.[37] The painting is called *Jesus Said Love Everyone* and has Jesus wearing a robe with rainbow colors.[38]

Allison later posted the painting and this message on Facebook:

Thank you J. Kirk Richards for this beautiful painting we gave to our darling son Jake, who is gay, and for letting me pick it up on Christmas Eve. Don't you love the way that Christ is cradling all of us in his arms? Kirk's understanding of the Gospel of Christ is so evident in this painting "Jesus said Love Everyone." I am so grateful for the embracing love of our families and friends and for our Latter-day Saint family, who have literally showered Jake Dayton and our whole family with endless love and support. I am so proud of my brave son and all that he is and will become. And I'm grateful for Father in Heaven for teaching us what it truly means to have Joy in our posterity.[39]

Jake Dayton shared his feelings on receiving this painting:

> When I opened my present Christmas morning, I . . . immediately recognized J. Kirk Richards's style. Then I started to take in the details. The rainbow colors first; that year was just after coming out, so my wish list included the line "rainbow stuff." Then the Christ arms holding the people. I felt a real strong feeling of joy. I knew that my family loved every part of me and that my sexuality didn't detract or affect our relationships. But the painting felt like something more than that. It felt like they were saying, "This part of you is something that not only are we okay with it, it's something we have no problem showing." So now a rainbow hangs in our front room proudly on display, reminding me I have people who love me at home and that our home is a place for any and everyone else too.[40]

Allison Dayton and Kirk Richards later joined me on my podcast to share more about this experience. Kirk shared these insights about the painting:

> It's called *Jesus Said Love Everyone*, and it's a painting of Jesus, and His robes are the colors of the rainbow, and if you look closely, there are little people within those colors. Jesus has His arms kind of cradling or wrapped around this rainbow full of people. The painting has—there are actually seven colors in this rainbow and there are seven sides to the painting. That number seven in Christian symbolism has meanings associated with perfection. The idea behind that for me was that the body of Christ is perfect with the vast variety of people within it, as represented by the colors of the rainbow. A second, not secondary, meaning of the use of seven is that our LGBTQ siblings and friends are perfect in their own right, that God has created them, that they are God's creation, and they are not less than seven or perfection.
>
> None of us are perfect, obviously. That's something that we hear a lot at church. But I don't feel like any of the people that I know, and I have met a lot of especially gay friends, and I don't feel that they are any less in terms of what God meant them to be than I am or any of my cis-heterosexual friends. I just think that God intends for them to live a rich and fulfilled life, and a life that has faith and love in it. And I think that it's incumbent on us to allow them to live that life, to have that love, and to exercise that faith. As a culture, as a community, we have a history of not allowing those people to exercise faith and to be part of our community, and I think that is a huge opportunity for us to repent. As people who want to follow Christ, call ourselves disciples of Christ,

> we shouldn't be afraid to look at that thing that needs repentance squarely in the face and move towards repentance, to turn ourselves to the right. That can be painful to acknowledge—that we have changes to make or that we have caused hurt. But I know that's what Jesus wants us to do. We need to be reborn in the love of Christ, and we try to do that every week with the sacrament. We are baptized, but that's an ongoing process. We need to keep examining and keep extending love, and allowing people to exercise faith in our community.[41]

Alyssa Edwards, a high school seminary teacher in Utah County, has a copy of the same painting hanging in her office. She joined me on the podcast to talk about the painting signaling to her LGBTQ students that she is a safe person for them to discuss their feelings. This also allows her cishet students to feel safe talking to her if needed about complicated things in their lives. Alyssa is not trying to replace the role of a parent or local leader but wants to be a safe person for her students as she helps them come unto Christ.[42] As a parent, I've been glad when my own children felt safe opening up with a seminary or institute teacher.

In June 2018, Eric Kirby, an active Latter-day Saint and an assistant vice president at Southern Utah University, shared his feelings about the importance of pride month in a tweet that went viral: "I'm a straight, male, Mormon. So what does Pride Month have to do with me? Actually, a lot. Happy Pride Month to all who agree to: Treat others with fairness and dignity. See all as God's children. Appreciate diversity. Provide more safe and welcoming spaces, and show more love."[43]

During pride month of June 2019, Willy and Kristy Donahoo wanted each person in their Sandy, Utah, neighborhood to know they are accepted unconditionally. To do this, they decided to work with their neighbors to display pride flags. This neighborhood, with many active Latter-day Saints, displayed more than sixty flags. The story was covered broadly by the local media, including Church-owned KSL News. One of the quotes in the KSL article was from David Brown, a former stake president: "I hope it will help people to recognize with all of the diversity within our community, that there is still reason to focus on supporting one another."[44]

Willy and Kristy joined me on my podcast to share all the positive things that had occurred because of this effort and how they hope to scale this effort in the future to other neighborhoods.[45]

On my morning walk, I pass two Christian churches not of our faith. Often these churches are displaying the rainbow flag with the message "all are welcome here." I have wondered what Jesus would say about the rainbow flag being displayed at a church. While I don't know how He would respond, my feeling is He would welcome anything on the exterior of a church that helps create a welcoming feeling so more of His children would enter to hear His message of hope, healing, and coming unto Him. His ministry was focused on marginalized groups and breaking social norms to help them feel welcome. I also believe that helping marginalized groups feel welcome results in an umbrella message that everyone truly is accepted. No, I'm not suggesting that we post rainbow flags outside of Latter-day Saint buildings. I leave those kinds of decisions to our leaders whom I sustain and support. But I am pointing out the welcoming feeling the flag may create.

In 2019 two Utah communities, Heber City and St. George, had pride flags flown along city streets. This was a first for both communities and generated significant community discussion and press.[46] Mayor Kelleen Potter of Heber City, a Latter-day Saint mother of two LGBTQ children, joined me on the podcast to share more about this decision.[47]

Mayor Jon Pike of St. George posted this message on his personal Facebook page in September 2019 about the pride flags in his city:

> I'm actually happy for the discussion that is occurring in St. George about Pride of Southern Utah's events this week along with their banners highlighting them. I hope we can keep the discussion civil and respectful.
>
> I realize we're not all in the same place or of the same opinion on these or many other issues. But I view these banners and the rainbow flags differently than I used to. I view them as a celebration of all people and of acceptance, inclusion and love.
>
> We'll still have differences. We won't understand everything. But I hope we can agree on one thing: People are awesome! I enjoy getting to know many people in my role as mayor, and I love it! I hope we will all simply enjoy and respect every individual for the person they are and what they can contribute to our community and to our lives. We need EVERYONE!"[48]

I agree with Mayor Pike—people are awesome! Mayor Pike, an active Latter-day Saint, later joined me on the podcast to share more of his thoughts including his desire to "be the mayor for everyone."[49]

CHERYL SMITH (MOTHER OF GAY SON)

I wear a rainbow bracelet. I do this to show that I am a safe person for any of my LGBTQ brothers and sisters.

LAURA STURM (MOTHER OF BISEXUAL SON)

I remember having a conversation with my sister years ago about how annoyed she was that the beautiful rainbow had been hijacked by LGBTQ people, and I mostly agreed with her. Anyway, it was a thing that I was reluctant to embrace when we entered this world of having an LGBTQ child because it seemed to run so counter to everything the gospel stands for. As time has passed though, I've come to see that the message is the same when utilized by either group—God's love for *all* his children. That's the message I see in the rainbow: love.

CHRISANN RICHINS TOELUPE (MOTHER OF GAY SON AND TRANSGENDER DAUGHTER)

I wear my Mama Dragon shirt and/or other pride gear to show the LGBTQ community that I see them, I love them, and I support them.

I also wear LGBTQ clothing/jewelry as a protection. Being a mom of LGBTQ children is wonderful, but it can also be full of fear and anxiety. Wearing LGBTQ clothing feels like a shield to protect my family and me. It protects us from people making derogatory comments, and lets them know as they stare in awe at my family's queerness that my kids have loving and supportive parents who will do whatever needs to be done to protect them.

CAROL M. COLVIN (MOTHER OF GAY SON AND BISEXUAL DAUGHTER)

I tell anyone who asks that I wear rainbow pins, bracelets, and other items to show any closeted youth or adults in my vicinity that I support them and they can feel free to live openly and to be themselves around me. I also wear the rainbow to show other straight people that it's a good way to show support and love for all. I've had other parents contact me after their child came out because they knew I could help them learn what to say and do to show love and support and acceptance for their child.

EVAN SMITH (FATHER OF GAY SON)

A few months ago, I started wearing a rainbow flag lapel pin to church (and I now occasionally wear a rainbow-themed tie). I decided to start doing so following a negative experience I had with a church leader whose comments (which he apologized for later) made my wife and me feel like we had to choose between loving our son how we know he needs us to or being good Church members. We chose to walk away from the opportunity to continue serving in a leadership calling ourselves because we didn't want to feel like we had to pretend to be ashamed of our son's chosen path. I don't wear the pin (or tie) now to be antagonistic or to promote a political agenda though. Rather, now that I have more freedom to express my opinion than I did when I was in leadership callings, I think it's good to remind everyone who sees me at church that my first priority is to love my family. I also wear it to remind people how important it is to love the marginalized and vulnerable and be a safe person for them to speak with about anything. I wear it to show people that diversity of thought and opinion is not a bad thing in the Church—that the body of Christ is improved when we open our hearts and minds to be more loving to people who aren't like us. I just wish I had had the guts to wear the lapel pin/tie before, when I was a bishop or in the stake presidency, because I think those messages are very important for leaders to communicate more openly.

JODY ENGLAND HANSEN (MOTHER OF QUEER CHILD)

I have been wearing my rainbow pin and pendant constantly (especially at church) for nine years. It starts many conversations. People of all ages have felt safe coming out to me. Others have asked me for resources or help with greater understanding for loved ones.

HEATHER ROBERTSON (MOTHER OF GAY DAUGHTER)

To many, the rainbow symbolizes something they don't understand and feel is wrong. I used to feel that way. It made me very uncomfortable. By supporting it, it meant I was less than faithful and not perfectly obedient. When my daughter came out as gay, suddenly I couldn't turn away from the discomfort. I had to learn, pray, study, and fast to understand. It has been painful but necessary growth.

What does the rainbow mean to me now? It means my daughter is seen. Her presence among us is valued and needed in our family. Like a rainbow, the "colors" that make her unique and different are the very things that make her beautiful. I want her to feel those same feelings at church. I want her to know she belongs and that her perspective is valuable as another member of the body of Christ.

I love rainbows.

MARION MCCLELLAN (MOTHER OF GAY SON)

We fly our rainbow flag for the LGBTQ+ children and teens in our community. We fly it so that the kids who walk or drive past our home know that we love them. We see them.

We fly our flag for these precious children's parents. We fly the pride flag so that after their child musters all of their courage and bravery and comes out to them, those parents know that they have friends they can reach out to.

We fly this beautiful rainbow flag so that one child sees it, that one child who [feels] there is no place for them in our community or in their family or in their congregation absolutely knows they *always* have a place next to us.

Our flag is for that one LGBTQ+ person who is certain there is no place for them in this life. It is for the one child who isn't sure they can live for one more day. It actually matters. It actually can help to save a life.

MARK NELSON (FATHER OF GAY SON)

I wear lots of things with rainbows. I wear them a lot. I typically wear my rainbow-colored bracelet every day. I also wear one of my six hats that has a rainbow on it every chance I get. And on occasion I wear a rainbow tie to church. First reason I wear them is so my gay son knows each and every day that I love and support him.

Second, I wear them to let other people that see me know I am safe and that I love them. It's not about any agenda or sticking it in people's faces. The rainbow is a beautiful symbol of love. God gave us a rainbow after he flooded the earth as a symbol of love. Well, I wear them to show my love as well.

STACEY NERDIN (MOTHER OF PANSEXUAL DAUGHTER)

During the Face to Face about the new children and youth program, I was struck by the announcement on the new "emblems of belonging."[50] Of all people, I feel like Church members should understand the idea of a visual symbol that represents and unites a community. We've been doing it forever with CTR rings, but also silly things like the RULDS2? license plate frames I've seen, and even the proliferation of BYU paraphernalia. Members love to use signs like this to identify themselves as members but also to sort of "seek out" or give a wink and nod to others like them. I try to explain that wearing anything rainbow is not so different—for me, it's a way I can display my association with the LGBT community and also give a signal to other people who might be associated or who might want to know more. For me, it's not really a political statement but more an "emblem of belonging."

JODY ENGLAND HANSEN (MOTHER OF QUEER CHILD)

There is a painting just inside the main entrance of the Salt Lake Temple. It shows a pastoral landscape, with a rainbow appearing over it. It is an old master painting. The rainbow is a symbol of hope and promise from God that They love us and are not looking to destroy us. I choose to see this amazing symbol of hope, depicted as a full spectrum of visual color, as a way to recognize that God's love and grace are most evident when we recognize the vast, endless variety of the countless beings that create the body of God's universal family. All are priceless and known and loved, in all their infinite variety. God offers us a symbol of that variety as a means of reminding us of Their love for us and to remind us to love each other as we are loved. My rainbow pin and flag and any other similar emblem is a reminder to me of God's unconditional love, as well as the great commandment to love one another, as we are loved.

LIISA LOWE FREI (MOTHER OF GAY SON)

I live in a very conservative community. During Southern Utah Pride week, from my front door, I could see four rainbow flags, and I knew of eight others within a few blocks of me. What this felt like for me was a community moving towards the inclusion of all of God's children. Not only was this a visual sign of support to LGBTQ individuals, it also gives comfort to their families, knowing that many of our friends and neighbors love and support our children for who they are. This is what the gospel is about—everyone feeling God's love. I don't worry too much if this makes others feel uncomfortable, because we should feel uncomfortable if we aren't showing love to those individuals who have been pushed to the margins. Flying the rainbow flag in front of my house started some great conversations with some of my neighbors. I also wear a rainbow ring and bracelet. It is my quiet way of showing love and support. I don't think it is necessary for everyone to fly flags or wear rainbows. I know some LGBTQ kids don't want their parents to do this. To other kids, seeing their parents support in this way means the world to them.

SUMMER SPACKMAN (MOTHER OF GAY SON)

We were able to see firsthand the effects of the rainbow during pride week down here in St. George. There were four flags put up in my ward boundaries (including mine and my sister's). All of our flags were thrown down, and two were stolen. My sister's flag was burned and thrown in a porta-potty in the empty lot next door. It was heartbreaking. We ended up having a community gathering at her home and used chalk to cover her driveway/sidewalk in painted rainbows. It was a wonderful outpouring of support. The two individuals who burned the flag were eventually identified (she had a security system that captured them on camera), and they ended up being two young kids who live in our stake. She was able to meet with the parents of both of the kids and have a great discussion on what the flag represents and what it means to love your neighbor. It drew media attention and ran on a couple of news sites. All in all, I will say it was a good experience. I was shocked to see the negativity that these flags generated but found much hope in the greater good. I had multiple people reach out to me after my flag post telling me of loved ones who were gay—and even another young woman in our ward came out privately to my daughter. I only had one neighbor that was bothered enough by it to message me about taking it down. If anything, the rainbow can start a discussion on love and inclusion—and the difficult road these kids have ahead of them.

CAROL ANN MOODY (MOTHER OF GAY SON)

I wear one or more LGBTQI bracelets every day in support of my beloved family. And I wear my rainbow earrings often as well—actually I only get complimentary comments from people I see on errands.

SHERRY PROFFITT MACNAB (MOTHER OF QUEER DAUGHTER)

I wear a rainbow ring. Sometimes I think I should wear something more obvious. But every time I raise my hand at church or in the temple, it's visible.

Statistically speaking, there are probably a few LGBTQ folks in our ward. At least one. But no one is out.

My hope is that anyone in my ward who is closeted feels safe next to me. They see it as a signal, that they have an ally. That someone in church accepts them as they are.

I hope they see it. Though I often feel like I should be doing more.

NANCY AYRE (LGBTQ ALLY, ACTIVE LATTER-DAY SAINT)

I used to see a rainbow flag and feel unsettled. Threatened. Concerned. Unconvinced. Now when I see the rainbow colors, I feel understanding. Love. Peace. Empathy. Gratitude. Some ask, "How can you be a devout person of your faith and be an advocate for the LGBTQ community? How do those two intersect?" It's easy. I believe they can intersect beautifully. I have been taught that all are alike unto God. That where love is, there God is also. I have made covenants to "mourn with those that mourn and comfort those that stand in need of comfort" (Mosiah 18:9). In essence, I have been taught to empathize and to gain understanding. I have been taught to be like Jesus who ministered to those who were not always understood or valued in society. What a blessing it has been to be in this space and more fully understand the road of my dear LGBTQ brothers and sisters. The rainbow colors remind me of my faith and the beauty and diversity of God's creations and his love for all his children.

ENDNOTES

1. "Same-Sex Attraction," Gospel Topics, The Church of Jesus Christ of Latter-day Saints, accessed November 20, 2019, churchofjesuschrist.org/study/manual/gospel-topics/same-sex-attraction.
2. M. Russell Ballard, "Questions and Answers" (devotional address, Brigham Young University, Provo, Utah, November 14, 2017), speeches.byu.edu/talks/m-russell-ballard/questions-and-answers/.
3. "President Nelson Shares 5 Truths in Address to Young Adults; Says Love behind LGBT Policy Changes," *Church News*, The Church of Jesus Christ of Latter-day Saints, September 17, 2019, churchofjesuschrist.org/church/news/president-nelson-shares-5-truths-in-address-to-young-adults-says-love-behind-lgbt-policy-changes.
4. Brené Brown has pointed out that one of the first stages of the Holocaust was the dehumanization of the Jewish people by Nazi Germany, which gave them subhuman names. Brené Brown, *Braving the Wilderness: The Quest for True Belonging and the Courage to Stand Alone* (New York: Random House, 2017), 73.
5. Schilaty, "What I Wish People Understood."
6. Patrick Kearon, "Refuge from the Storm" (general conference address, Salt Lake City, April 2016), churchofjesuschrist.org/study/general-conference/2016/04/refuge-from-the-storm.
7. Tad Walch, "National Media Attention Overwhelms BYU Valedictorian Who Came Out During Convocation Speech," *Deseret News*, April 29, 2019, deseret.com/2019/4/29/20672023/national-media-attention-overwhelms-byu-valedictorian-who-came-out-during-convocation-speech.
8. Matt, who is a close family friend, and I visited about his speech in episode 134 of the *Listen, Learn & Love* podcast.

9. Lauren Jackson, "Devotion and despair: The lonely struggle of a gay Mormon", CNN, July 19, 2016, cnn.com/2016/07/16/living/gay-mormon-struggle/index.html
10. "'I'm Not Ashamed of Who I Am': Studio C Member Comes Out as Gay, Shares Touching Message for LGBT Youth," *LDS Living*, December 19, 2018, ldsliving.com/Studio-C-Member-Comes-Out-As-Gay-Shares-Touching-Message-for-LGBT-Youth/s/89990. Stacey Harkey later joined me on episode 77 of the Listen, Learn & Love podcast.
11. Charlie Bird, "Guest Opinion: Everyone Loved Me as Cosmo the Cougar, but Would They Love Who I Was behind the Mask?" *Deseret News*, February 26, 2019, deseret.com/2019/2/26/20666826/guest-opinion-everyone-loved-me-as-cosmo-the-cougar-but-would-they-love-who-i-was-behind-the-mask#byus-cosmo-the-cougar-performs-with-the-byu-cougarettes-during-the-2017-homecoming-football-game-against-boise-state-oct-6-2017. Charlie Bird later joined me on episode 96 of *Listen, Learn, & Love* podcast.
12. "Berta Marquez," Obituaries, *Deseret News*, June 28, 2018, legacy.com/obituaries/deseretnews/obituary.aspx?n=berta-marquez&pid=189406898.
13. "Purpose of This Website Video," The Church of Jesus Christ of Latter-day Saints, accessed February 20, 2020, churchofjesuschrist.org/topics/gay/videos/purpose-of-this-website of Elder D. Todd Christofferson at 10:50.
14. Having your sexuality and romantic relationships be the norm is a part of "straight privilege." See "Recognizing Heterosexual Privilege," Campaign for Positive Space, University of Calgary, accessed February 15, 2020, ucalgary.ca/positivespace/node/38.
15. "The Conversation I Wish We Were Having," *Ben There, Done That* (blog), June 20, 2017, benschilaty.blogspot.com/2017/06/the-conversation-i-wish-we-were-having.html.
16. Hear Brian's story in episode 79 of the *Love, Listen & Learn* podcast.
17. Brené Brown, *Daring Greatly: How the Courage to Be Vulnerable Transforms the Way We Live, Love, Parent, and Lead* (New York: Avery, 2015), 232.
18. "Perceived burdensomeness" is a component of Joiner's "Interpersonal-Psychological Theory of Suicidal Behavior." Thomas Joiner, "The Interpersonal-Psychological Theory of Suicidal Behavior: Current Empirical Status," Science Briefs, American Psychological Association, June 2009, apa.org/science/about/psa/2009/06/sci-brief. This topic is discussed by Dr. Jeff Case in episode 86 and Dr. Scott Braithwaite in episode 193 of the Listen, Learn & Love podcast.
19. Some transgender individuals take on plural pronouns (they, them). See "Pronouns: A Resource Supporting Transgender and Gender Noncomforming (GNC) Educators and Students," GLSEN, accessed February 12, 2020, glsen.org/sites/default/files/GLSEN%20Pronouns%20Resource.pdf.

20. "Same-Sex Attraction," Gospel Topics, The Church of Jesus Christ of Latter-day Saints, accessed November 20, 2019, churchofjesuschrist.org/study/manual/gospel-topics/same-sex-attraction.
21. "Same Sex Attraction," Church Leaders, The Church of Jesus Christ of Latter-day Saints, accessed February, 2020, churchofjesuschrist.org/topics/gay/leaders.
22. "Same-Sex Attraction," Individuals, The Church of Jesus Christ of Latter-day Saints, accessed February 19, 2020, churchofjesuschrist.org/topics/gay/individuals, emphasis added.
23. The missionary in Elder Holland's talk is Preston Jenkins, now a returned missionary, who shared his story on the *Listen, Learn & Love* podcast. See episode 237.
24. Jeffrey R. Holland, "Behold Thy Mother" (general conference address, Salt Lake City, October 2015), churchofjesuschrist.org/study/general-conference/2015/10/behold-thy-mother, emphasis added.
25. Tom Christofferson, *That We May Be One: A Gay Mormon's Perspective on Faith and Family* (Salt Lake City: Deseret Book, 2017), 16–17.
26. Dallin H. Oaks, interview by Jennifer Napier Pearce, TribTalk, January 29, 2015, video, 17:39, youtube.com/watch?v=UIJ6gL_xc-M, emphasis added.
27. For more information on the Genesis Group, see ldsgenesisgroup.org/.
28. Schilaty, "What I Wish People Understood."
29. See northstarlds.org/.
30. See encircletogether.org/.
31. See affirmation.org/.
32. See mormonsbuildingbridges.org/.
33. "Rainbow Flag (LGBT)," Wikipedia, accessed February 17, 2020, en.wikipedia.org/wiki/Rainbow_flag_(LGBT_movement).
34. Ezra Taft Benson, "Beware of Pride" (general conference address, Salt Lake City, April 1989), churchofjesuschrist.org/study/general-conference/1989/04/beware-of-pride.
35. Dallin H. Oaks, *Pure in Heart* (Salt Lake City: Deseret Book, 1988), 89.
36. Ben Schilaty, "Pride Is the Opposite of Shame," *Ben There, Done That* (blog), July 2, 2019, benschilaty.blogspot.com/2019/07/pride-is-opposite-of-shame.html.
37. Allison is the founder of the LGBTQ support organization Lift and Love; see liftandlove.org/.
38. See an image of the painting on Rosemary Card's Q.NOOR website, accessed February 17, 2020, qnoor.com/products/jesus-said-love-everyone.
39. Allison Dayton, "Thank you J. Kirk Richards," Facebook, January 29, 2019, facebook.com/allison.dayton/posts/10156329796603380.
40. Jake Dayton to Richard Ostler, email, December 29, 2019.
41. Episode 170 of the *Listen, Learn & Love* podcast.
42. Episode 165 of the *Listen, Learn & Love* podcast.

43. Eric Kirby, June 3, 2018, twitter.com/ericmkirby/status/1003458251059417089. Eric shared his story on Episode 38 of the *Listen, Learn & Love* podcast.
44. Jenny Rollins, "'Each Person Is Accepted Unconditionally': Sandy Neighborhood Lines Streets with Rainbow Flags for Pride Week," KSL.com, June 2, 2019, ksl.com/article/46565141/each-person-is-accepted-unconditionally-sandy-neighborhood-lines-streets-with-rainbow-flags-for-pride-week.
45. Episode 138 of the *Listen, Learn & Love* podcast.
46. See Gretel Kauffman, "LGBT Pride Flags Spark Controversy, Support in Utah City," *Deseret News*, June 10, 2019, deseretnews.com/article/900074800/lgbt-pride-flags-heber-city-utah-spark-controversy-support.html and Ryann Richardson, "Rainbow Banners Line St. George Streets for Southern Utah Pride Festival," *St George News*, September 9, 2019, stgeorgeutah.com/news/archive/2019/09/09/arh-rainbow-banners-line-st-george-streets-for-southern-utah-pride-festival.
47. Episode 149 of the *Listen, Learn & Love* podcast.
48. Jon Pike, "I'm actually happy for the discussion," Facebook, September 16, 2019, facebook.com/jon.pike.988/posts/10214245372195049.
49. Episode 207 of the *Listen, Learn & Love* podcast.
50. "A Face to Face Event with Elder Gerrit W. Gong," Broadcasts, The Church of Jesus Christ of Latter-day Saints, November 17, 2019, video, churchofjesuschrist.org/broadcasts/face-to-face/children-and-youth-gerrit-w-gong.

CHAPTER 6

THE ROLE OF THE ATONEMENT OF JESUS CHRIST

I have a deep testimony of the Atonement of Jesus Christ and its ability to both cleanse people from sin and give hope and healing during difficult mortal challenges. The power and effects of the Atonement are impossible to overstate. That is why I like the term "the infinite Atonement"—it indicates that the Atonement's reach and Christ's love are endless and limitless. One of my favorite books is the *Infinite Atonement of Jesus Christ*, by Elder Tad R. Callister, which teaches about the completeness of the Atonement of Jesus Christ.[1] Elder Callister teaches that in addition to making repentance and receiving forgiveness possible, the Atonement gives us hope and heals broken hearts. During my younger years, I mostly understood the ability of the Atonement to remove sin. However, in my older years, I better understand the power of the Atonement to heal our pain that is unrelated to sin, such as pain cause by the death of a loved one, difficult relationships, the actions of others, loneliness, and other difficult mortal challenges.

The Atonement not only allows us to survive the pain and trials of mortality but also provides healing to make us better, happier, and more Christlike people. This is evident in the lives and testimonies of many LGBTQ Latter-day Saints who have used the Atonement to ease the burdens of loneliness and frustration. Feeling the full effects of the Atonement requires us to be humble, vulnerable, and honest with ourselves, to admit we need the Savior's help and grace. This kind of honesty can be particularly difficult for our LGBTQ Church members who often feel shame, self-loathing, or fear because of messages in society about people like them. By expressing openness and love to our LGBTQ members, we may make it easier for them to accept that our Savior loves them too. My friend Kurt Nielsen, a gay Latter-day Saint, shared this quote from Henri Nouwen, a gay, celibate Catholic priest:[2]

> Over the last few years I have been increasingly aware that true healing mostly takes place through the sharing of weakness. Mostly we are so afraid of our weaknesses that we hide them at all cost and thus make them unavailable to others but also often to ourselves. And, in this way, we end up living double lives even against our own desires: one life in which we present ourselves to the world, to ourselves, and to God as a person who is in control and another life in which we feel insecure, doubtful, confused, and anxious and totally out of control. The split between these two lives causes us a lot of suffering. I have become increasingly aware of the importance of overcoming the great chasm between these two lives and am becoming more and more aware that facing, with others, the reality of our existence can be the beginning of a truly free life.
>
> It is amazing in my own life that true friendship and community became possible to the degree that I was able to share my weaknesses with others. Often I became aware of the fact that in the sharing of my weaknesses with others, the real depths of my human brokenness and weakness and sinfulness started to reveal themselves to me, not as a source of despair but as a source of hope. As long as I try to convince myself or others of my independence, a lot of my energy is invested in building up my own false self. But once I am able to truly confess my most profound dependence on others and on God, I can come in touch with my true self and real community can develop.[3]

Being LGBTQ is not a weakness, but by sharing our pain and struggles with those who love us and with God, we can find hope even as we recognize our shortcomings and strive to become better. Our shortcomings are meant to guide us to our Savior's grace, which offers hope and healing (see Jacob 4:7). One of my favorite scriptures is D&C 88:6–7: "He that ascended up on high, as also he *descended below all things*, in that he comprehended all things, that he might be in all and through all things, the light of truth; which truth shineth" (emphasis added). I love that Christ "descended below all things" because it means He understands us, has felt our pain, and can heal us from that pain. For our LGBTQ members, this doctrine is critical—a loving Savior understands their road and therefore can walk with them, heal them, and give them hope.

In the following statements, LGBTQ Latter-day Saints and LDS parents of LGBTQ children explain how the Atonement of Jesus Christ helps them navigate their road. Some of these statements mention pain resulting from Church experiences. I share these not to be critical but to give insights on how we can do better. I certainly would have welcomed reading these comments or attending an LGBTQ sensitivity training meeting before my YSA service so I could have better understood and met the needs of our LGBTQ members.

Thoughts on the Atonement of Jesus Christ from LGBTQ Latter-day Saints

JOEY SHEPPARD (QUEER INDIVIDUAL)

One thing that has brought me peace is stated in *Preach My Gospel:* "All that is unfair about life can be made right through the Atonement of Jesus Christ."[4] I don't know what fair means, but I know if I stick with Christ, it will all be okay.

RJ RISUENO (GAY MAN)

I personally believe that the Atonement has helped me forgive those who treat me unfairly. In the same way Jesus was spat upon before His Crucifixion, I feel that I have been spat upon. I look to Christ's Atonement as suffering for my sins as well as understanding my pain from hurtful comments.

DAVID DOYLE (GAY MAN)

As I understand it, the Atonement is a series of events performed by Jesus that allow us to be unified with God—taking on our pains and sins in the Garden of Gethsemane, dying on the cross, and exiting the tomb as a resurrected being.

The part of the Atonement I think most relates to being queer is that Jesus experienced all our hurts, sicknesses, weaknesses, and imperfections so that He would have mercy on us and know how to nourish us. (Just to be clear, I'm not saying that me being queer is a sickness or imperfection).

Jesus knows the pains and trials I experience, including things like loneliness and betrayal. He knows the ways in which I am weak. He perfectly understands me and my circumstances. With that knowledge, Jesus knows how to succor me and strengthen me. He helps me be strong enough to love and to forgive.

I get messages that are affirming, such as that I'm not broken, God loves me as I am, and I am not unworthy simply for being gay. Jesus mourns with me over the homophobia I encounter in this life.

The Atonement changes our desires to be more in line with God's. I used to plead for God to turn me straight, and that was always answered by spiritual silence. Accepting that this is part of who I am has brought peace, and my understanding of how God views homosexuality has changed.

I believe that I increase my access to the blessings of the Atonement when I am active in living the faith I have. I'm directed to where I can be used. There are people who are hurting, and I try to help them see hope, to challenge the negative messages they've internalized, and to help them feel God's love and that they are worthy of it. As I do so, I feel the love of the Savior for me.

BOO TINLING (LESBIAN WOMAN)

I find myself faced with critical questions for my life that currently don't have answers. So often the burden of trying to reconcile seemingly irreconcilable things sends me into a tailspin of frustration, anger, and depression. But my mind and heart always come back to the Atonement of Jesus Christ, and I feel hope. I hold onto this hope graciously and fiercely! This undeniable hope in a loving God and a perfect Savior is what gets me through my darkest days.

JOHN GUSTAV-WRATHALL (GAY MAN)

Jesus Christ has helped me to navigate this road, first of all, by communicating His love to me in very direct and personal ways and by helping me to see the way He sees me, which is not the way the world sees me. He helped me to understand that no atonement is needed for my gayness.

Through Christ I am forgiven for the rebellion, sin, and error I've committed and the harm that I've done. Also—importantly—I experience healing that enables me to forgive others who have harmed me. In fact, it is the healing power and presence of Christ in my life that makes so much else possible, and that gives me hope that everything in this life that is broken (including the things that are broken because of homophobia and ignorance) will be fixed and healed and made perfect.

Through Christ, I can have a relationship with the Father and with the Holy Spirit and receive the guidance and love that I need in order to perfect myself and become like the Father. Through the peace I find in Christ, I'm also granted the gift of patience—which as an LGBTQ Latter-day Saint, you need lots of. I'm okay with not having all the answers to every question. I'm able to trust that what God has for me is so much greater than what I can imagine.

JOSEPH ELDREDGE (GAY MAN)

Through Christ's Atonement, I can realize my full potential as a queer son of God. My queerness is given to me by Him, and Christ helps me navigate that. I've also learned that being queer and LDS [is] like a rope being held by Christ that you just have to hold onto. Do I know if I'll be eternally happy married to a woman? No. Do I trust that God has told me it'll all be worth it? Yes. So I keep holding onto the rope that Christ is holding.

BEN SCHILATY (GAY MAN)

I always share Alma 33:23[5] and then say: "I used to think the Atonement of Jesus Christ was supposed to make me straight, but instead it healed my broken heart."

CRAIG NEWSOME (GAY MAN)

For me, the act of Jesus coming to earth and paying the price for my life and everyone else's is just something I can never comprehend. I was raised in another faith to hate myself for being gay. But since joining the Church and coming back to God, I feel like [the Atonement] is about reconciliation and [having a] relationship with my Father and Jesus. I love how the restored gospel teaches that God loves me as I am! That He's not requiring me to change my orientation—that orientation is not the sin.

There have always been aspects of me, some kind of inner self condemnation, that I have never been able to present to God. But when we did the *Come, Follow Me* section on Jesus washing the disciples' feet, I had this huge realization that it's those icky bits of myself that the Savior wants to minister to. It has changed how I relate to Heavenly Father and the Savior. I feel like I can bring before Them my most unpleasant things. I know They want to love me.

JUSTIN TRAASDAHL (GAY MAN)

When I came out, I thought that through the Atonement of Jesus Christ *all* things could be made possible, including being made straight. I was taught over and over [that] *all* things could be made possible through the Atonement of Christ. For ten years I went through conversion therapy, worked with Church leaders to change my sexuality. I think when I realized that the Atonement of Christ was never meant to fix me but to help me be the best gay I could be in my Latter-day Saint community, I finally found my peace. I just wish the Church leaders had helped me realize this sooner. I don't think I'm broken. I'm not perfect, just as a straight person is not perfect. But I was not built to change my sexuality through the Atonement of Christ, just like a straight person was not asked to change their sexuality through the Atonement of Christ.

STANLEY ALVEY (GAY MAN)

When I first came out, I was fully expecting to be changed or "fixed." I was praying morning and night and all throughout the day. I was preparing for a mission. I was doing everything I was supposed to be doing. The Atonement of Jesus Christ was the only thing keeping me alive. I remember feeling like there was no way anyone understood what I was going through, but there was a video from Elder Jeffery R. Holland that always hit so close to home and comforted me. He talked about how through Christ's Atonement, [Christ] understands the individualized pain and suffering of each individual.[6] "The Son of Man hath descended below them all. Art thou greater than he?" (D&C 122:8). No matter how dark it gets, Christ has seen that darkness. No matter how alone you feel, Christ has felt that.

CALVIN BURKE (GAY MAN)

For years I prayed that I would be made straight. One day after church, after having faithfully served a mission, studied scriptures, prayed multiple times a day, and faithfully kept my covenants for years, I was so upset I hiked a mountain and prayed for the first time in anger. "Why won't you take this away from me?" I asked. "I have done everything I can. You are all powerful. Why will you not make me straight, Heavenly Father?" The answer that came back hit me so powerfully, I jumped up off my knees: "You have not done the work required of me to understand my feelings about the way that I created you." I walked down the mountain humbled, having realized Heavenly Father was right. I hadn't humbled myself enough to understand what

His plan was for me, or for the way that He felt about me, His gay child. I leapt into the scriptures, this time asking the right questions—and I watched and wept in awe as I learned of Heavenly Father's love for me, exactly as I am, for the first time. With Nephi, I testify, "I know that he loveth his children; nevertheless, I do not know the meaning of all things" (1 Nephi 11:17).

KURT NIELSEN (GAY MAN)

There was something powerful for me in thinking that Christ descended below all things. That meant he descended below my things. Could there actually be someone who really understood what I was experiencing? Could there be someone who would keep knocking on the door of my heart, seeking me to open it up regardless of my shame? Could there be someone who would keep pursuing me, [who] found me desirable and beautiful? Could I really be loved? The Atonement has answered all these questions for me in the affirmative. The Atonement has relentlessly sought my heart and declared it good. The Atonement has filled that deep pit of emptiness, [of] pain, and of longing that I tried to fill in so many important ways. I love Christ because as the scriptures say, "He loved me first."[7]

I had a dream. In the dream, I was standing in front of the Savior. In between us was a hologram image of myself. The hologram was speaking, praising Christ, and saying all sorts of flowery/eloquent things. As the hologram spoke, the Savior became more and more agitated until He finally had enough and said to me: "I don't want him. I want you." He then reached through the hologram, which evaporated the moment He touched it, and pulled me into His arms. After that dream, I knew that God wanted all of me, the true me, and not the façade that showed up each week to church pretending to be straight in order to fit in. I learned that God doesn't want His children to fit in—He wants them to belong to the body of Christ.

DALE LARSEN (GAY MAN)[8]

When I look back on my life of nearly sixty-five years and how the Savior's Atonement has blessed my life, I am brought to tears. Tears because of how intimately He knows me, how fiercely He loves me, and how determined He is to be with me. He has been with me and understood my pain, my loss, my loneliness at times, my fears, my failures, my weaknesses, my sin, as well as my joy and happiness. He has sustained me during my darkest days, through my trials and addictions, and has brought me through them into the light. He still pursues me and is there at every turn in my life.

Though He has been there always, steady and firm, He has never taken away my agency. He has taught me His voice and how to hear it. He has also taught me the voice of the adversary by allowing me to experience the good from the evil, . . . patiently waited upon me to make the right choices, and has given me space to correct the wrong ones because of His suffering for them in Gethsemane. He has stood at every juncture of my life and accepted me just as I am and then each time pleaded for me to become a little better. He blessed me to be free from the powerful urges of same-sex attraction (SSA) during the years I served in Church leadership callings, which allowed me to totally focus on His children and give my all to those over whom I was called. He also allowed those feelings to return when I was released so I could continue to learn and draw even closer to Him.

He blessed me to find the one woman to whom I could be attracted, the one who would become my best friend, my lover, my wife, and my companion with whom I made eternal covenants. He knew me completely so as to know who that person would be and to direct my life in such a way as to find her, win her heart, and be sealed to her for time and all eternity. He gave both myself and my wife deep spiritual impressions that led us to each other far before our time of meeting. He gave me the blessing to have children and grandchildren who now bring me my greatest joy. He has completely been there to bless our marriage during both the hard and good times.

He especially showed his understanding and love for me at a turning point in our marriage, at a time when I was considering leaving my wife and children. His voice came to me through the Spirit and in a way specific to my needed tutoring, which brought into my mind and heart the true choice that I was about to make. The voice said, "If you continue down the path you are following, and you can, and you can be happy, you will lose them." Although my family was not present in front of me, I looked at a family sitting near me, and there displayed before my eyes was my wife and our two sons. All my life, from the young age of eight years old, my greatest desire was to be a father and raise a family, my family. Because of His atoning love and understanding of me personally, He was able to present the choice to me in a way that changed the course of my life.

Because of His suffering, He now shows me the intimate compassion He has for me, He has shown me my worth to Him and the Father and has helped me to visualize that eternal worth in myself. He has not only taught me to love others completely without judgment, but to completely love myself as a son of God.

Later in my life, still feeling shame for my same-sex attractions, still feeling less than in my own mind and believing that God must see me in the same light, I was brought to my knees in earnest prayer to ask God if He knew I would struggle with SSA and if so, how He now saw me. After being prompted to follow up on a previous impression that I had ignored for a time, and after returning to my knees again, I was told that I was just as He intended and just as we had agreed in the pre[mortal] existence. That changed my life; for the first time I was able to love myself as much as I loved others. I was finally able to be me, a true son of God. From that time on, how I viewed myself and my standing before God [has] forever changed.

[The Savior] has taught me to know the best questions to ask Him and the Father to create the greatest impact upon me for good. He has answered each one in turn in His own way and time. He has and is continuing to help me to allow my will to be swallowed up in His will, which brings me so many blessings and the opportunity to bless others.

Because of His Atonement, because of His suffering, He knows and has felt everything I have and will yet experience in this mortal life. Though this life is not yet complete for me, I trust in Him completely. He has always been with me; He will be with me to the very end. I love Him, and He loves me.

Thoughts on the Atonement of Jesus Christ from Parents of LGBTQ Children

TAMMY BITTER (MOTHER OF GAY SON)

Because of the Atonement, I know that Christ also feels the hurt at the insensitive and sometimes cruel comments made about my gay son, and I take comfort in knowing that I'm not alone in this pain. Because of the Atonement, I know that my warm, loving, intelligent, motivated, gay son will have his life validated and accepted in the next life, even if sometimes that doesn't appear to happen on earth. Because of the Atonement, I know that the Savior loves my son as much as I do, and that sustains me even on my lowest days and brings me joy and happiness on my good days. Because of the Atonement, I have hope that I will have my son in the next life. Finally, because of the Atonement, I can feel happy in loving and supporting my gay son while still being active at church.

DEBRA OAKS COE (MOTHER OF GAY SON)

The Atonement is one of the greatest blessings we have to help us through the huge challenges in this life. The Atonement is for all the hurts and struggles and loneliness we experience. The Atonement has helped hold me together and brought light when I have only been able to see darkness. Having the Atonement has given me help with carrying burdens and replacing those with hope and love. I couldn't have walked this path without my Savior. He has healed my broken heart from the many hurtful things that have happened because of people who don't understand having this challenge. He helped me know how to help my son as well. I have seen the difference the Atonement has also made to our son. Like I said, it is the greatest power and blessing we could have been given.

HEATHER ROBERTSON (MOTHER OF GAY DAUGHTER)

The Atonement has become more tangible and personal as I've labored in my own Gethsemane, coming to terms with this new reality as a parent of a gay child. I've experienced and witnessed a tiny fraction of what Jesus must have felt as he was "rejected by His own." As I experience pain and anguish deeper than I thought possible, I understand just a little more the pain Jesus suffered for me—for my child. The deeper the pain, the more gratitude I feel for His infinite Atonement that helps me to know I am never alone. He is always there with perfect understanding.

DIANE CALDWELL CARPENTER (MOTHER OF GAY SON AND BISEXUAL DAUGHTER)

The Atonement of Christ has given me the freedom to simply love my son and daughter as they are. Christ has already carried this burden for me, so I don't need to. I can just love without judgment.

JULIE WOOLLEY (MOTHER OF GAY SON)

The Atonement has given me the strength to stay in the Church because I know I need this relationship with my Savior. The Atonement has shown me His love and the love of our Father in Heaven, not only for me but also for my son. The Atonement has helped me forgive those who say words that have hurt me, even those in the leadership of the Church. The Atonement has helped me love all kinds of people, no matter what their circumstances, and not judge them. My heart still breaks at times, but because of Christ, I know I can carry on.

KARL STUM (FATHER OF GAY SON)

The Atonement of Jesus Christ and the endless love, mercy, and fairness I have hope and belief in are the principles that give my life peace when thinking about the outcome in the next life for my gay son and our family. When my mind is coupled with the Atonement, I am calm and my mind is unfettered about outcomes. He was made this way. He is seeking divine guidance and moving through life making noble choices based on the light given him. Though some are incongruent with current Church policies—and even amidst his unbelief because of irreconcilable contradictions in his mind and heart—I am confident relevant truths will be made known to him and all God's children in due time in this life or the next, and they will be able to make choices relative to the gospel without deterrence from inadequacies in mind, emotions, and spirit they have little or no control of now. And, relating to the future in eternity he has as a gay man, I'm not convinced that when we are all brought out into the full light of day, that sons and daughters of God who were attracted to their own gender on earth will change or even need to. I feel that it is more likely that we are "seeing through a glass darkly" (1 Corinthians 13:12) and that our theology is just incomplete right now. I have no real worries because of the love of our Heavenly Parents and of our Savior.

ANNALEE WOLFORD KELLY (MOTHER OF TRANSGENDER SON)

The grace aspect of the Atonement has been a powerful tool in our journey parenting our transgender son. It enables us to receive our daily manna. His grace gives us everything we need just for a day at a time—the energy and revelation needed for raising our son on a daily basis. Never much more [than that]—but just enough.

LAURA STURM (MOTHER OF BISEXUAL SON)

One of the best things I heard when I went to the North Star conference in the spring was, "You are not your child's Savior . . . they already have one of those. You are their parent, and your job is to love unconditionally. The saving part is on Jesus."

My bisexual son is the oldest of five children, and I'm so glad I learned this important thing through parenting him. I used to obsess about all my children making correct choices, thinking that it was on me to get them all to heaven. Now I just have so much faith in the process of mortality and free agency. We are meant to struggle and make mistakes, and we all have a Savior to help us grow and learn through the process and fill in the missing pieces.

MARGARET STEWARD (MOTHER OF GAY SON)

The Atonement is for everyone, every moment of every day. In Mosiah 2:21, it says that no one is a profitable servant. No one. We are each dependent on Christ for loaning us breath and for sustaining us from moment to moment. So no matter what shape and form our lives take, no one needs the Savior more or less than their fellow brother or sister. Also, . . . the "strait and narrow" path is actually not linear.[9] *Strait* means "situation of perplexity or distress, difficult to navigate."[10] So the path to the tree of life is fraught with difficulty and distress—that applies to everyone. So we shouldn't feel shame when we realize that we all need the Savior equally.

People who experience anything on the LGBTQ spectrum are in no more of a "dire strait" than anyone. The same love is available to them and the same help. We should never view the Savior's infinite gift of love as anything less than it is, and [we] should not view some people as needing Him more. We make a serious error when we assume that He can't love us when we make mistakes and missteps; it is precisely the necessity and possibility of misstepping that brought about the need for the Atonement in the first place.

We can't learn and become what Father intended without experiencing opposition and taking missteps as a result. Christ understood this perfectly and accepted the awful arithmetic of every misdeed and misstep. We often project our limited understanding of our life here on the Savior. Others' actions may cause us to feel less inclined to love them, but not so for the Savior. His love is infinite. His patience in this process of mortality is infinite. One of Satan's greatest tools is to cause us to question our or another's worth in the sight of God.

I wish we had a perfect way to describe the Atonement. That word is beautiful, but it sometimes gets equated with a program or procedure. The Atonement is love—the Father's love, Jesus Christ's love. It was lovingly conceived, accepted, lovingly suffered, and lovingly extended. It isn't a system of salvation. It is pure and complete and inexhaustible love.

EVAN SMITH (FATHER OF GAY SON)

The Savior's ability, through the Atonement, to comfort me in my suffering has helped me learn to love and support my twenty-year-old gay son more fully. I'll share a recent experience as an example.

Recently my wife and I felt it necessary to walk away from a meeting with a Church leader (in which he was extending me a calling). We left because when I said I was not sad about our son returning a bit early from his mission and choosing to step away from the Church a few months [prior] so he could date men to try to find a husband, the leader's response was not supportive. I said our son had received strong and clear personal revelation about his decisions and that we knew his keeping the Church at a distance was the only way for him to maintain good mental health. But the leader's words made us feel like we had to choose between being genuinely and emotionally supportive of our son and being truly faithful disciples.

It felt like the Church was asking me to not just sacrifice family time for Church service but to actually place my emotional loyalty to the Church ahead of my love for my family and their well-being. It was a very painful experience. But I'm glad it happened because a few days later the Spirit told me the whole thing occurred so I could empathize with my son, even if just a tiny bit—so I could understand a little bit better how painful it was for him to have to choose between having a future family and having full fellowship in the Church. In the moment the Spirit spoke to me, I felt the Savior's love comfort me, and I seemed to catch a glimpse of the empathy that He has for my son—and of the Lord's ability to love and console him so much more than I can. And I saw how important it was for me to always try to show that same type of pure love, without mixed emotions or qualifications, to my family.

I'm so thankful God blessed us with a gay son. My understanding of the comforting power of Christ's Atonement and of His matchless love and empathy have been deeply enriched because of the challenges our son has faced. Because of his belief in Christ, he has forgiven so many people who say hurtful things to him. The Atonement has similarly helped me forgive that church leader. I know his words aren't reflective of the Savior's views. I'm eternally thankful for the Atonement's ability to alleviate my pain and to teach me how to best support my son by loving him as Christ loves me.

BECKY EDWARDS (MOTHER OF GAY SON)

For me, the Atonement covers the unanswered questions. It brings trust that the answers will come, and it brings peace in the meantime. Many LGBTQ people feel there is no plan of happiness for them in our church, but I have come to believe that God does have a plan for my son, that he is beloved and precious to God, and that all questions will be answered at some point. Another way the Atonement has helped me in this journey is giving me the strength to forgive people who have hurt my son with rejecting or homophobic comments made at school, seminary, and church. At first, we struggled with the fact that our son stopped attending church and seminary, but once he let us know the comments and teachings were causing self-loathing and suicidal thoughts, of course we chose his mental health as the top priority. Part of using the Atonement for us is that we have turned all of this over to God. We know that God has our son, that He understands our son's heart of gold, and we are grateful that our son is living his life guided by prayer and personal revelation. The Atonement is applicable in every step of this journey.

ENDNOTES

1. Tad R. Callister, *The Infinite Atonement* (Salt Lake City: Deseret Book, 2000).
2. Kurt Nielsen's story is told in episode 147 of the *Love, Listen & Learn* podcast.
3. "Sharing Our Weakness," Meditations, Henri Nouwen Society, accessed December 19, 2019, henrinouwen.org/meditation/sharing-our-weakness/.
4. "Lesson 2: The Plan of Salvation," *Preach My Gospel: A Guide to Missionary Service* (Salt Lake City: The Church of Jesus Christ of Latter-day Saints, 2019), churchofjesuschrist.org/study/manual/preach-my-gospel-a-guide-to-missionary-service/lesson-2-the-plan-of-salvation.
5. "And now, my brethren, I desire that ye shall plant this word in your hearts, and as it beginneth to swell even so nourish it by your faith. And behold, it will become a tree, springing up in you unto everlasting life. And then may God grant unto you that your burdens may be light, through the joy of his Son. And even all this can ye do if ye will" (Alma 33:23).
6. Jeffrey R. Holland, "The Savior Understands Me," The Church of Jesus Christ of Latter-day Saints, October 21, 2016, YouTube video, 0:47, youtube.com/watch?v=EUhgBU3coPY&t=47s.

7. See 1 John 4:19: "We love him, because he first loved us."
8. Please see episode 154 of the *Listen, Learn & Love* podcast for Dale's full story.
9. See Matthew 7:13–14: "Enter ye in at the strait gate: for wide is the gate, and broad is the way, that leadeth to destruction, and many there be which go in there at: Because strait is the gate, and narrow is the way, which leadeth unto life, and few there be that find it."
10. See Merriam-Webster, s.v. "strait," accessed December 18, 2019, merriam-webster.com/dictionary/strait.

CHAPTER 7

MINISTERING TO LGBTQ LATTER-DAY SAINTS

In April 2018, Elder Holland explained a "bold, new, holier way" of ministering:[1]

> Brothers and sisters, as the work of quorums and auxiliaries matures institutionally, it follows that we should mature personally as well—individually rising above any mechanical, function-without-feeling routine to the heartfelt discipleship articulated by the Savior at the conclusion of His earthly ministry. As He prepared to leave His still-innocent and somewhat-confused little band of followers, He did not list a dozen administrative steps they had to take or hand them a fistful of reports to be filled out in triplicate. No, He summarized their task in one fundamental commandment: "*Love one another; as I have loved you. . . . By this shall all men know that ye are my disciples, if ye have love one to another*" (John 13:34-35).

Some of the first steps we must take to show that Christlike love described by Elder Holland in ministering to others, especially LGBTQ individuals, are to learn to withhold judgment, to act in love and not fear, and to treat them not as enemies and outsiders but as fellow siblings in the gospel.

Ministering Based on Love, Not Fear

When Ellis and Katie Ivory arrived to preside over the England Manchester Mission in July 1979, they felt the mission was too focused on a message of "us versus the Church of England." President and Sister Ivory believed the missionaries were demonizing the Church of England, inhibiting their efforts to take the positive message of the restored Church to the English people. They wanted to change the culture of our mission and after thought and prayer decided to hold a mission conference at a prominent Church of England parish church called the St. Michael and All Angels Church, in Hawkshead, England.[2]

During the mission conference, both President Ivory and the vicar Reverend Norman Scott spoke. We felt Christ's Spirit while sitting in that chapel and listening to the vicar, and our hearts were softened toward the Church of England and its members.

This event changed the direction of our mission. We learned that the positive message of our restored Church could stand on its own merits and not on the backs of those who believed differently. They were not the enemy. Fact-based discussions on our doctrinal differences and bearing testimony with the Spirit did help many join our restored Church. We did not need to turn to negative, emotionally charged statements about their faith to lift our position. The result of our changed outlook was dramatic. Heavenly Father opened the windows of heaven, and many joined our Church. In some months, over three hundred people were baptized, and at times, our mission was the top baptizing English-speaking mission in the Church.

In 2016, thirty-seven years later, one of our missionaries, Brent Brown, visited this same church in Hawkshead and learned they were raising money to save the parish's tower bell. He decided to return the courtesy extended to us in 1979 and raised about twenty thousand dollars from our group of missionaries. In 2017, a check was presented at an event with President and Sister Ulrich of the England Manchester Mission, Reverend John Dixon of St. Michael and All Angels, missionaries, and members of the parish congregation. The story was covered by BBC and our church.[3]

This kind of outreach to another religion was seen more recently in March 2019 when President Nelson visited Rome. I was glad to see him shaking hands with Pope Francis at the Vatican.[4] My heart has been similarly warmed when I've seen instances of these two faiths engaging in common work, such as the Church's support for Catholic charities.

These stories bring me joy because they illustrate how people can come together, even with their differences, to support a common goal. We didn't compromise our doctrine in helping the parish's fundraising efforts. In fact, by offering assistance we lived up to our covenants and followed the example of Jesus Christ, who brings us all together.[5] President and Sister Ivory's outreach effort in 1979, as well as the later fundraising event, were also consistent with the teachings and example of our Church leaders. In Elder Uchtdorf's April 2017 talk in general conference, he invited us to live a higher law based on love and not a lower law based on fear and manipulation:

> Fear rarely has the power to change our hearts, and it will never transform us into people who love what is right and want to obey Heavenly Father. . . .
>
> One of the ways Satan wants us to manipulate others is by dwelling on and even exaggerating the evil in the world. . . .
>
> Let us serve God and love our fellowmen. Let us do this with a natural confidence, with humility, never looking down on any other religion or group of people. . . .
>
> I don't believe God wants His children to be fearful or dwell on the evils of the world. "For God hath not given us the spirit of fear; but of power, and of love, and of a sound mind" (2 Timothy 1:7). . . .
>
> I pray with all the strength of my soul that we may become liberated from this fear by the divinely appointed antidote to fear: the pure love of Christ, for "perfect love casteth out fear" (1 John 4:18).[6]

One way in which we as Church members may inadvertently act out of fear is by being critical of other faiths. Perhaps we do this to create a sense of solidarity or to improve our self-image. Sometimes I hear comments on the decline of other faiths as a way to prop up our Church (for example, "Their churches are empty on Sunday"). Pointing out the struggles of other faiths may help us make our point, unifying us as Church members, but prevents us from living a higher law of love, as taught by Elder Uchtdorf. We may even cast LGBTQ people as an outside enemy—viewing their existence as a sign of the last days. This mindset, however, is motivated by fear, not by love or by God. I know many Church members find the "us versus them" narrative to be off-putting, and they are looking for a more positive message. Let's save the "us versus them" for the only real "them": Satan, his followers, and the fear that he engenders.

Brené Brown refers to humans' tendency to create a common enemy in her book *Braving the Wilderness*: "Common enemy intimacy is the opposite of true belonging. If the bond we share with others is simply that we hate the same people, the intimacy we experience is intense, immediately gratifying, and an easy way to discharge outrage and pain. It is not, however, fuel for real connection."[7] True connection with others is based on understanding and love.

To develop a love and understanding of others, we need to withhold judgment and try to see things from different perspectives. In Elder Robert C. Gay's October 2018 general conference talk, he reminded us of what the Prophet Joseph Smith taught: "While one portion of the human race is judging and condemning the other without mercy, the Great Parent of the universe looks upon the whole of the human family with a fatherly care and paternal regard," for "His love [is] unfathomable."

Brigham Young also encouraged the Saints to show compassion and avoid judging others: "I wish to urge upon the Saints . . . to understand men and women as they are, and not understand them as you are. How often it is said—'Such a person has done wrong, and he cannot be a Saint.' . . . We hear some swear and lie . . . [or] break the Sabbath . . . Do not judge such persons, for you do not know the design of the Lord concerning them . . . [Rather,] bear with them."[8]

How do these teachings apply to our treatment of LGBTQ Latter-day Saints? Sometimes in church discussions, we may be tempted to talk negatively about LGBTQ people. Our polarized and emotionally charged political environment thrives on these negative remarks that cast whole groups of people as outside threats. However, there may be LGBTQ Latter-day Saints (and families with LGBTQ members) within the sound of our voices, and these statements could cause them to feel unwelcome and conclude there is no place for people like them in our Church. Our LGBTQ Church members sitting in the pews need to hear positive, inclusive messages about them, not messages that treat them as a different group.

For example, I heard a member of the Church say, "I can remember when gay was a positive thing" (referring to a time when gay meant being happy and not a sexual orientation). A few days earlier, I had given a priesthood blessing to a gay BYU student and felt Heavenly Father's love for His gay son. As I heard that comment, I thought about that BYU student doing his best to stay in the Church and how messages like these cause him to feel that people like him are not fully welcome at church.

Following the counsel and example of our leaders, we can learn to live a higher law, teaching the beautiful truths of our Church on their own merits and not at the expense of others. For example, I've learned to say my marriage can stand on its own merits—without talking negatively about individuals in same-sex marriages. Yes, same-sex marriage is outside of the Church's doctrine, but those couples are still our spiritual siblings, children of the same Heavenly Parents, and inside the circle of God's love, as taught by President Thomas S. Monson: "Heavenly Father loves you—each of you. That love never changes. It is simply there. It is there for you when you are sad or happy, discouraged or hopeful. God's love is there for you whether or not you feel you deserve love. It is simply always there."[9]

ODDBJØRN STRAND-ANGERMANN (GAY MAN)

Many years ago, amid the controversy about legalizing same-sex marriage in Norway, I will never forget an older brother bearing his testimony of how grateful he was for being a member of a Church where "people like that" have no place. That was the first time I considered leaving the Church. I don't know why I stayed, but I did and still do.

ANNIE HOLLIS (BISEXUAL WOMAN)

I overheard someone in my singles ward bluntly state, "Gay people shouldn't be allowed here." I was the only "out" queer in the ward, and he was new and didn't know me, but I was standing right behind him and within earshot were two other LGBTQ members who were still in the closet. I spent most of that Sunday in tears. I've heard a lot of little comments over the years, but I had never heard someone say it quite so harshly as that.

MATTHEW AYDELOTTE (QUEER MAN)

I've heard things from people saying straight up that "gay people shouldn't be allowed at church" to vague comments about how "we all know there are people out there threatening the Proclamation and the sanctity of the family." Some stuff is said straight out, but most of the time it's vague, general comments that everyone understands . . . Those are generally even worse because everyone feels safe agreeing to those "vague" comments.

JEFF CASE (GAY MAN)

When I hear members use "threat to the family" as a euphemism [for] the LGBTQ community's seeking civil rights, I remind them of what the actual threats are to their families. The families

> of those sitting in the room that day were at risk [for] a different set of reasons than [the ones] they were implying: excessive debt, domestic violence, various forms of abuse, infidelity, etc. [The threat is] not, in fact, the pursuit of civil rights by the LGBTQ community. The only threat that I am to my congregation by being out and vocal is that sometimes I push people into evaluating their assumptions.

Creating a Culture of Inclusivity and Nonjudgment

Many local leaders have told me they don't feel the need to address LGBTQ issues because "there are no LGBTQ people in the ward." I felt the same way until a few of my own ward members opened up to me about being gay. According to a Gallop poll from May 2018, 4.5 percent of the US population identifies as LGBTQ.[10] If a typical ward reflects the general population and has three hundred members, then each ward would have, on average, thirteen LGBTQ members.

I suggest that we assume there are LGBTQ members in each ward and they are listening very closely to every comment about LGBTQ people. In one case, Kurt Nielsen's stake president believed there was no need to address this topic in their stake until Kurt prodded him to do so. During the adult session of stake conference, the stake president asked the congregation to raise their hands if they had an LGBTQ family member or friend who they loved. Almost all hands were raised. Those leaders realized that this topic probably impacts all Latter-day Saints, and we need to learn to have loving conversations about LGBTQ individuals at church. Further, the decision to speak about this subject in a church setting gave everyone else permission to speak about it as well. According to Kurt, that was the most significant thing his stake president did that day.

In my last year as a bishop of a young single adult ward, I began to post kind things about LGBTQ people on social media (often linking to Church resources) and a picture of me having dinner with some LGBTQ friends. What happened stunned me. Many of the YSAs (including those who didn't attend church) concluded that if I was a person who was open about sensitive topics and said positive things about LGBTQ people, then perhaps they could open up to me without fear of being judged. No additional LGBTQ people came out to me, but many of the ward members felt safe for the first time sharing with me complicated issues that weighed on them.

As a parent or local leader, we can act on our impressions to create a culture in which our children and ward members feel safe telling us about things going on in their lives. Some of my most meaningful moments in either parenting or Church service are when someone opens up and we work together to solve a difficult challenge. As we create a culture of nonjudgment and make an effort to say kind things about others, people around us know they can safely talk to us about difficult things; when they need a trusted friend, parent, or Church leader, they will be more likely to turn to us. If we are a local leader, we can prepare in advance what we'd say if someone were to come out to us (more of this below).[11] We can't really minister to others until they feel safe sharing how they are truly feeling and what they are actually experiencing.

Part of creating a safe culture is helping others not feel marginalized. Saying and doing things that helps them feel needed and welcome as described by Carol F. McConkie, former first counselor in the Young Women General Presidency: "The Gospel of Jesus Christ does not marginalize people. People marginalize people. And we need to fix that."[12]

One of best examples I've seen of following Sister McConkie's counsel occurred at a stake conference in the California Long Beach East Stake in January 2019. In the Saturday-night adult session, Stake President Emerson Fersch invited Michael Secrist, an interventional radiologist and gay member in the stake, to share his journey. He wanted Michael to speak because, in the president's words, he desired to "create Zion" where no one felt marginalized, but where all members felt valued and welcome. As I sat in the congregation, I watched Michael on the stand next to the stake presidency. President Fersch, sensing that Michael was nervous since he was about to come out to the entire stake, traded seats with his counselor to sit by Michael. That simple act of kindness brought tears to my eyes. I thought, "That is what the Savior would do."

After Michael's powerful talk in which he came out to the entire stake, he began walking back to his seat. President Fersch got up to give his concluding remarks, and as the two men passed one another on the stand, President Fersch stopped and gave Michael a huge hug—not a polite handshake but a huge hug. I thought of the stake members witnessing that hug. If they needed to open up to a leader, they would know President Fersch is a loving and safe person to help them. If I were a local leader in that stake, I would see President Fersch's example as a way to better minister to my ward members. After the meeting, I was pleased to see a long line of stake members eager to thank Michael for his remarks. I wish every LGBTQ Latter-day Saint could have that kind of experience in their stake.[13]

Another example of following Sister McConkie's counsel was in 2019 in the Oklahoma, Oklahoma City Mission, as told by Elder Dashiell Miner who was serving there:

> During one leadership conference for our mission, the subject came up about how we could improve. I raised my hand and talked about how we could be more sensitive to our LGBTQ brothers and sisters by stopping gay jokes. "We are missionaries of Jesus Christ and his restored Church. Our example as missionaries set the stage for the way the community sees us. Shouldn't we be the archetype of his love for all of his Children?"
>
> Another missionary commented that they had a gay brother that dealt with cruel jokes from other members of the church.
>
> The mission president, President Darren Mansell, then reaffirmed the comments by saying that he had had some gay missionaries in the mission, many of whom were some of his best missionaries. Moreover, he mentioned that some gay LDS members can be examples to us, such as the recent BYU valedictorian, Matt Easton.
>
> That day, there seemed to be a resolve to repent and be more sensitive to the silent majority of those who have gay family members and friends.

LGBTQ People Are *Our* People

I used to hear the term *LGBTQ community* and think of a different people on a different road—a people separate from my Latter-day Saint family and a group I didn't have any responsibility to help or serve. That all shifted when I was a YSA bishop. I had a priesthood responsibility to the LGBTQ Latter-day Saints in the ward and began to see LGBTQ people as *our* people.

As mentioned, about 4.5 percent of the US population identifies as LGBTQ. If we apply that percentage to the entire Latter-day Saint population (16,313,735 at the end of 2018),[14] that means 734,118 of Church members would identify as LGBTQ. If all of those individuals were to sit in LaVell Edwards Stadium at BYU, with a capacity of 63,470,[15] they would fill it eleven times over. That's almost two full seasons of home games.

These people are *our* people, *our* family members. These are people who worship with us at church. They are not relegated to a different community; they are a part of *our* community. As my thinking shifted along these lines during my YSA assignment, I began to feel a deep responsibility to say and do things that helped our LGBTQ ward members and recognize the difficult road they walk. Perhaps these words from Rebecca Simpson Craft, mother of a gay son, illustrate how to talk about LGBTQ members as our people:

> Teachers, please be aware that you likely have an LGBTQ student or two in every class. Please let them know that being gay is not a sin and is not a choice. Be aware that our LGBTQ youth and their families often feel alone. Let them know that you love them, and listen to their experiences. Ask them how you can help. We now have openly gay missionaries serving missions, and they are some of our finest young adults! How wonderful! We can do better at supporting and loving them and recognizing their talents and gifts as part of the body of Christ. Let's make sure that all of God's children, regardless of their sexual orientation or gender identity, know they are loved and needed. All of our youth need encouragement and understanding.

I love the words of Elder Holland in his April 2017 general conference talk, titled "Songs Sung and Unsung." Magnificent choirs have different voices that come together to create beautiful harmony. Each member of the choir is needed: "There is room for the single, for the married, for large families, and for the childless. There is room for those who once had questions regarding their faith and room for those who still do. There is room for those with differing sexual attractions."[16] If one of these individuals is missing, the choir's song is not as beautiful. Beautiful harmony is possible as we assure our LGBTQ members that they do belong with us.

The choir analogy is similar to Paul's words in the New Testament about the body of Christ: "And the eye cannot say unto the hand, I have no need of thee: nor again the head to the feet, I have no need of you. Nay, much more those members of the body, which seem to be more feeble, are necessary: And those members of the body, which we think to be less honourable, upon these we bestow more abundant honour; and our uncomely parts have more abundant comeliness" (1 Corinthians 12:21–23). Just as choirs need all parts sung, a body equally needs every part. One body part can't look at another and conclude that the latter is less honorable or less necessary.

The center of the body and soul of the choir is the heart, and leaders in my own ward are following the example of Elder Holland to create a feeling of unity. My former bishop, Lane Summerhays, and current elders quorum president, Steven Sharp Nelson of the Piano Guys, both use the words in

Mosiah 18:21 to share a vision of inclusion: "their hearts knit together in unity and in love one towards another." When I think of *knit together*, I picture different colors and textures of yarn skillfully intermeshed to form a magnificent finished article that is strong, beautiful, and resilient. When I consider our wards, I see all of us working to "knit together" our hearts as we bring our different gifts, attributes, and contributions to intermesh this diversity into a ward culture of acceptance, kindness, and inclusion to help all of us come unto Christ. It allows the love spoken of in this scripture to develop, to cover and be felt by every ward member.

I believe that we cannot become the Latter-day Saints God wants us to be without our LGBTQ members. And when LGBTQ individuals stay in the Church, they are not the only ones who benefit—we benefit as well. They are vital to our Church community because of their gifts, attributes, and contributions.

The Importance of Listening

In early 2019, I attended a training meeting about our LGBTQ members in Salt Lake City, hosted by LDS Family Services. The meeting was packed. The speaker was Ben Schilaty, a gay Latter-day Saint doing an internship at LDS Family Services. Ben later presented this same training on our podcast. His is the first episode I suggest local leaders listen to if they want to learn more about ministering to their LGBTQ members.[17] One of the highlights from the training was a question that Ben answered during the Q&A portion. His answer later became one of his blog posts:

> I was asked by a bishop what resources the Church has for same-sex attracted members. I mentioned the churchofjesuschrist.org/topics/gay site and then was about to say that the Church really doesn't have many resources. In an unusually clear moment of inspiration, I knew exactly what to say. I was prompted to say something I'd never said before. "You are the resources," I said. "The Lord has placed you in your callings so that you can be the resource for any member who feels marginalized." And then I requoted a line that I had shared a few minutes before from a ministering resource website for local leaders: "The most important thing you can do after a member discloses feelings of same-sex attraction is to listen and help them feel welcome."[18] The resource I've needed the most in my life is to be heard, validated, and understood.[19]

Ben's answer and the Church resources he mentions highlight the importance of listening. Bonnie H. Cordon, Young Women General

President, shared similar advice: "Our sheep may be hurting, lost, or even willfully astray; as their shepherd, we can be among the first to see their need. We can *listen* and love without judgment and offer hope and help with the discerning guidance of the Holy Ghost."[20] Similarly, Jean B. Bingham, Relief Society General President, invites us to minister as the Savior ministers: "He also smiled at, talked with, walked with, *listened to*, made time for, encouraged, taught, fed, and forgave . . . Those 'simple' acts of service and love provide a template for our ministering today."[21]

Later in this chapter are suggestions from Latter-day Saint parents of LGBTQ children to local Church leaders on how to help. A recurring theme in their answers is simply to listen. In my own life, one of my biggest regrets is not being a better listener to family members, friends, and fellow Church members. My insensitivity has caused pain to others I love. I recognize I have a long way to go to fully develop this Christlike attribute.

As I reflect back on my Church service, I can't recall a single training meeting in which the main focus was on the importance of and developing better skills for listening. I don't think listening is an attribute that is valued enough in our Church culture, especially among men. For example, we often revere effective Church leaders by referring to their public service; we compliment their great talks, teaching moments, or lessons rather than their ability to listen. Observing the honor given these people, younger Church members may work on developing these more public attributes instead of quieter qualities, such as listening, which often go unnoticed, even though they are often the most effective means of ministering. (In saying this, I'm not diminishing the public attributes to help people come unto Christ or implying that people with strong public attributes lack these quieter ones). At the beginning of my YSA assignment, my wise brother Steve, who was serving as a stake president, told me I would help change more lives in the bishop's office than over the pulpit. I found his insight to be true.

Stephen Covey has given similar advice with his counsel to "seek first to understand, then to be understood." He expanded on that statement, explaining:

> If you're like most people, you probably seek first to be understood; you want to get your point across. And in doing so, you may ignore the other person completely, pretend that you're listening, selectively hear only certain parts of the conversation or attentively focus on only the words being said, but miss the meaning entirely. So why does this

> happen? Because most people listen with the intent to reply, not to understand. You listen to yourself as you prepare in your mind what you are going to say, the questions you are going to ask, etc. You filter everything you hear through your life experiences, your frame of reference. You check what you hear against your autobiography and see how it measures up. And consequently, you decide prematurely what the other person means before he/she finishes communicating.[22]

After reading Stephen Covey's statement, I realized that becoming a good listener takes effort. It may not come naturally, but I believe the capacity to become a good listener lies within all of us. Listening is an attribute that gets suppressed, however, when we hear a person's problem and immediately go into "fix-it mode." We are quick to offer advice and solutions, missing the chance to fully minister by listening and striving to understand. I believe strongly that effective listening is one of the most desirable Christlike attributes, something we all can learn, and is often the very best thing we can do to help another person.

This principle is illustrated in a letter I received from a gay Latter-day Saint, not in my ward, who had reached out to me and I agreed to meet with him. I share this not to bring attention to me, but to share the positive impact listening can make: "I had my letter typed and ready to give to my bishop to have my name removed from the church last week. I remember staring at the letter for about 2 hours asking myself if I was ready for it. I ended up throwing the letter away and just couldn't seem to do it. I thought of you when I did that. That fact that you can listen to understand helped me and wanted you to know the positive impact it had on me. One day, I believe I will look at this and be glad I kept my name in the Church."

During my mission in England, most of my interactions with others involved my teaching and testifying about our restored Church. Teaching, testifying, and public speaking are all needed skills. How else will others hear our message? However, as I matured as a missionary, I learned that using multiple open-ended questions often encouraged people to open up about their faith and feelings before talking about the restored gospel. As they opened up, we learned to trust one another, and I was able to receive more spiritual impressions on how the Church's doctrine could meet their needs.

As my YSA service progressed, I shifted to more listening in my interviews. I tried to resist the temptation to use these interviews as a platform to share my life stories and doctrinal insights. I found I needed to really listen to understand the road these young single adults were on and how to minister to them. In some cases, acquiring this understanding took multiple interviews. Listening helped them feel validated and, in some situations, that was really all they needed. When they directly asked for my advice, I sometimes turned the conversation back and asked for their suggested solutions. Their responses were often the same thing I would have said. Sometimes the conversation needed very little input from me. As they spoke and I listened, the YSAs recognized spiritual impressions and realized the correct course of action. Regardless, once I fully understood their situation and they felt heard, I felt that I had more help from Heavenly Father in giving them guidance and direction. Because I better understood the totality of their situation, I often felt inspired that now was the right time to offer them a priesthood blessing.

I thought about this principle during a home teaching visit (before the ministering program was instituted in April 2018) and realized I would be more effective if I approached this as "home listening" instead of home teaching—I actually changed the name of the program in my mind to focus on this goal. Listening is how we really learn the needs of those for whom we have stewardship. Yes, a gospel message is helpful and needed, but often the optimal message can be delivered once we understand someone's needs and gain their trust. I believe ministering visits are the most effective and enjoyable when we encourage those we visit to do most of the talking. I'm grateful for Elder Hans T. Boom reminding me that I still need to work on being a better listener: "I remember and still experience situations where I have been too quick to judge or too slow to listen."[23]

When Someone Comes Out to You

I believe one of the greatest honors a local leader or trusted adult can have is when someone comes out to them as LGBTQ. I encourage everyone to prepare in advance for these conversations. This preparation will provide the necessary skills to better minister to our LGBTQ members as well as others who open up about their lives. I wish I had prepared in advance for these types of conversations. In episode 102 of the *Listen, Learn & Love* podcast, Ben Schilaty (who has come out as gay to multiple bishops) shares six questions that Church leaders should ask when someone comes out as LGBTQ.[24] Ben adds, "I think that if every bishop asked these questions when someone came out to them, almost everyone would have a positive experience." The questions include:

- Will you please tell me more about your experience?
- What is this like for you?
- How have these feelings affected your life? How have they affected the lives of your friends and family?
- How can I help you?
- Would you like us to meet regularly to discuss this?
- Labels have different meanings for different people. What do the words *gay*, *lesbian*, *bisexual*, *SSA*, and so on mean to you?

Note that none of the questions lead to reminders to live the law of chastity or to study "The Family: A Proclamation to the World." My experience is that our LGBTQ members are often near experts on those topics. If needed, those conversations can come later, after a foundation of trust has been established. I love the humility one of Ben's recent bishops showed when Ben came out as gay: "Ben, what do I need to know and understand so that I can serve you better?" Wow! What a great response.

A few years ago, I wrote this poem (the only poem I've written) about listening:

Listen
Listen deeply
Listen to understand
Listen without judging
Listen without reacting
Listen and bring hope and relief
Listen to hold their pain and sorrow
Listen to learn the roots of their suffering
Listen and take notes of impressions
Listen and ask follow up questions
Listen and become a true friend
Listen and don't turn it to you
Listen to learn what is unsaid
Listen and keep listening
Listen without agenda
Listen and validate
Listen

Advice from Latter-day Saint Parents of LGBTQ Children to Local Leaders

In the focus group of Latter-day Saint parents of LGBTQ children, I asked what advice they would give to local leaders. I wish I had known these responses before my YSA service. They provide insights that can help us be more sensitive to others and to welcome all people into our congregations.

KATIE HARRIS (MOTHER OF GAY SON)

I would ask them to make it clear in their training that no jokes or unkind comments about LGBTQ people will be tolerated. So many hurtful things were said to my son by youth and leaders who didn't know he was gay but thought it was funny to tease him about it. Some of the comments were truly vile with offensive words I never thought the "good kids" in my ward would use. My son didn't tell me and my husband about his sexuality or share these painful incidents with us until over a year later. During that year, he was depressed and suicidal and started pulling away from church activity. I would plead with Church leaders to remember that you never know which child in your class is contemplating ending their life or leaving the Church because of their "secret." Youth and youth leaders need to be educated about the harm their comments can cause. Please have a meeting—a fifth Sunday lesson, a youth fireside, or an adult stake conference session—talking about compassion and love. We haven't had anything like this in our stake yet, and I am hoping to facilitate that soon to spare other youth what our son endured.

ANNALEE WOLFORD KELLY (MOTHER OF TRANSGENDER SON)

Please welcome them no matter their appearance! Including trans kids!

JILL HAZARD ROWE (MOTHER OF GAY SON)

Respect the answers that we get to our prayers. Let us be the stewards of our children.

CALEB JONES (FATHER OF GAY SON)

As our gay son turned twelve (still closeted at the time), he got a streak of color in his hair that he was very excited about. Sadly, leaders communicated that he could not pass the sacrament because of it. His first experience with the Aaronic

Priesthood came in the form of rejection. Far too many of the qualifications enforced for participation or service are based on norms that disregard many forms of modest gender expression. After some discussion with local leadership, our son was later able to pass the sacrament. I fear that experience internalized for him that priesthood participation is counter to his divine nature.

JENNIFER ATKINSON (MOTHER OF GAY SON)

Educate yourself by reading or listening to the stories of LGBTQ people.

DREW ARMSTRONG (FATHER OF TRANSGENDER SON)

Make sure you know that the Church does not see being gay or trans as a choice any longer.

JOE PIERSON (FATHER OF GAY SON)

Get educated on the topic before passing judgment or speaking for God. Spend time with LGBTQ kids, and really get to know them. That will do more to change their hearts and minds than anything else. Forget everything they ever thought they knew about the topic. Until they are truly educated, they will inadvertently cause serious harm and trauma to our kids!

LANCE SWEETEN (FATHER OF TRANSGENDER DAUGHTER)

One of the most important messages to bishops and stake presidents for me would be . . . when someone is experiencing something in their life that you are not and have no comprehension of . . . please don't tell them that they are not living worthy of the blessings of God. When these people, at their most vulnerable point, express to you their deepest, darkest pain and sadness and express their frustration and anger toward leaders whose words and actions hurt them or the ones they love, please, please do not threaten them with taking away their membership because they are speaking from pain! Listen, listen, listen with an open heart and a contrite spirit.

MONICA PHILLIPS (MOTHER OF TRANSGENDER SON)

My advice to them would be that the first thing that comes out of their mouth should sound something like this: "Thank you for trusting me enough to share this part of your life with me. I don't have all the answers, but I know your Father in Heaven loves you dearly, and so do I. Please help me to understand what it's like to be you. I want you to know that I'm going to walk this journey with you as your bishop/leader/friend." I would also advise them to not let their LGBTQ friend or ward member leave without first wrapping their arms around them and thanking them and expressing their love for them. I'd then encourage them to follow up again soon, even if it's with a text, letting them know they appreciate them being vulnerable. This follow up is so important!

STACEY NERDIN (MOTHER OF PANSEXUAL DAUGHTER)

I would ask leaders to give grace in allowing members to come for what they need from church and be wildly happy to see them there, no matter what. There are going to be many things at church, for one reason or another, that do not resonate with LGBT youth and members. And yet there are many other aspects of the gospel and Church involvement that do. Let people come for what they need, and see that they get it. I can't imagine a better leader than that.

MARION MCCLELLAN (MOTHER OF GAY SON)

Remember that loving and listening to the child and their family is essential. How [a leader] behaves and advocates for the child and the family with the ward will have a huge impact on whether the family can stay [in the Church] or not.

The bishop must make room for the child and their family.

Love and compassion is always the answer.

Jesus will never fault us for being too compassionate or too loving. Always err on the side of compassion and love.

HEATHER ROBERTSON (MOTHER OF GAY DAUGHTER)

One of the best ways to build trust is by responding to hard questions with the words "I don't know." Past generations may have felt comfort in the knowledge and security of an all-knowing authority figure, but today's kids are different. They crave honesty and truth above all. Aren't they wonderful?!

Please avoid speculation. When talking about the plan of salvation, always combine it with the fact that God loves all of His children and has a place for them and that we don't know all the answers.

Lastly and most importantly, show love. No "except" or "only when" phrases when discussing LGBTQ issues. They won't feel the love if it comes with a disclaimer. If our kids can feel unconditional love from their leaders and parents, it helps them believe God can love them too. That is the most important message! Once they have a relationship with God,

He can work in them greater miracles than we ever could. Let's trust Him.

WHITNEY FRANK (MOTHER GAY SON)

My husband and I are both strong and present in our kids' lives. We have two straight kids and one who is gay. The fact is that straight parents are continually giving birth to kids who are LGBTQ. I can tell you what has been absent in our lives—support from our ward. After my son came out, the young men in the ward stopped talking to him, so he stopped attending. There had been too many jokes and disparaging comments. No leader reached out until six months had passed. I was grateful for that. However, it was not nearly enough to convince my son to return to a place where, still, none of the young men were talking to him.

CAROL WHEELOCK GARNER (MOTHER OF GAY SON)

I just met with my bishop two Sundays ago, and I practically begged him to open his heart and mind. I asked him to read Tom Christofferson's book or to listen to Ben Schilaty's podcasts[25] so he could begin to see a new perspective. All I needed for him to do for my son and the other LGBTQ youth in our ward was to be open to the idea that he might be wrong and to be willing to educate himself. Bishops just need to love these kids and be willing to learn more about what life looks like from their point of view.

KATE SHERMAN (MOTHER OF GAY SON)

All ward leaders and teachers need to be trained in LGBTQ [issues]. My adult daughter's ward gathered all the youth in a BYD (bishop youth discussion), and the bishop told them he loved them all: You vape? I love you. You are sexually active? I love you. You are LGBTQ? I love you. I will listen. I will help you find the way. You are welcome here.

They also need to teach the congregation to be open and loving. When my son came out, my bishop wasn't talking to him about sin—it was about keeping him alive. He took him for dinner every Thursday for months!

SHERRY PROFFITT MACNAB (MOTHER OF QUEER DAUGHTER)

My advice would be to tell them to assume they are talking to members of the LGBTQ community every time they speak. Because they are, whether they know it or not. Maybe include [this principle] in a teacher training. All teachers need to know that what they are saying is being heard by LGBTQ kids or adults. Many of them are not out yet.

ANGIE WAITES LEAVITT (MOTHER OF GAY SON)

Read *That We May Be One* by Tom Christofferson.[26] Read *Love Boldly* by Becky Mackintosh.[27] And then find a way to sit down and listen to LGBTQ members. And if you don't know someone who identifies as LGBTQ and Latter-day Saint, at least listen to parents of someone who is LGBTQ. Don't sit down with them to tell them why they're wrong. Sit down and listen. Just listen. And listen some more. Listen to the podcast with Michael Secrist. Listen to the podcast with Scott Osmond.[28] And don't try to defend the Church and what happened to these men. Just listen to the pain. And then make sure you train your ward leaders to do better.

NECA ALLGOOD (MOTHER OF TRANSGENDER SON)

Take the time to imagine what church is like for an LGBT kid. Our bishop did that when [our son] told him he was transgender. He thought, "What would it be like for one of my priests to have to wear a skirt to church every Sunday and to have to stand and recite the Young Women theme each week?" I sincerely think this was a profound manifestation of the gift of discernment, and because our bishop took the time to let that gift work in him, my son continued to feel welcome and respected at church. Eight and a half years and three bishoprics later, the impact of that spiritually sensitive and compassionate bishop still makes my ward a more Christlike place than many other wards in the Church.

BARB WILLOUGHY (MOTHER OF GAY SON)

Tell them *not* to say, "It will all be made right in the next life," which makes the person feel like they are a mistake and an abomination . . . that phrase is what leads so many to commit suicide, hoping that they will be "made right" sooner. Also, just love them. Love them for who they are, and don't assume that they are doing immoral stuff just because they are gay, and don't tell them they can't have a temple recommend just because they are gay.

KIM CRUMP (MOTHER OF GAY SON)

To all the leaders, especially Young Men and Young Women leaders, please be mindful of siblings of LGBTQ children. Not only do your words effect the LGBTQ person but they [also] have a great and lasting impact on a sibling. These words . . . may make the sibling feel they have no place and want to leave the Church as well, if the words and messages are negative.

Please, please be careful not to use the word "gay" to indicate that something is less than. For example, saying "that's so gay!" is not acceptable and can really harm our LGBTQ youth and [their] siblings.

Know that most people in your ward have an LGBTQ person in their immediate or extended families, and please don't forget about the fact that there are most likely closeted LGBTQ people right now in your ward. Please be mindful of your words and actions; you never know the lasting positive or negative effects of them.

BECKY EDWARDS (MOTHER OF GAY SON)

I would give them the advice that statistically speaking, every ward has closeted LGBTQ people, most or all of them being youth, and those LGBTQ youth are likely in a stage of a lot of self-loathing, shame, depression, and even suicidal ideation, so be proactive in creating a safe space for them. This could be inviting active Latter-day Saint LGBTQ people to come and speak in a fifth Sunday combined meeting or a fireside. Another way is when the Family Proclamation comes up in a lesson, for teachers to say something like this: "I know that families come in many shapes and sizes, and God loves all families." Those lessons can make families with LGBTQ people feel unwanted and "othered," so it's important to intentionally say things to help them feel welcomed and included. My son receives prejudice from Latter-day Saint teens daily. They need education on how to be less judgmental and more loving.

PAM KEENY (MOTHER OF GAY SON)

Take a moment to pray before reacting or responding. So often it's the knee-jerk reactions that cause pain. Pray with the family. Ask for a moment to pray; just listen without responding until you pray!

COLLEEN DARCAS HARRIS (MOTHER OF GAY SON)

Please don't take the time after someone has come out to bear . . . your testimony of the Proclamation [on the Family]. That just serves as a reminder that my child does not fit into the gospel. Make sure to try and help the family still fit into your ward. The LGBTQ family member is highly likely to leave the

Church, and it is so difficult for the remaining family to feel they have a place as well.

REBECCA SIMPSON CRAFT (MOTHER OF GAY SON)

It may take time, even years, for some individuals to clarify [their] sexual orientation or gender identity. Taking time to clarify one's identity or orientation, regardless of the outcome, does not mean someone is making a choice to be (or not be) LGBTQ.

Many leaders misinterpret [youth taking time to understand their gender identity or sexual orientation] as "some people do make a choice," and so they may share anecdotal stories of a young adult who once told them they were gay but then went back into the closet or chose to never disclose these feelings to [the leaders] again, or of a young adult who entered a mixed-orientation marriage . . . The leader will say, "Well, they weren't gay after all."

DON COE (FATHER OF GAY SON)

Our experience has been very different than dozens, or even hundreds, [of other stories] we have heard about. We have had a four-year plus ongoing dialogue with our stake president. We have met with him at least a dozen times. He has never tried to threaten us (release us from callings, take away our temple recommends), counsel us, or chastise us. I have been very honest with him and told him where I think the leaders have gotten things wrong. He asked us to coach him and teach him. You don't find that attitude in many organizations—including the Church. He asked us to send him information. I think we have given him hundreds of pages of materials. He reads them and comments on them, so I know he reads them. He asks good questions. He came to an event hosted by Tom Christofferson and Richard Ostler, which was great (we also had another stake president, two stake presidency counselors, and a state representative come to the same event). The stake president used a stake conference to talk about LGBTQ issues. This is all very refreshing and different. He never asked us to choose between the Church and our family and friends. He came to our gay son's wedding reception. This has allowed us to remain participating in the Church, while most of our peers have left.

DEBRA OAKS COE (MOTHER OF GAY SON)

My advice would be to focus on Christ and the first two great commandments. Let love be your guide in helping LGBTQ members and their families. What the Church teaches about the importance of families is absolutely true—families are the backbone of society. Help the families of LGBTQ people stay strong and united. Parents and relatives need to only worry about the love and unity of their family and not about what is a sin. Read what the Church has available for priesthood leaders on ministering to these members and follow those suggestions.[29] Meet with [LGBTQ people], and ask them to teach you about their struggles and personal experiences. Go out of your way to make them feel welcome, loved, and wanted in your ward and stake.

JOY SOUTHERN (MOTHER OF TRANSGENDER SON AND BISEXUAL SON)

What was helpful for our family was having leaders who very lovingly and willingly used my transgender son's preferred pronouns and name when talking to him and praying for him. That was huge for us. [They greeted] him warmly without judgmental looks when he first showed up to church dressed up in a suit instead of a dress. Also realize that, as leaders, you set the tone for the rest of the ward. As you show love unconditionally towards all, it helps to set the example for the rest of the ward. And allow LQBTQ members and their families to share their stories. It helps us all to better understand one another when we do that.

REBECCA SIMPSON CRAFT (MOTHER OF GAY SON)

This is for other ward members who work with the youth:

Being LGBTQ is not a worthiness issue. If you find out through your interaction with youth in your ward, that one of them identifies as LGBTQ, perhaps through other kids telling you that this teen disclosed this to another youth, there is no need for you to "out" that young person to their parents or others. Keep confidences. Let that individual determine how and when they decide to come out. Great damage can be done to that youth and their relationship with the Church when a teacher or Church leader outs them without their permission and before they are ready.

We do not "confess" that we are straight, and gay kids and adults do not need to "confess" that they are gay. Do not assume that a kid who identifies as gay is sexually active or has something to repent of.

As an example, . . . a kid in your ward [who is] drinking and driving creates a dangerous situation for himself and others, and a responsible adult would disclose that to parents so they can protect their child and others. In contrast, simply being LGBTQ is not an immediate danger that needs to be reported to parents or ward leadership. Many parents of LGBTQ children have reported negative and hurtful instances where a youth leader or teacher has outed their child to others.

Being told by others that a teenager in the ward is LGBTQ is not the same as having that teen "come out to you." Respect their privacy and keep confidences. Do not pass on gossip.

Listening to and Honoring Parents' Revelations about Their LGBTQ Children

Parents have the primary responsibility for raising their children, and we should work to support families. This is consistent with the home-centered, Church-supported approach initiated in 2018. In the words of Elder Tad R. Callister, "As parents, we are to be the prime gospel teachers and examples for our children—not the bishop, the Sunday School, the Young Women or Young Men, but the parents. As their prime gospel teachers, we can teach them the power and reality of the Atonement—of their identity and divine destiny—and in so doing give them a rock foundation upon which to build. When all is said and done, the home is the ideal forum for teaching the gospel of Jesus Christ."[30]

Latter-day Saint parents of LGBTQ children have spent countless hours on their knees praying, attending the temple, fasting, serving, reading general conference talks, and studying the scriptures—all in an effort to receive answers from Heavenly Father on how to raise their LGBTQ children. Because of their faithful efforts, they are receiving personal revelation for their LGBTQ children and on how to keep the family circle together.

President James E. Faust taught that parents receive revelation for their children: "Latter-day Saints, having received the gift of the Holy Ghost by the laying on of hands, are entitled to personal inspiration in the small events of life as well as when they are confronted with the giant Goliaths of life. If worthy, we are entitled to receive revelations for ourselves, parents for their children, and members of the Church in their callings."[31]

I believe we need to honor the personal revelation that Latter-day Saint parents of LGBTQ children are receiving and implementing in their families. If these parents are at peace with their LGBTQ child stepping away from the Church, we shouldn't tell them that they are "not standing up for the doctrine of our Church" or that they will "lose their eternal family." We don't want to communicate that active Latter-day Saint parents are doing the wrong thing, lack faith, or are being deceived by Satan if they support their LGBTQ child who steps away from the Church. We don't want to create a false dichotomy that members need to choose either the Church or their LGBTQ child. Rather, the family needs an increased measure of our love and support. We should not withdraw or pass judgment. If they feel criticized for the way they are supporting their LGBTQ children, they may also leave the Church.

Within the following stories of personal revelation that parents are receiving about their LGBTQ children, you may notice that many include an LGBTQ child choosing to leave the Church. It was not my goal to gather and share only responses of those with a child who steps away. Though many can and do stay in the Church, it is unfortunately a reality that many LGBTQ members do leave, which is why we must work harder at creating a loving and welcoming environment in our Church. When facing this situation, you'll also notice that the most consistent guidance parents receive from Heavenly Father is to "love your child."

ANNALEE WOLFORD KELLY (MOTHER OF TRANSGENDER SON)

The peace and guidance comes on a daily-only basis, much like manna. I can't tell you how I'll parent tomorrow or let alone next week, but God is good and feeds me daily concerning my trans child.

CHER PETERSON MCCOY (MOTHER OF GAY SON)

When I first found out that my son was gay, I . . . heard [a] voice say to me, "This is your new quest." I remember saying that I didn't need a new cause. It was crystal clear that I had one. I prayed for weeks and months that [if] the Lord made him this way, [then] He could "fix" this. I pleaded that [if] He could move mountains, why not fix this situation. I just knew the world would treat [my son] differently, so I desperately wanted him to avoid that. The Lord answered time and again that he was perfect and all we had to do was love him.

SUE ZWICK HENDRICKS (MOTHER OF QUEER DAUGHTER)

My answer came first as an overwhelming peace in my heart and an increase of love for my amazing daughter, whom I already loved so much. Then as I saw her relationship progress,

I felt an immense, unconditional love for my future daughter-in-law. As we began their wedding preparations, my heart grew heavy from the weight of the messages I was hearing from the Church. Things my soul didn't really believe but I was expected to believe if I was going to "toe the line." Every time I tried to attend the temple, I would break down in tears in the parking lot. After several months I finally made it through the doors and into a session. As I sat crying in the celestial room, I received a most magnificent and affirming answer. Essentially the answer was that my daughter was Theirs before she was mine. They created her as an incredible, eternal spirit just as she is, with all of her gifts and talents and love and everything that makes her amazing and unique and special, and They loved her then, and They love her now. My responsibility to her is here in mortality, and my responsibility as her mother is to see that she is happy and healthy and thriving, and the rest is up to Them. She is mine for mortality (and, I believe, eternity). More importantly, she is Theirs for eternity, and it's not my responsibility to worry about the eternal part. Ever since then, I haven't looked back. I do not believe They are displeased with her marriage. I don't understand how that fits into our doctrine, but I don't need to.

AMANDA SMITH (MOTHER OF BISEXUAL DAUGHTER)

When it first came to our knowledge [that our daughter was bisexual], I was very weepy, and it was heavy. But even though it was heavy, I felt very close to my Heavenly Father and Savior. Closer than normal. Maybe it was more like being held up or being carried. I was finding so much peace in prayer—pretty much opposite to the fear I felt that stemmed from worries about what others would think, how she might be treated, or how this conflicted with Church teachings. I kept a list of tender mercies that happened that first week that were just too out of the blue to be coincidences. One of those tender mercies was the hymn "How Firm a Foundation." It kept coming up at random times. One example is, I teach early-morning seminary, and two different students picked this song two days in a row [for the opening hymn]. This never happens. I found myself playing it on repeat. Especially verse 4. As I have continued to pray and fast and go to the temple with regard to my daughter, some of the things I have learned are a greater understanding of allowing agency and then loving. I have felt strongly that God is bigger than all this and has a plan. I have found greater hope in the statement that "we believe that He will yet reveal many great and important things pertaining to the kingdom of God" (Article of Faith 9).

The ironic answer to prayer in all this is that just a few months before we found everything out, I had been praying for my children, that they would recognize God's hand in their lives and the Savior's role in their lives. Then the thought came that that means hard things. I'm not sure if my kids have noticed a greater relationship with the Savior, but I have. It is at a whole new level, with a completely new understanding of Him.

ANABEL HITCH (MOTHER OF GAY SON)

As I felt the constant oppression of learning that my baby boy wanted to spend the rest of his life with the man of his dreams, I felt as if I had a constant open dialogue going on with my Father in Heaven. I heard and felt many thoughts come to my mind that were instrumental in what I can only explain as a mighty change of heart. This all transpired while he was home for Christmas, so the first message to me was simply from the story of Mary when she found out she was to bear the son of God: "and she pondered these things in her heart" (see Luke 2:19). I knew that I needed to make sure I thought before I spoke. So that is what I did, I did *a lot* of thinking and continual prayer. The next [message] came shortly after, while I was driving one day about a week later. That was quite simply that *all* of God's children will receive a kingdom of glory; and that my son would receive that as well. Within a few more days, as I continued my journey to accept and love my son *and* his choice, both the choice he was making with his lifestyle and the man he was choosing, I was given more knowledge and assistance. Very clearly to me came the words "the first and greatest commandment is to love. Your son is *my* son and I love him too. Simply love him and love his choices without stipulations."

LYNETTE BRADDOCK (MOTHER OF TRANSGENDER DAUGHTER)

Which name and pronoun does God want me to use for my transgender child? This was the question I had when my child wanted me to use female pronouns and a female name. I had called this child my son for seventeen years. Learning of the gender dysphoria came as a surprise to me, and I didn't really understand or know what to do. Following Heavenly Father's will was important to me, so I sought His guidance through prayer, fasting, and temple attendance. The answer has been feelings of peace as I've honored her request to use her female name and pronouns. Never has it felt wrong—just peace and the assurance that it's okay. The Spirit has been strong as Heavenly Father has helped me to understand that keeping this child, His child, safe and alive is of utmost importance to Him, and supporting the decisions my child was making was the way I could help Heavenly Father do this. As I have learned about the high suicide-attempt rate for transgender kids who are not supported by their parents, I have understood Heavenly Father's wisdom. As my husband and I have called her by her female name and used female pronouns, she has felt our love and support, and this has resulted in her wanting to maintain a relationship with us.

I have met other transgender young adults who don't want to visit home because they don't get the love and support they need from their parents. We need our trans daughter in our lives so we can help guide her on the safest and healthiest paths possible. And, more truthfully, we need her in our lives because she is a blessing to us. The Family: A Proclamation to the World teaches us to base our families on a foundation of love and respect, which is what we are doing when we respect and support our transgender daughter. When our family is together, showing respect and love toward each other, and I feel God's peace, I am grateful to Heavenly Father for guiding the way.

REBECCA SIMPSON CRAFT (MOTHER OF GAY SON)

Our son came out to us (his parents) when he was in high school. None of us knew exactly how his orientation would play out in his life at that time. It was only after he finished high school, served a mission, and completed a couple of years of college, that he told us that he hoped to someday marry a man, so this was a gradual process of clarity for him.

As he shared those hopes with us, I felt a deep sense of peace. He had not let himself set any personal, relationship, or family goals, and he felt that needed to change. I can't explain it, but I feel at peace with his life and with his hopes to someday meet an honorable man. That sense of peace just permeated my being, and it has remained with me. The comfort I feel has been unexpected and also just a gift that I cannot fully explain. I often think of the scripture in John chapter 14, verse 27: "Peace I leave with you, my peace I give unto you: not as the world giveth, give I unto you. Let not your heart be troubled, neither let it be afraid."

SHAUNA EDWARDS (MOTHER OF LGBTQ CHILD)

I learned in January 2016 that my then thirteen-year old-daughter (AFAB [assigned female at birth]) was transgender when I opened a notebook sitting on her desk and saw what she had written. (She has since felt that her gender is actually nonbinary. She continues to use female pronouns, and she is bisexual). I was completely devastated. She did not want to talk to my husband or me about it. We prayed continually and sought guidance from a therapist about how to parent her. She had been obviously depressed and anxious for some time but would not engage in therapy or accept treatment. I'm a medical doctor, and I feel fortunate that I have enough education that I knew gender identity is biologically based and not a choice or something we could change. For me, the predominant concern was how to keep her active in the Church and progressing in her testimony. I prayed constantly and have kept her name on the temple prayer roll continually since then.

I received clear guidance in the first few months after learning my child is a gender minority. I joined a North Star parent group online and read many stories of LGBTQ Latter-day Saints. I was filled with an overwhelming love for LGBTQ people and a very high regard for them. Any time I would meet someone who was or seemed to be LGBTQ, especially transgender people, I would feel overjoyed, as if I were meeting the Savior Himself. It was like they were VIPs. At the same time I felt deep sorrow and pain knowing the terrible suffering that is inflicted on them by Church members, including leaders. This sorrow and pain and clarity regarding the wrongness of how they are treated was accompanied by a feeling of no condemnation of Church leaders. I felt no anger. My sorrow was "swallowed up" in Christ (Alma 31:38). This feeling lasted a few weeks and then left me. I think of it often as I have subsequently felt the anger so familiar to most parents of LGBTQ that I know. It helps me avoid condemning others, especially Church leaders.

During these first few weeks, as we were discussing our desire to try to keep our child in the Church with the therapist we met with, she said, "She may need to distance herself from some aspects of LDS culture." When she said this, I had a powerful spiritual confirmation and [received] clarity again. It was obvious, and the conflict I felt decreased. Also during this time, I had a strong spiritual message that "it is not safe to be 'out' to priesthood leaders." I was warned by the Spirit to not discuss my child with our bishop or any other leaders. As I sat in sacrament meeting during those first few weeks, a man in our ward got up to bear his testimony. The Spirit said to me, "He will be your next bishop, and [it] . . . will be safe to discuss her with [him]." This man was sustained as our bishop about four months ago. My child has not attended church in three years, and I now support her decision, but I feel our current bishop may be an important person in her life at some point in the next few years.

DUKE ALVEY (FATHER OF GAY SON)

Our son is gay and came out to us, and I struggled finding out how to help and support [him]. I didn't know how to feel or what to do. I couldn't seem to get any answers. One day our son wrote a blog post that talked about him driving home alone and not having anyone in the passenger seat with him. Was he not going to have anyone in his passenger seat for the rest of his life? He didn't know if he could handle that. My heart hurt so bad for him. I poured my heart out to Heavenly Father to let me carry some of the burden and heartache our son was carrying around with him. As the tears in my eyes kept coming, Heavenly Father told me: "I've got this. He is in my care. You can love him and support him, but you can't take it from him." Since that day, I have taken a role in our son's life that brings me happiness every single day. I know that his struggles are still there, and he hurts, but my Savior is there for him and me through it all.

KIM PEARSON (FATHER OF GAY SON)

I received a very simple answer to my prayers when my gay son came out at [age] twelve: love him, and don't try to change him.

ERIC CANFIELD (FATHER OF TRANSGENDER NONBINARY CHILD WHO USES THEY/THEM PRONOUNS)

We ended up finding another Christian church for our kid to attend. It is an affirming church where gender and orientation don't cause any problems or concerns. We have felt confirmation many times that this was the right thing for our kid. We never expected that God would give us an answer that would take our kid out of the Church, but that is what happened. We know that many people won't understand that, but we felt this was what they needed. One heartbreaking comment our kid made to us was, "I hate that my existence subverts the plan of salvation." We are happy with where they are now and that they have a safe place where they are loved and accepted and can feel the love of God in a supportive faith community. Our vision of what the kingdom of God is has expanded, and we have been blessed so much in our participation with another church in addition to our Latter-day Saint ward.

PAM KEENY (MOTHER OF GAY SON)

My immediate response to finding out my son was gay was tears. I went instantly to fear that he was going to get beat up and live his life in fear. I prayed every night for his safety and that society wouldn't hurt my child. I also went to the temple a couple of times to pray for protection and safety for him. This summer, he came home for six weeks between semesters, and we were able to attend the temple together. As a returned missionary, he spent more time in the temple than I did. The first time we went together, I was still wrapping my head around this new reality. We were asked to be the witness couple, which was surprising to say the least. It was a great experience, and every word was absorbed as I knelt next to my son. I felt a sense of peace and calm but no big experience. Our somewhat rebellious but amazing daughter had recently gotten married after six years of living with her boyfriend. She was now fully able to participate in Church activity, and no one would ask about her need to repent or comment on past behavior. She could come back and be welcomed and loved. Why was it so different for my son, who had never dated or kissed anyone?

[Later we returned to the temple], and I was in the celestial room with him and these thoughts, and asking what his future would be. I had a very clear impression. The words came to me: "Your son is going to leave the Church, and it's okay. I know him and have created him, and he's going to be just fine."

My husband is on his knees every night, and I know that our son is a main topic. This homophobic man has been moved to love [and] acceptance and [has welcomed our son's] boyfriend into our home. My husband is gentler, calmer, and more nurturing than I have ever seen him in thirty years of marriage. He's a great man, but it took a gay son to move his heart way past what I had ever envisioned. The transformation in my testimony of the Savior and my husband's open heart only came because of the blessing of having a gay child. That is something I think most of us never thought was possible when these wonderful children of God revealed themselves to us.

JENNIFER ATKINSON (MOTHER OF GAY SON)

I truly believe that coming from a religious background and parenting an LGBT child can initially be one of the most confusing and overwhelming situations a parent can face. I also believe that the Lord is extra generous with the revelation He gives us if we seek Him. And that may be because I had a lot to learn. I can't write all the direction I have received but will include a couple of things.

When my son initially came out to us, during his senior year of high school, I was completely overwhelmed and had no idea how to parent an LGBT child. He would be the first in my extended family of fifty plus, and I just had no experience with this. I was praying and asking what I needed to do, and the words "Your job is to love him. I will take care of the rest" came very clearly to my mind. A few days later, as I was grieving over what seemed to be an impossible situation for my son, I heard, "You need to have more confidence in your son."

I have received reprimands when I have said the wrong thing, such as when my son first told me that he was going to marry his boyfriend, and I told him I wasn't sure I wanted to support that financially. The Lord slammed the story of the prodigal son into my brain, without me even asking for an answer. I knew right then that the Lord wanted me to support his wedding. This answer was confusing to me, since I had witnessed our Church so strongly oppose same-sex marriage. The Lord taught me when I asked about this that worldwide policies are sometimes different than how He needs us to minister to the individual.

After we attended the wedding in Hawaii, we put photos up on Facebook, which was also our son's coming-out post to most of the people in our ward. My husband is currently serving in our bishopric and had an assignment to speak on the Sunday after we returned. I really didn't even want to go to church after our big announcement and couldn't imagine how he would pull off giving a talk. I was complaining to the Lord about why he had to be serving in this calling at this time, and the reply I got was "I need leaders to show how to love and support their families through all circumstances." He gave a beautiful talk and shared some of our journey and how we had learned what it really means to love someone unconditionally.

I just want to end with my testimony that parenting an LGBT child has strengthened my relationship with our Savior and Heavenly Father to a point that I could not deny They exist, because They have so carefully guided and directed me and blessed me with answers to almost every question I've asked. I totally recognize that this is an experience filled with ambiguity, but I know that the Lord will answer the questions we need answered as we are partners with Him in raising these beautiful souls.

MONICA PHILLIPS (MOTHER OF TRANSGENDER SON)

I wish everybody I share my story with could know my transgender son—the kind of person he is and always has been despite what pronouns he uses. Growing up he always just "got" the gospel. He didn't have a rebellious spirit and never has. He was every seminary or Sunday school teacher's dream. He loved the Lord and the gospel with all his heart, and he still does. He was a kid that I never worried about. He turned to the Lord in prayer in all things and was no stranger to the Spirit. The reason I share these things is not to boast about my kid, but so many assumptions are made when people find out I have a transgender child. They often assume he can't have a testimony, that he was a rebellious kid, that he came from a dysfunctional family, that he was abused or had a traumatic childhood (I know I once thought these kinds of things about people who were transgender!).

Because I knew him so well, when he came out to us all I could feel was love for him. I didn't know what gender dysphoria was, but I trusted that he was looking for help and love and support, and that's what I wanted to give him. I immediately received confirmation that our Father in Heaven loved him so much, but it sure didn't take long before the fear, confusion, anger, and panic set in. I feared for his future, his safety, his salvation.

I had a brief period of anger at Heavenly Father. How could He possibly allow this to be happening to one of his most valiant children—one who served and loved Him from day one? I had no idea how one could be transgender and be able to remain active. This just didn't seem fair! I realized quickly that the fear, confusion, and anger were not of the Lord. These are Satan's devices, so I gathered myself together and laid it at the Lord's feet. I stopped praying for Him to take this away. I stopped asking why, and I focused on praying to know how to navigate this as a family in the gospel. I prayed to know what I was to learn from this.

I knew Heavenly Father knew my child even better than I did. I also knew I had to trust my child (age eighteen, almost nineteen at this point) to seek and find his own answers. I know he knew how to be led by the Spirit, and so I promised myself I would trust his ability to pray and receive answers for his life. When I did these things, an unexplainable peace came flooding in. It pushed out the fear, confusion, anger, and panic. This kind of peace I know only comes from God. It was then that I began to learn things I didn't know I needed to learn and grow in ways I didn't know I needed to grow.

Over and over my husband and I have received confirmation that our son is loved, that it's all going to be okay, and that it's okay for us to not have all the answers just yet. We know someday we will, but for now, we are okay with trusting Him. We've been taught recently that we will not be able to survive the last days without personal revelation. Personal revelation. We should honor people's personal revelation, especially when they are navigating in uncharted waters. My son hasn't made any decision without taking it to the Lord, but others will say things like, "Well, you don't need to know the answer right away. Just keep praying." As if they know that the Lord wouldn't ever answer my son's questions in a certain way. I have seen my son act on the answers he has been given, and I have seen him continue to move toward his temporal and spiritual goals.

There was a great talk given in my sacrament meeting recently. The sister giving the talk shared how she always brought mazes in her purse to sacrament meeting so her kids could sit quietly. She was explaining to her young son that the goal was to get from the starting point to the finish point without crossing any lines. He stared at it for a while. When she looked down to see his progress, she noticed that he had drawn a line from the starting point, around the outside of the maze (in the margins), and around to the finish. This made her stop and think. Indeed, he had gotten from the start to the finish without crossing over any lines. It just was not how the average person thinks a maze should be solved.

We need to stop passing judgment on other people's personal revelation. There are different ways to get from the start to the finish. Personal revelation might look "outside the box" to others, but that doesn't mean the Lord cannot answer in ways we might not have once expected. This journey has been amazing because I have been able to watch the Lord unfold His plan for my son and we have felt the Lord's peace along every step of the way. Each path is different, but I believe He has a plan for each of His children. Let's step aside and let Him do His glorious work.

EVAN SMITH (FATHER OF GAY SON)

Our oldest son came out as gay to my wife and me during his junior year of high school (in 2015). For over a year before then he was depressed, angry, and distant, and we couldn't get him to open up and tell us why. I had been serving as branch president/bishop for four years at the time when he came out to us.

What made him finally decide to talk to us was a presentation I had made as bishop in our ward (just a couple months before) in response to the First Presidency's instruction that all bishops and branch presidents read a statement from them that the Church's position on homosexual behavior had not changed, notwithstanding the US Supreme Court's legalization of gay marriage. I dedicated an entire third-hour meeting to that [subject] because I wanted to be especially sensitive to a couple individuals (including a youth) in my ward who had been counseling with me about their same-sex attractions for a year or two before then. So I spent five minutes reading the First Presidency's statement and forty minutes reviewing churchofjesuschrist.org/topics/gay and discussing how we can love, accept, and include gay people better.

The ward members were great, and we had a wonderful discussion where love was the focus and the Spirit was strong. I made sure to be discreet so as not to "out" the individuals I had been counseling with, but I was so glad they got to hear so many members of our ward be publicly affirming and loving toward LGBT individuals in general. Little did I know my own son was also listening intently and benefiting from hearing the same messages—garnering the courage to speak with us about his sexual orientation.

I will forever be grateful for the individuals (especially the youth) who came to speak with me as their bishop about their homosexuality before my son was ready to come out. Because of the priesthood stewardship I had over them, I researched homosexuality and the Church's then recently revised position on it (i.e., that the attractions are not a choice) extensively. I had been pretty ignorant about homosexuality before then and had said negative things about gays in front of my son at home on occasion. But the duty I had as bishop to lovingly counsel with those individuals—and seeing their tears and desires to do what God wanted—helped prepare me for when my son came out to us.

The Spirit led me to research the topic and really ponder on it more than anything else I ever had before as bishop. I'm glad God prepared me that way because I think I would have reacted differently if my own son had been the first person [to come] out to me as gay . . . All the research I had done (to figure out what to say in counseling as a bishop) and love I had felt for those other individuals made the response I gave to my son [when he came] out a no-brainer. I told him I loved him and would support him in whatever path he chooses in life.

He then decided to go on a mission over a year later. He had some very hard experiences on his mission (with people saying cruel and hateful things about gays). We asked him every week if he was mentally healthy (there was a real concern he would get depressed again and hurt himself while away on his mission). He ended up coming home after serving nineteen months because he received an answer from the Lord that His path for him was outside the Church. I prayed to receive confirmation of that answer and had the Spirit whisper clearly to me that my son was following God's unique will for him and that my job was just to continue to love him. I have felt the Spirit confirm that over and over since then—that my job as his father is just to love him, unconditionally.

CHERYL SMITH (MOTHER OF GAY SON)

I have prayed often to know how to parent our gay son and what path is best for him. When he came out to us, I felt a strong feeling that whatever his path would be, God would be okay with it. I also felt the Spirit tell me . . . "Tell him you will leave the Church for him if necessary." I told him that, but he said he didn't want me to do that for him.

More recently, when [my husband] and I were in the temple, we both felt an overwhelming sense that God was happy with us—that we had done enough as parents and we should be happy for our gay son (who had chosen to leave the Church at that point to find a husband).

There were other times when I was teaching the youth in seminary when I felt constrained by the Spirit to teach things differently or skip lessons. I didn't know why at the time, but now I realize it was because I had a gay student in my class.

The Lord is mindful of His LGBTQ children, and if we listen closely to the Spirit, He will guide us in a way of love and support for them.

LIZ MACDONALD (MOTHER OF GAY SON)

When our son was a teenager, we had a few discussions, and at one point I asked him point blank if he was gay. He vehemently denied it and spent the next six years being the "perfect" kid to make sure he wasn't gay. After that first discussion, I, as a mother, went to my Heavenly Parents in prayer and called down the powers of heaven to keep Satan away from my son. I am sad to admit that now, but that is where I believed his feelings were coming from—temptations from Satan.

Over time my prayers shifted, not from my own reasoning, but through the Spirit, to help my son find a woman who would love him (just as he is) and that he could love her (just as she is). While he was on his mission, my prayers again shifted, to help me be the best mother to my son I can be and help him feel the love of his Heavenly Parents.

I wish I could take credit for that change in my heart, but I can only give credit to myself in that I kept praying. My heart was changed through the process of the work of prayer with the help of my Heavenly Parents through the Spirit.

KELLI STEPHENSON (MOTHER OF TWO GAY SONS)

I have two sons who are gay, and they came out to us about two years apart. Both boys were fifteen when they came out. I was surprised the first time but not the second (for that child, I had always known deep in my heart that he was gay). I've had a very close friend for several years who is gay and active in the Church. She prepared the way for my children to come out to a mom they knew loved them no matter what. [My friend is] very spiritual, and we spent many hours hiking and running in the mountains discussing the Latter-day Saint faith and LGBTQ issues. I've never felt the Spirit quite as strongly as when I am with her. I know she's a daughter of God, sent here to be just the way she is. I've never had a doubt. Knowing her paved the way for me to fully understand the love and immediate acceptance my kids would need when they were brave enough to tell their truth.

My prayers are quiet prayers sent daily for my boys to know they are perfect the way God made them and that our love for them will never change or leave or be withheld. My husband always says that I have the simple faith of a child. I just believe because I know. I don't require proof. I don't need everyone to agree with me. My faith is not shaken when I hear something contradictory in a lesson or from the pulpit. I just know. And I just know my boys are exactly how they are supposed to be. I just want them to be happy and healthy, and if that happens in or out of the Church is not what is most important. God knows them the best. He knows their hearts and sees all of the good inside of them. I worry far more about their lives on earth and how they are judged and mistreated here than I do their eternal salvation. God has them. They were His before they were mine, and He will take care of all in the next life (what that looks like, I don't know, and I don't worry about it. It will be what is right, and it will be perfect).

TAMMY BITTER (MOTHER OF GAY SON)

When my gay son was about twelve, he started to have behaviors that we didn't understand. He was not out at the time, but I suspected he was gay. He curled up in a ball, stopped going to church, acted out, was angry, and many other things that were not like him. I attended the temple often and often felt very strong promptings about what to say and to do. We started seeing a counselor to help us understand his behaviors and to know which ones were things to be afraid of. [The counselor] was often impressed by our words and actions, and I knew without a doubt that it was because of the inspiration I felt in the temple.

Then a few years later another of our sons announced, after going to the temple and within a few days of reporting to the MTC, that he was not going to serve his mission and no longer believed in God . . . Once again we went to the temple, and this time instead of the help and guidance I had felt, I felt immense loss. I kept attending and kept feeling the loss, which started to be accompanied by a sense of guilt that somehow our son's lack of belief and our gay son's decision to eventually lead a gay lifestyle instead of live a life of celibacy were my fault. (Good grief, I'm in tears as I write this).

I needed all the help I could get, so I continued to go to the temple, but not nearly as often as I had been. At times I'd be fine during a session and [then] be in tears as soon as I got into the celestial room because I knew that in this lifetime I would not have all of my kids there ever, and that pain was intense. I felt conflict over knowing that I was loved by my Heavenly Father and [also] feeling a slap in the face at all of the things I had to say goodbye to, [a feeling that] seemed to be intensified in the temple.

I also saw huge conflict between how I knew the Savior to be and those members who chose to say damaging and hurtful comments about LGBTQ people and their families. Eventually, after hundreds, if not thousands, of hours in prayer, fasting, [and] oceans of tears, and through the Atonement, my spirit started to heal. I have started to feel the Spirit [in the temple]—sometimes I am calmed. I still don't feel the profound detailed promptings that I did during those earlier years, and sometimes the pain is still intense, but [it's] less often than before, and I am not afraid to just pass through the celestial room if needed. More often, though, I feel that I am loved and belong there, that my sons are both loved and known to my Heavenly Father, and more importantly, that I will not be alone in the eternities—somehow I will have my children.

. . . Just before we left for Argentina (since January 2020, my husband and I have been serving a mission in Argentina), Mark and I taught the temple prep classes and were escorts for a couple we taught when they went for their endowments. We then accompanied them for their sealing to their three sons, one of whom was my seminary student. I was extremely and genuinely happy for them; I felt the Spirit strongly and was grateful for the experience. Then I cried in my husband's arms as soon as we got to the car because of all the times I had envisioned my family being together in the temple someday, but I was still grateful for the experience.

A few days later we went with friends to do sealings for my ancestors. At one point the sealer stopped, and with tears in his eyes, said that he wanted us (there were others in the room also) to know and understand that our children will be sealed to us for eternity regardless of their decisions in this life. He said he even asked those who told him this, how it could be. No answer was given, and it doesn't matter because while months before, I would have doubted and maybe even laughed at this, the Spirit told me it was true. All sadness I felt left, and I was filled with gratitude for having been there that day.

MICHELLE SHERWIN (MOTHER OF GAY SON)

I have a son who is gay. He's almost eighteen now. I started realizing that he might be gay when he was fifteen. He never talked about it and was in a very dark place. He was reserved and had pulled away from our family. Some months after figuring out that he is gay, I approached him and let him know that if he was gay, I would still love him and would accept him. He still didn't want to talk about it. I knew that he felt like if I and our family knew that he was gay, he would be shunned, and I wanted to start planting seeds in his mind that that wouldn't be the case. I still loved him and always would.

I struggled intensely with wanting to know Heavenly Father's view of my son and how I could accept him—and also [to know] if I could continue to believe the doctrines of the Church but also support my son. Issues that had seemed so black and white no longer were. I spent a lot of time on my knees in prayer. I also made these questions part of my fasting and temple attendance. Another question that I struggled with was, has he chosen this, or was he born this way? And why is he gay? I've come to peace with the fact that our LGBTQ members are born that way and that they are loved dearly by their Heavenly Father and Jesus Christ. I don't know why my son was born gay, but I have learned so much because he is.

A year or so after learning that my son was gay, he got a boyfriend. One time as I was praying specifically about how to parent him, a feeling came to me that I should parent him just like I parented my older kids when they had boyfriends or girlfriends. In other words, give him the same rules and talk to him about the same expectations. This helped me a lot to normalize the situation and realize that I could still teach and guide him.

Another time as I stood and pondered in the celestial room of the temple with a specific question in my heart regarding gay marriage, I was given a feeling of peace and a feeling that God wants all of His children to be happy, and He loves all of us. That answer has helped me remember that our Heavenly Father has a plan for all of His children, that Jesus Christ atoned for all of us, and that I need to leave judgment to Them and that my role is to love them and keep learning.

PAULA NICHOLSON EDMUNDS (MOTHER OF TRANSGENDER CHILD)

My child was born female in the early 1980s and raised in a small southern town. Little was known about homosexuals or transgenders . . . We called this child a tomboy [from a young age]. As she got older, she said she wanted to be a boy, dressed like a boy, and wanted us to call her by boy names. Being a strong Latter-day Saint family, we treated this as a phase [and] accepted this as part of her personality. Gradually, as puberty hit, we vaguely thought [she was] homosexual and lesbian. We even questioned her when she was an older teenager. When she finally came out as lesbian, we had been aware of it for a while. Her testimony had always been missing something, and she stopped going to church by the time she was eighteen.

We had no knowledge of what any of this meant. I spent many years praying for understanding. I attended the temple regularly. I read what the Church had, mostly in secret. I felt I had an understanding—that she was choosing to disobey the commandments. It saddened me. But I prayed to love and understand her.

Eventually she realized that the feelings she had felt most of her life were actually gender dysphoria. As we learned more, talked more, it became clear that she felt much more masculine than feminine. She asked me to start using "they" pronouns. They did not come out to anyone but close family and friends. But suddenly I could see a light in them. As I continued to pray and attend the temple, my understanding blossomed. Suddenly new avenues of knowledge, such as North Star, were opened to me. I began to understand from my child and others what my child had been feeling—all the emotions they had been holding in for so long. Suddenly they began to progress in ways I could not have imagined! We fought less. They actually prayed, occasionally attended church for family events, smiled more, [and] held down a full-time job! I began to see that only by living as their true self could they truly feel the Spirit of God in their life, feel their own self-worth, and progress. I am still praying for understanding and still receiving answers every day on how I can help my child. It is a lifelong journey.

JULIE WOOLLEY (MOTHER OF GAY SON)

I have a thirty-year-old son who is gay. We've known for about fifteen years, but his desire was to keep it private. Two years ago he came out, and life has changed! Some people we know treat us differently, but we carry on. Sometimes it's hard, but I'm still in the Church, wanting to serve and lift others.

Last week I was in Utah for a family reunion. We went to the Bountiful temple. Beforehand, I prayed, "Heavenly Father, if you are in the temple, will you let me know today?" As we sat during the film, about the time right before man is created, I felt a huge warmth start at my feet, and it spread all the way to my head. Never happened to me before. Tears ran down my cheeks. I looked at the screen, and there were images of people from all lands and races. Only this time, for a second, I saw the face of my son. I looked at my sister-in-law, then back at the screen. It was gone.

I sat very still and waited. I felt a voice say, "I love you. And I love your son." I've never had anything like that happen to me. I had tears throughout the session. I'm very grateful.

I don't know what will happen with the Church in the future, but I do know God loves my son and so do I. I pray I live long enough to see a change toward acceptance and equality in the Church for our LGBTQ brothers and sisters.

JEFF FOWLER (FATHER OF GAY SON)

Our son was in his late twenties when he came out to us. We relied on prayer, hope, and faith in the Savior and a few close friends. Our parenting experience was enriched through open communication and heartfelt communication with our other children and their spouses. What became clear in our thoughts and mind was overwhelming love for our son and a desire to keep our family together. We also realized he was the same thoughtful, hardworking, caring, incredible son we have always loved.

HEATHER ROBERTSON (MOTHER OF GAY DAUGHTER)

We've always had great relationships with our kids. My youngest would frequently talk to me about spiritual impressions she was having. She begged to go on pioneer trek early. She was counting the years before she could serve a mission. She would come home from church frustrated to the point of tears that other kids wanted to laugh and goof off when she so desperately wanted to be learning the gospel every single minute she was there.

At age thirteen, she became increasingly private and withdrawn. When she came out as gay at fifteen, it all started making sense. The pain, dissonance, fear, shame, and self-loathing had been destroying her. I prayed every day in the car on my way to work that Heavenly Father would help her see a way to stay on the straight and narrow path. I prayed that she'd recognize Satan's temptations and have the strength to resist them. Those prayers changed me. I've come to understand that taking away her "gayness" would also be erasing all that makes her unique, talented, and beautiful.

Being gay is not all of who she is, but it's intertwined with every part of her being. As I've come to understand this, I've watched her blossom into a happy, grateful, kind young woman. By loving her, all of her, exactly as she is, she's coming to accept this part of herself, and I'm seeing hope return. I have never felt closer to her.

Within a few months of her coming out, she attended EFY. I fasted and prayed so intensely that she would have a good experience that would give her the strength to stay in the Church. Heavenly Father answered those prayers—again, very differently than I had expected. He let me see the pain and loss of hope and self-worth my daughter felt when hearing that there was no place for her. Hearing that marriage between a man and a woman is the only way to receive exaltation did not sound like happiness to her. She felt that God didn't care about her. She was home within a day.

I know this child. I know her heart and her desire to be close to her Heavenly Father. I could see so clearly, in a way only communicated by the Spirit, that the messages she was hearing at church were destroying that relationship. I'm at complete peace with her stepping away. I know with absolute surety that this is His will for her right now, as counterintuitive as that may sound to faithful members of the Church.

Coming to the understanding that there are different paths for people that will ultimately bring them the closest to Heavenly Father has brought me so much peace. I've learned to trust people and their journeys. I've learned to respect different points of view. I no longer feel the need to control. I can turn things over to the Lord. I find this makes it much easier to love and minister to people in a way I've never been capable of before.

I don't know what the future holds for my daughter, but I trust that Heavenly Father will guide her. As I pass through moments of fear, I continually hear the words, "I have not asked you to be her savior. I'm only asking you to be her mom." Turns out love really is the most important thing.

BRYCE COOK (FATHER OF GAY SON)[32]

Having a gay son was something so far out of our range of experience as parents. And combined with the fact that the Church had no answers or programs at the time, it absolutely required us to turn to Heavenly Father for answers. As we learned and progressed in our knowledge and understanding, we found ourselves having greater compassion toward all our LGBTQ brothers and sisters and, indeed, toward all people who tend to be judged and pushed to the margins.

When our gay son told us he wanted the same thing my wife and I had, the thing we had taught all our six kids to desire and aim for: a loving companion and family—but with a man—we could understand and accept that desire. In fact, the way he expressed it and explained how that desire had come with much thought, struggle, and prayer, it felt like a righteous desire to us. Our son had always been a uniquely spiritual and obedient child. He had always tried to live a moral and upstanding life and, as the oldest child, was a superb example to all our other children. Now that he was a young man in his mid-twenties, I could see that he had really thought this through; and knowing the good person that he was, I felt that I could trust his judgment without having to worry about his standing with God. This was something I could trust that the Savior's Atonement could handle.

Around this time he even asked me for a father's blessing. In giving that blessing, I felt inspired to simply bless him to follow the Spirit as he had always done and that as he did this, and lived according to the principles we had taught him from the time he was a child, he would be in God's hands. I did not feel impressed to give any specific guidance on how to live his life other than to follow the Spirit and live according to the principles he knew to be true.

From this point on, I felt at peace and reconciled to whatever path my son took and that we would be a happy and united family who would handle all this silently and in private. I had just finished serving on the high council for five years and was newly called to be the ward Young Men president. But I soon found that being silent was not an option. More than any time in my life, I felt strong promptings from the Spirit that I needed to speak out and be a voice for our LGBTQ brothers and sisters, that I needed to share what I had learned to help make our Church a more welcoming place for them. These promptings were strong and persistent. So I acted on them. I wanted to do so in a way that was respectful of the Church and would not cause division or contention. My wife and I met with our stake president to share our thoughts with him and to let him know of our intent to help start an LGBTQ support group, along with a host of other ideas.

The more we became involved in this "calling" from the Spirit, the more we continued to learn and grow in understanding and compassion for our LGBTQ brothers and sisters. All along the way, we both prayed constantly that we would act in accordance with God's will and not make any missteps. I always prayed for discernment and wisdom that if I was going astray in any way, Heavenly Father would let me know. The positive fruits we have witnessed from our involvement in this work have provided us with more than enough spiritual confirmation. It has brought a peace and Christlike love into our lives that we never would have known otherwise. It has expanded our family to include so many wonderful LGBTQ people and their families and friends. These fruits, along with the answers I have received through study, prayer, and observing and loving my LGBTQ brothers and sisters, have probably been the most significant personal revelation I have ever experienced.

JODY ENGLAND HANSEN (MOTHER OF QUEER CHILD)

For months after my child came out (when he had asked me not to tell anyone), I took all my conversation to God. And I had felt a need the year before to attend the temple weekly, so I was often pleading for help there. Many of my questions and pleas were about wanting God to somehow "fix" things—please keep my child safe, make sure they know they are loved, make sure no one hurts them, make sure they don't do anything destructive, make me say the things so they know I love them no matter what. I had not considered these fix-it questions, but I was never feeling as if God was answering. I was spending hours a day, for many many days, wanting God to make things happen the way I desperately wanted.

Finally, I stopped asking and just knelt in stillness. I was exhausted and wondered where I could turn. In the stillness, the words came: "Ask a different question." It was suddenly clear that I had been asking questions God can't answer because God does not micromanage behavior. I had not been open to seeing things in a new way. I had wanted God to make my life and my child's life somehow work out in a way similar to what I had always envisioned. I let go of needing God to do that, and a new question came to me. "Is he loved?" I was immediately overwhelmed with such a powerful feeling of complete, unconditional love. I don't have adequate language to describe it, but that is all I can think to come close. It was so physical, I opened my eyes, thinking I would see it pouring over me and spilling over the floor. My child, as precious as he was to me, was infinitely more precious to God, right now and every moment. They were so aware of him and with him in all things, no matter what.

It was the beginning of me letting go of trying to make things turn out a certain way. It was a moment of God showing me a type of love that transforms life because there is no limit or condition. And I felt an invitation to live it, even when I didn't know where it might lead. It was like making room for an unplanned, unknown miracle—and the miracle was that my child's life might be more than I could imagine. All I needed to do is have space to love him and be there to see the life he was creating as his own.

In the following weeks, as I thought about this in the temple, I began to see the covenant to sacrifice in a new way. Giving time and money and service is one type of offering. I realized that I had been clinging to something—refusing to let go of it even though it was getting in the way of experiencing God's love for my child, for me, and for everyone. I had been hanging on to my idea of how I thought things should be—how my life was supposed to be, what kind of life my child was supposed to live, what was "right" or healthy or safe.

By clinging to those ideas, I had no room in my heart or mind for anything that was different from what I already knew or planned on. I had no room for revelation or inspiration or any new paradigm about love . . . I began to practice laying on the altar, over and over and over . . . my idea of how things should be. Each time I do that, I have room for God to show up in greater ways. I have room for love to be beyond words or condition. I have room for miracles that I can't describe, but I let go of needing to limit the possibilities by setting boundaries on them before they can occur.

When I have sacrificed my idea of what my life should have looked like, the life that I experience is stronger than death. Even when there is indescribable pain or difficulty and seeming insurmountable challenges, the love is greater, the joy is deeper. The focus is on what works, and energy does not go to reaction or panic or . . . blaming. I feel inspired by that unconditional love, and that is what leads my actions. That is what makes the greatest difference [for] . . . my child and the world he lives in.

CAROL M. COLVIN (MOTHER OF GAY SON AND BISEXUAL DAUGHTER)

I was extremely afraid of finding out my son was gay. I was in denial for a long time despite the evidence. After he told us he was gay, I switched to thinking that it was fixable. I listened intently to every speaker at every [General] Conference session, hoping to hear things that justified my belief that it was a temporary condition that would be fixed or cured. But all that time (2007 to about 2014) God was telling me that everything would be fine and that I just needed to love my son.

Whenever I went to the temple and my mind would drift from the movie, visions of my son holding hands and kissing another man would pop into my head. I got upset and wondered how God could allow these thoughts to invade my mind in such a sacred place. I never directly asked for personal revelation about whether it was okay with God that my son was gay. I only looked for revelation on how to change him. I looked for confirmation that I was right about homosexuality being an affliction. All along, God was telling me that my son was just fine the way he was and that everything would be okay and just to love.

JOY SOUTHERN (MOTHER OF TRANSGENDER SON AND BISEXUAL SON)

When my youngest came out as transgender, I prayed for answers. How should I react? Which pronouns should I use? So many questions as I poured my heart out in prayer. The answer that I received was simply one word, pure and simple: "Love." I knew that I could do that. It also confirmed for me, in the strong feelings [that came] with that answer, of the incredible love that Heavenly Father has for my sweet child . . . That answer . . . helped enormously with the many discussions that I had with my son later to better understand what he was going through and how best to support him.

CALEB JONES (FATHER OF GAY SON)

My story is a bit out of order chronologically. When the policy excluding children of same-sex parents came out, I did some deep soul searching, fasting, and praying to ask God if this policy was right. I got two powerful personal answers: (1) no, this is not my will; and (2) it is good for you to be in this Church.

The years that followed were a journey for me to better understand our LGBTQ+ siblings. Little did I know that at roughly the same time, my then twelve-year-old son began privately wondering if he was gay. He and I walked separate but parallel paths understanding this space—him living it and I coming to better understand it from the outside—until these paths converged a few years later when he came out to my wife and me just one week before that same policy was rescinded. Because of the personal revelation God graciously gave me, I was in a position to welcome and accept him for how God created him. And I see now how God has been walking with both of us on our paths, preparing us for this moment, and will be there for us on the paths ahead.

LYNETTE BRADDOCK (MOTHER OF TRANSGENDER DAUGHTER)

My first spiritual experience regarding my transgender child was when she was born. When the doctor placed her into my arms, I was filled with this immense love for her. I loved all my newborn babies, but this was much more than normal, and I knew it was from heaven. I felt that God knew something significant and special about this child, and as she grew, I wondered what it was. When I learned she is transgender, I felt this godly love again. I knew then that the love I felt was the love Heavenly Father has for her, and He wanted me to feel this love and know she is His precious child.

At seventeen, she wanted to start taking hormones, and because she was not yet eighteen, she needed my help to get them from a doctor. My child was born with a male physical appearance but has an inner female awareness and identity. This gender incongruence is also called transgender. She struggled with this gender incongruence for many years, trying to "fix" it through lots of prayer, fasting, scripture reading, and obedience. After years of trying to fix herself and suffering under the shame and self-hatred she had for something about herself she didn't choose and didn't want, she came to understand [that] the gender incongruence wasn't going away, and [she] didn't want to fight it anymore.

I didn't really understand transgender, and I didn't know what to do. I was hesitant to help her get hormones because I wasn't sure that was what God wanted her to do. Seeking Heavenly Father's guidance was important to me, so I spent a lot of time praying, fasting, and attending the temple. I remember the clear impression that came to my mind and the feeling in my soul. Heavenly Father told me that she was going to start hormones one way or another, and I needed to help her so she got them from a legitimate doctor. The message I got that day was [that] keeping her alive and safe was of the utmost importance to Heavenly Father, and to do this, I needed to be by her side, respecting and supporting her journey, so I could help her navigate it as safely as possible.

As I have pondered on the spiritual guidance I've received about my child, and as I've read about the spiritual guidance from Heavenly Father given to other LGBTQ people, I've come to realize the lines of what is right and what is wrong are not as black and white and rigid as I had thought. What is right is following Heavenly Father, and what is wrong is not following Him. He will guide us on the path that is right for us individually, and the same answer may not be given to everyone. As long as we are seeking His guidance and following it, we are on the right path for ourselves. Rather than judge another, I try to encourage people to seek God's will for themselves and then trust they are following it.

JULIE SAUER AVERY (MOTHER OF GAY DAUGHTER)

I have a gay daughter. I wish I would have just said, "It's okay. I love you." But I didn't. I said, "Are you sure?" I spouted Church teachings and tried to convince her otherwise. I was in the Relief Society presidency at the time. My best friend, the Relief Society president, had a husband that talked horribly about anyone LGBTQ. I felt conflicted. I knew I loved [my daughter]. I wanted her to live a good life and be happy. I talked to Church leaders. They all told me not to tell anyone so when she changed her mind, she wouldn't have to deal with those that knew. I did that but found it wasn't working for me or her.

I went to the temple a lot. I feel lots of peace in the temple. I receive answers in the temple. I went one day and just knew that Heavenly Father loved me and that He loved my daughter. From then on I knew it was my job to love her. Heavenly Father can work out the details. Since I changed my outlook, all of us became happier. Our relationship is really good. She just got married, and we celebrated just like we did with our straight children when they married. The only difference is that only a handful of our Church friends even recognized her marriage. Thank heavens we have lots of supportive extended family and close friends who celebrated with us. So I look at the world and my Church with a bigger lens. I try to help others do the same. I want to make room in pews for all of us.

DIANE CALDWELL CARPENTER (MOTHER OF GAY SON AND BISEXUAL DAUGHTER)

I have a gay son and a daughter that is bisexual. I have known about my son for the past fifteen years and my daughter for about eight years. Through the years, I have spent countless hours praying, fasting, and attending the temple. In the beginning I prayed that this could somehow not be, that my son would not be gay, and that I could raise him to be a strong member of the Church. As time passed and I knew he was definitely gay, I changed my prayer. I prayed that if it was God's will, that He might lift "gayness" from my son and help me raise him to know the gospel. As more time passed, I changed my prayer again. I prayed for strength and peace, for us as parents and for him. I also prayed that I might help him gain a meaningful relationship with his Savior.

About this time . . . my daughter (his older sister) came out to us, and honestly my first prayer to our Father was something like this: "Are you kidding me? I'm barely managing with one gay child, plus the other five, and now you made one of them bi?" I did calm down, and my prayers became requests for understanding and [to know] how I could help my children navigate this reality we were living. I also continued to pray that they would have a close relationship with their Savior. Now when I pray, I give thanks for these amazing souls just as they are. Oddly enough, as I think back on my prayers and my fervent search for answers on how to parent my kids, my answers were all pretty much the same. They were "Just love him"; "I hear you, and I'll carry all of you through this"; "Be there for them." I had asked for the Lord to change my son. Instead He helped me to change to accept that this is not a curse but . . . just part of our path back to Him.

My answer to why my child is gay is one I searched hard for. After all my searching, the answer I clearly received one day started with a few questions: "Would I love my child any more if he were straight?" "Do I believe my son will not have the right to any of the blessings promised to him?" "Do I believe the Lord will take care of all things?" My answers were a resounding "no," "no," and "yes," after which I was told to love my kids as they are and trust God. I know that might not be enough for others, but it was enough for me.

ADAM SKINNER (FATHER OF TRANSGENDER CHILD)

Since my child came out as transgender, I have had two distinct impressions that came through fasting, prayer, and temple worship. The first is that my child's birth identity is correct—she is a female spirit born into a female body. The second is that I need to support them in living their transgender, nonbinary identity. I have asked the Lord why and what this means for my child's mortal and eternal future. Those answers have not come, and I find myself needing to just trust in the Lord one day at a time. It's very lonely because I'm out of alignment with the LGBT-affirming community and the mainstream Church culture.

ANDREA PARKS (MOTHER OF GAY SON)

I have never received answers in my life like I have regarding my gay son. I have seen this as an evidence of my Heavenly Parents' love for my son and the importance of this. The first [time I got an answer] was the moment I received the message from my son telling me that he was gay. I had a clear and distinct message in my mind: "This is my son. He is perfectly created, and you are not to try and change him." The next [answer] came weeks later when I was talking to my son and asked him if he felt any better now that he'd come out to us. With tears in his eyes, he told me that he didn't—that he wanted a family and didn't want to spend his life alone. I remember feeling helpless, knowing the Church's policy on same-sex marriage. Later that night, as I was praying, I felt again the clearest answer—that my son's desire was righteous, that we should support him in this desire, that a marriage or family was a good thing for him, and [that] God was pleased with my son's heart. More times than I can count, I have felt the reassurance from God that my son is loved, that all is well, and that I get the privilege of having this boy—he is a gift.

ENDNOTES

1. Jeffrey R. Holland, "Be With and Strengthen Them" (general conference address, Salt Lake City, April 2018), churchofjesuschrist.org/study/general-conference/2018/04/be-with-and-strengthen-them?lang=eng.

2. See "St Michael and All Angels, Hawkshead," The Benefice of Hawkshead with Low Wray and Sawrey and Rusland and Satterthwaite, accessed January 6, 2020, hawksheadbenefice.co.uk/hawkshead.htm.
3. See BBC Cumbria, "A Gift from a Church in Utah to One in Hawkshead," Facebook Watch, June 18, 2017, facebook.com/watch/?v=1403777303050327; Nicholas Read, "Mission Fundraises for St Michaels," United Kingdom & Ireland, The Church of Jesus Christ of Latter-day Saints, accessed January 6, 2020, lds.org.uk/mission-fundraises-for-st-michaels.
4. See Sarah Jane Weaver, "President Nelson Meets with Pope Francis at the Vatican," *Church News*, The Church of Jesus Christ of Latter-day Saints, March 9, 2019, churchofjesuschrist.org/church/news/president-nelson-meets-with-pope-francis-at-the-vatican.
5. President Ivory, President Ulrich, and Brent Brown share more in episode 18 of the *Listen, Learn & Love* podcast.
6. Dieter F. Uchtdorf, "Perfect Love Casteth Out Fear" (general conference address, Salt Lake City, April 2017), churchofjesuschrist.org/study/general-conference/2017/04/perfect-love-casteth-out-fear.
7. Brené Brown, *Braving the Wilderness: The Quest for True Belonging and the Courage to Stand Alone* (New York: Random House, 2017), 136.
8. "Redemption for the Dead," chapter 35 in *Teachings of Presidents of the Church: Joseph Smith* (Salt Lake City: The Church of Jesus Christ of Latter-day Saints, 2011), churchofjesuschrist.org/study/manual/teachings-joseph-smith/chapter-35?lang=eng; Brigham Young, "Personal Reminiscences, &c," April 6, 1860, in *Journal of Discourses* 8:37, jod.mrm.org/8/37; Discourses of Brigham Young, sel. John A. Widtsoe (1954), 278, archive.org/stream/discoursesofbrig028407mbp/discoursesofbrig028407mbp_djvu.txt; all quoted in Robert C. Gay, "Taking upon Ourselves the Name of Jesus Christ" (general conference address, Salt Lake City, October 2018), churchofjesuschrist.org/study/general-conference/2018/10/taking-upon-ourselves-the-name-of-jesus-christ.
9. Thomas S. Monson, "We Never Walk Alone" (general conference address, Salt Lake City, October 2013), churchofjesuschrist.org/study/general-conference/2013/10/we-never-walk-alone.
10. Frank Newport, "In U.S., Estimate of LGBT Population Rises to 4.5%," Politics, Gallup, May 22, 2018, news.gallup.com/poll/234863/estimate-lgbt-population-rises.aspx.
11. For more, read Ben Schilaty's blog post on his coming out to his bishops; "Coming Out to Church Leaders," *Ben There, Done That* (blog), March 30, 2017, benschilaty.blogspot.com/2017/03/coming-out-to-church-leaders.html.
12. Carol F. McConkie, "Lifting Others," The Church of Jesus Christ of Latter-day Saints, Topics: Same-sex Attraction, 1:45–1:54, churchofjesuschrist.org/topics/gay/videos/lifting-others?lang=eng.

13. Michael Secrist shares his talk and journey in episode 168 of the *Listen, Learn & Love* podcast.
14. "Facts and Statistics," Newsroom, The Church of Jesus Christ of Latter-day Saints, accessed January 11, 2020, newsroom.churchofjesus-christ.org/facts-and-statistics.
15. "Football Facilities Info," BYU Athletics, accessed January 11, 2020, byucougars.com/facilities/football.
16. Jeffrey R. Holland, "Songs Sung and Unsung" (general conference address, Salt Lake City, April 2017), churchofjesuschrist.org/study/general-conference/2017/04/songs-sung-and-unsung.
17. See episode 102 of the *Listen, Learn & Love* podcast.
18. "Same-Sex Attraction," Counseling Resources, The Church of Jesus Christ of Latter-day Saints, providentliving.churchofjesuschrist.org/leader/ministering-resources (only accessible to members of ward and stake councils).
19. Ben Schilaty, "You Are the Resources," *Ben There, Done That* (blog), March 18, 2019, benschilaty.blogspot.com/2019/03/you-are-resources.html.
20. Bonnie H. Cordon, "Becoming a Shepherd" (general conference address, Salt Lake City, October 2018), churchofjesuschrist.org/study/general-conference/2018/10/becoming-a-shepherd, emphasis added.
21. Jean B. Bingham, "Ministering as the Savior Does," Ministering, The Church of Jesus Christ of Latter-day Saints, April 2018, churchofjesus-christ.org/study/manual/everyday-ministering/ministering-as-the-savior-does, emphasis added.
22. As quoted in "Habit 5: First Seek to Understand, Then to Be Understood," The Seven Habits of Highly Effective People, Franklin Covey, accessed February 26, 2020, franklincovey.com/the-7-habits/habit-5.html.
23. Hans T. Boom, "Knowing, Loving, and Growing" (general conference address, Salt Lake City, October 2019), churchofjesuschrist.org/study/general-conference/2019/10/52boom.
24. "Same-Sex Attraction," Counseling Resources, The Church of Jesus Christ of Latter-day Saints, providentliving.churchofjesuschrist.org/leader/ministering-resources (only accessible to members of ward and stake councils).
25. Episodes 10 and 102 of the *Listen, Learn & Love* podcast.
26. Tom Christofferson, *That We May Be One: A Gay Mormon's Perspective on Faith and Family* (Salt Lake City: Deseret Book, 2017).
27. Becky Mackintosh, *Love Boldly: Embracing Your LGBTQ Loved Ones and Your Faith* (Springville, UT: Cedar Fort, 2019).
28. See episodes 168 (Secrist) and 162 (Osmond) of the *Listen, Learn & Love* podcast.
29. See "Same-Sex Attraction," Counseling Resources, The Church of Jesus Christ of Latter-day Saints, providentliving.churchofjesuschrist.

org/leader/ministering-resources (only accessible to members of ward and stake councils).

30. Tad R. Callister, "Parents: The Prime Gospel Teachers of Their Children" (general conference address, Salt Lake City, October 2014), churchofjesuschrist.org/study/general-conference/2014/10/parents-the-prime-gospel-teachers-of-their-children?lang=eng.
31. James E. Faust, "Communion with the Holy Spirit," *Ensign*, March 2002, churchofjesuschrist.org/study/ensign/2002/03/communion-with-the-holy-spirit?lang=eng.

CHAPTER 8

TRANSGENDER LATTER-DAY SAINTS

In our conversations about LGBTQ Latter-day Saints, much of the focus is on our gay and lesbian members. Transgender Latter-day Saints, however, are often overlooked. Already members of a marginalized group, they often feel further marginalized by people's inattention and lack of understanding. Stories of transgender Latter-day Saints and their parents are found throughout this book, but this chapter specifically highlights transgender Church members so we can better understand their experiences and how to minister to them.

Readers should not infer from the short length of this chapter that the importance of transgender Latter-day Saints is somehow secondary. I also recognize that there are other groups within the LGBTQ spectrum who deserve their own dedicated chapter, including our pansexual, intersex, and asexual members. These individuals were not well represented in my LGBTQ focus groups, which is why their specific experiences are not explored thoroughly here. Their stories, however, are just as important and valid and should be the focus of other projects.

Definitions

- **Transgender:** the term used to describe a person whose gender identity or gender expression does not match their biological sex
- **Gender Dysphoria:** distress a person feels when their gender identity does not match their biological sex

Further, these definitions help us understand that being transgender is separate from sexual orientation. Someone can identify as transgender and consider themselves either heterosexual or homosexual—just like a cisgender person.

Neca Allgood, an active Latter-day Saint, uses the words of her transgender son, Grayson, to explain the distress/pain of gender dysphoria during her guest lectures to college classes:

> Have you ever gotten carsick? Carsickness, like many other forms of motion sickness, occurs when your inner ears and your eyes disagree about whether you're moving. Gender dysphoria is like that. Awful, nauseating, headache-inducing wrongness from the disagreement of your mind and body. And you feel it every time you wear the wrong clothes, or are called by the wrong pronoun, or hear your own voice, or someone looks at you and sees something you aren't; every time you look in the mirror, every time you think about yourself it's like a knife in the gut because it's wrong wrong wrong. It's not you but it won't go away and it won't stop and it hurts, it hurts like nothing you can imagine and nothing I can describe. It's so bad that I would literally rather die than feel like that again, even for a day.

Neca adds: "Lots of times cisgender people describe gender dysphoria as a mismatch between brain and body, but that understates the reality that many transgender people experience. For my son it was distress; it was PAIN. And unlike carsickness, for four years he couldn't get out of the car."

The pain and distress Grayson experienced is not a condition of mental ill health. Indeed, in the latest International Classification of Diseases, called ICD-11, the World Health Organization moved transgender related issues out of the mental and behavioral disorders and into "conditions related to sexual heath" reflecting that "trans-related and gender diverse identities are not conditions of mental ill health and classifying them as such can cause enormous stigma."[1]

Sign of the Last Days?

Before meeting any transgender individuals, I had concluded that being transgender was a sign of the last days, of society going downhill, or of Satan's efforts to confuse God's children. My mindset was changed by getting to know several transgender Church members, and I echo the words of Monica Phillips (mother of a transgender son):

> I don't believe [Satan's] work has been to deceive people into being LGBTQ. Instead, he takes these precious children of God and tells them they are worthless. He tells them that there is no place for them in God's plan. He tells them God no longer loves them. He resides in their shame. He also resides in our fears, knowing that our fears will hinder our ability to truly love. His goal is to tear apart families and drive people away from the gospel of Jesus Christ. He is succeeding, but not because this group has been deceived and are now gay or trans. He is succeeding because he is keeping us from coming together as the body of Christ and loving with pure Christlike love. We could do better to help heal those members who are hurting and feel they have no place with us. Every member is vital—without them we cannot function as a Church to our fullest potential. The answer to overcoming Satan, strengthening family, and bringing people to Christ is LOVE.

In chapter 1, I mentioned how we can all fall into the "trap of unearned opinions," forming ideas about individuals without getting to know them, and I encouraged us to not form opinions about a group until we have met many people in that group. If we are tempted to dismiss the lived experiences of transgender Latter-day Saints, we should first listen to them with an open mind and heart.

Historical Perspective

When it comes to our transgender friends, perhaps we don't know everything yet. Perhaps the Church, as well as society, is still at the beginning stages of learning and understanding what it entails to be transgender. There have certainly been many times in the past when society didn't understand something and made incorrect assumptions and conclusions. Many Americans, for instance, once justified slavery because they believed Black people were mentally and physiologically inferior, and women were long denied the right to vote because some believed they did not have the aptitude to make such civic decisions; we now look back on these circumstances and cringe.

With the benefit of hindsight and up-to-date knowledge, we might suppose that if we had lived during those times, we wouldn't have made the same assumptions and mistakes as others did. As Sheila and I watched the movie *Harriet*,[2] I wondered, "If I had lived during her day, how I would have responded to Harriet Tubman's heroic work of freeing slaves? Would I have supported her or fought against her?" I have also recently wondered, "If I had lived in Salem Massachusetts in 1693, with only the knowledge of that day, how would I have behaved during the Salem witch trials?" In both situations, I'm not sure I would have made what I know now to be the correct choices.

Having a historical perspective—recognizing that we don't understand everything now and that what we don't understand will likely become clearer later—allows us to become humbler and more teachable, with a greater willingness to learn when we encounter complicated issues. Nephi, an exemplar of humility, said: "I know that [the Lord] loveth his children; nevertheless, I do not know the meaning of all things" (1 Nephi 11:17).

This perspective is consistent with remarks President Oaks made in 2015 to a reporter: "This question concerns transgender, and I think we need to acknowledge that while we have been acquainted with lesbians and homosexuals for some time, being acquainted with the unique problems of a transgender situation is something we have not had so much experience with, and we have some unfinished business in teaching on that."[3]

Elder Uchtdorf reminds us to be open to learning: "Brothers and sisters, as good as our previous experience may be, if we stop asking questions, stop thinking, stop pondering, we can thwart the revelations of the Spirit. Remember, it was the questions young Joseph asked that opened the door for the restoration of all things. We can block the growth and knowledge our Heavenly Father intends for us. How often has the Holy Spirit tried to tell us something we needed to know but couldn't get past the massive iron gate of what we thought we already knew?"[4]

One historical example that showcases the need for humility so we can "get past the iron gate of what we thought we already knew" occurred in 1967, when Kathrine Switzer became the first woman to register for the Boston Marathon. Kathrine's coach believed that marathons were too long for women to run, but he eventually agreed to take her to Boston if they ran a marathon together in a training session. In their practice marathon, they ended up running thirty-one miles, almost five miles longer than a traditional marathon. They checked the Boston marathon rule book, which said nothing about the gender of the contestants. The coach, two male athletes from Syracuse University, and Kathrine registered together to run the Boston Marathon, with Kathrine using only her initials.[5]

In 1967, society generally assumed that women were too frail to run such a long race. Seeing Kathrine in the marathon, a race official chased her through the pack of runners, grabbed her shoulder, and attempted to rip the bib number off her shirt. He was unsuccessful, and she finished the marathon. The media coverage of Kathrine's altercation with the race official became the catalyst of publicity to open long-distance races to women. In 2017, fifty years later, Kathrine again ran the Boston Marathon with the same bib number (261) and crossed the finish line as a celebrated finisher. At that time, Kathrine ran with thousands of other women, and no one questioned a woman's ability to successfully complete a marathon.

What changed between 1967 and today? Our knowledge of a group of people—in this case, women runners—changed. Scientific research has confirmed that, indeed, women are completely capable of running marathons, and most of us today personally know a female marathon runner.

In 1967, smart people were certain that women could not run marathons. But they can. They do. They did. The first notes of women completing marathons are as far back as 1896.[6] Perhaps those early female runners were dismissed as anomalies, and experts—with their overwhelming certainty—held women back. They were trapped by their own assumptions, unable to see beyond them.

We should use this example to temper our judgment about gender dysphoria, and pause. Most of us have little direct contact with someone who experiences gender dysphoria. Further, we aren't experts in a field of study that is just beginning to be examined. We don't know which of our assumptions will turn out wrong (for surely some will) and what we will discover tomorrow. But we do know that today's transgender people walk a difficult road that few of us understand, and that our responsibility is to love and show compassion.

In the future, maybe we will watch a movie about today's brave transgender people and leave with tears in our eyes. Maybe we will wish we could go back in time and better support them.

Transitioning

Many people who experience gender dysphoria undergo what is termed *transitioning*, in which they take steps to end their feelings of dysphoria. In my experience, Latter-day Saints who transition are not doing it out of rebellion or to engage in behavior outside the teachings of our Church; rather, they wish to end/cope with their dysphoria to feel better, whole, and complete. That said, each transgender person's experience is unique, and some feel no need to transition.

There are three general categories of transitioning for our transgender friends.[7] Examples of transitioning stages appear alongside each category listed below.

- **Social:** using a different name and/or pronouns, changing their dress and grooming
- **Legal:** legally changing their name, changing their gender marker
- **Medical:** using hormones, undergoing sex-reassignment surgery

In their efforts to end feelings of dysphoria, each transgender person who decides to transition does so in a way unique to them, completing (or partially completing) some or all of the stages. We shouldn't create a norm in society that to be an authentic transgender person, one must complete any or all of the stages listed above. And we shouldn't take one transgender person's degree of transitioning and prescribe that to others. As I've met with many transgender Latter-day Saints, I've learned there is a great deal of personal revelation and individual feelings regarding the right degree of transitioning to end or manage the distress of gender dysphoria.

One element of social transitioning is adopting a new name and pronouns. This step is often the "coming out" as transgender. For example, someone whose biological sex at birth is female (often called "gender assigned at birth") and was given the name of Nancy may identify as male and take on the name of Nate along with he/him pronouns. Nate's gender is not tied to his biology but to how he feels inside. While Nate is a transgender man (also known as female-to-male, or F-T-M), we can see him just as a man. He doesn't have to pass some hurdle to earn this level of respect. For me, as a disciple of Christ, that respect and recognition are freely given.

Some of my transgender friends identify as "nonbinary," which means they do not identify in either of the binary categories "male" and "female." To reflect this nonbinary identity, these individuals use they/them pronouns. They/them pronouns are grammatically plural, but these terms are now also employed in these cases to refer to a single person.

Some people may be uncomfortable or react negatively when they observe transgender Latter-day Saints in one of the transition stages. Understanding the different steps of transitioning, however, can help us develop more empathy and encourage us to reach out in love and understanding. Transitioning is often motivated by a desire to be authentic, to reduce or end depression and suicidality, and to find peace and harmony with who a person feels they truly are. Though we may struggle at times to understand those feelings, acknowledging that they are real and respecting transgender Latter-day Saints will go a long way toward making them feel more accepted and welcomed.

New Church Transgender Website

In February 2020, the Church launched a dedicated webpage focusing on transgender Latter-day Saints. The page includes a reminder of the importance of asking Heavenly Father to assist us in loving and supporting transgender Latter-day Saints: "If you have family members or friends who self-identify as transgender, pray for the love of Christ as you strive to follow the example of the Savior and love them. The commandment to love one another includes those who don't experience the world the same way we do."[8]

Certain degrees of transitioning may place restrictions on a person's Church membership. Outlining possible restrictions on Church members based on various degrees of transitioning is beyond the scope of this book. I encourage everyone to work with their local leaders and to refer to the General Handbook for current information on this topic.[9]

The Church's website includes this statement reflecting use of hormones to manage gender dysphoria:

> Some children, youth, and adults are prescribed hormone therapy by a licensed medical professional to ease gender dysphoria or reduce suicidal thoughts. Before a person begins such therapy, it is important that he or she (and the parents of a minor) understands the potential risks and benefits. If these members are not attempting to transition to the opposite gender and are worthy, they may receive Church callings, temple recommends, and temple ordinances.[10]

In episode 48 of the *Listen, Learn & Love* podcast,[11] Neca Allgood and her transgender son, Grayson, talk about how hormones—an answer to their prayer—became the "ram in the thicket" to help manage his gender dysphoria, reducing the pain of the "car sickness" Grayson described earlier. The appropriate use of hormones helps us understand this is a medical issue and not a mental ill health issue. I'm grateful for the Church's statement and Neca's and Grayson's experiences helping us learn to ease the pain of those experiencing gender dysphoria.

Further, the Church's website helps us understand how we should view and treat transgender Latter-day Saints: "Church members need you and want you. If you identify yourself as transgender, we know you face complex challenges. You and your family and friends are just as deserving of Christlike love as any of God's children and should be treated with sensitivity, kindness, and compassion."[12]

Go Slow

My advice for those experiencing gender dysphoria is to go slow, work with a therapist, involve your family and Church leaders, and seek personal revelation. There are some voices from society that prescribe a path that includes fully transitioning. Only hearing these voices may lead someone with gender dysphoria to conclude this is their path.

Detransitioning[13] is the cessation or reversal of transgender identification or gender transition. There are stories of those who have transitioned and later regretted this decision and detransitioned. Those who detransition may continue to experience gender dysphoria. Being aware of these stories is helpful to make a more informed decision and seek personal revelation, with an eye to the long-term.

Listening to Transgender Latter-day Saints

In addition to keeping a historical perspective, there is more we can do today to better understand our transgender friends. Just as we personally know female marathon runners, we need to get to know transgender Latter-day Saints by listening to them and hearing their stories. Most important, we should have open hearts and minds, believing that the feelings and thoughts of transgender Latter-day Saints are real and authentic.

This approach is consistent with what S. Michael Wilcox suggests: "In some matters, it is better to be intellectually uncertain rather than superficially sure. This will still leave us with a great deal to be certain about, while maintaining a humility to learn."[14]

By striving to listen and understand, we follow the example of Jesus, who reached out to the most marginalized in society first and invited them, literally and figuratively, to His table for dinner and conversation. As we hear stories from transgender Latter-day Saints and try to walk in their shoes, we will be in a better position to help lift their burdens by showing respect, sensitivity, and understanding.

Our greatest resources are transgender Latter-day Saints themselves. The podcast *Listen, Learn & Love* has many episodes with transgender Latter-day Saints and a dedicated landing page where these podcasts are listed.[15]

Supporting Both the Church and Our Transgender Friends

Our baptismal covenants are to bear, mourn, and comfort. As active Latter-day Saints, we can listen to transgender people, call them by their preferred names and pronouns, recognize their gender identity, and love and accept them as fellow human beings. These actions cost us nothing but mean everything to them.

We also need to understand the risk of suicide for transgender Latter-day Saints and follow the words of Elder Rasband to love: "Particularly vulnerable for suicide are those youth and young single adults who struggle with gender issues. They need to be encircled in the arms of their Savior and know they are loved. So often the Lord calls on us; He expects us to be His welcoming, loving arms. We need to encourage their friends to do the same."[16]

I have been deeply touched by the transgender people in my life and the things they have taught me about being a better disciple of Christ. I don't need to give up any of my beliefs in or my commitment to the restored Church to accept my transgender friends and honor their lived experiences. In fact, we are following in the Savior's footsteps when we choose to love and minister to these and all LGBTQ individuals.

ENDNOTES

1. World Health Organization, "Brief: transgender health in the context of ICD-11," euro.who.int/en/health-topics/health-determinants/gender/gender-definitions/whoeurope-brief-transgender-health-in-the-context-of-icd-11.
2. *Harriet*, directed by Kasi Lemmons, written by Gregory Allen Howard and Kasi Lemmons, featuring, Cynthia Erivo, released 2019 by Focus Features.
3. Dallin H. Oaks and D. Todd Christofferson, interview by Jennifer Napier Pearce, Trib Talk, *Salt Lake Tribune*, January 29, 2015, YouTube video, 10:05, youtube.com/watch?v=UIJ6gL_xc-M&t=619s.

4. Dieter F. Uchtdorf, "Acting on the Truths of the Gospel of Jesus Christ," Broadcasts, The Church of Jesus Christ of Latter-day Saints, accessed February 11, 2020, churchofjesuschrist.org/broadcasts/article/worldwide-leadership-training/2012/01/acting-on-the-truths-of-the-gospel-of-jesus-christ. Also Chapter 2, Footnote 28.
5. "The Real Story of Kathrine Switzer's 1967 Boston Marathon," Kathrine Switzer, Marathon Woman, accessed January 23, 2020, kathrineswitzer.com/1967-boston-marathon-the-real-story/.
6. Charlie Lovett, *Olympic Marathon: A Centennial History of the Games' Most Storied Race* (Westport, CT: Praeger, 1997.) Excerpt at marathonguide.com/history/olympicmarathons/chapter25.cfm.
7. For more information on transitioning, see "Transitioning (transgender)," Wikipedia, accessed January 24, 2020, en.wikipedia.org/wiki/Transitioning_(transgender).
8. "Transgender: Supporting," Topics, The Church of Jesus Christ of Latter-day Saints, accessed March 1, 2020, churchofjesuschrist.org/topics/transgender/supporting?lang=eng.
9. *General Handbook: Serving The Church of Jesus Christ of Latter-day Saints* (Salt Lake City: The Church of Jesus Christ of Latter-day Saints, 2020), churchofjesuschrist.org/study/manual/general-handbook/title-page.
10. Transgender: Understanding," Topics, The Church of Jesus Christ of Latter-day Saints, accessed April 6, 2020, churchofjesuschrist.org/topics/transgender/understanding?lang=eng.
11. See episode 48 of the *Listen, Learn & Love* podcast.
12. "Understanding Yourself," Transgender, The Church of Jesus Christ of Latter-day Saints, accessed March 1, 2020, churchofjesuschrist.org/topics/transgender/understanding.
13. "Detransition," Wikipedia, accessed March 10, 2020, en.wikipedia.org/wiki/Detransition.
14. S. Michael Wilcox, *Who Shall Be Able to Stand? Finding Personal Meaning in the Book of Revelation* (Salt Lake City: Deseret Book, 2003), ix.
15. For a list of episodes of the *Listen, Learn & Love* podcasts on transgender topics, see listenlearnandlove.org/transgender-podcasts.
16. Ronald A. Rasband, "Jesus Christ Is the Answer" (address, Salt Lake City Tabernacle, February 8, 2019, churchofjesuschrist.org/broadcasts/article/evening-with-a-general-authority/2019/02/12rasband.

CHAPTER 9

POTENTIAL PATHS FOR LG LATTER-DAY SAINTS

The purpose of this chapter is to provide a brief overview of the potential paths LG (also referred to those with same-sex attraction) Latter-day Saints can take in their lives and to share insights from those walking each road. Though this chapter focuses on LG Latter-day Saints, the principles discussed may also apply to bisexual Latter-day Saints.

There are generally three options for LG Saints:

1. Remain celibate and single for the rest of their lives.
2. Enter a mixed-orientation marriage.
3. Enter a same-sex relationship or marriage.

The first two options offer many challenges but allow individuals to retain their membership in the Church. The third road cannot be followed while maintaining full membership in the Church, but some choose this option because of the emotional fulfillment they find with a life-long partner. Each of these potential paths has trade-offs that cishet Latter-day Saints do not face. Understanding the choices that LG members must face and their perspectives can help others develop empathy and love in ministering efforts.

Celibacy

Many of our LG members have decided to be celibate and fully participate in the Church. Those who choose this path are often motivated by a love of the gospel, a desire to follow Church teachings and receive the associated blessings, make and fulfill temple covenants, and maintain community with other Latter-day Saints. Many also find purpose in reaching out to and supporting other LGBTQ Church members. Many of these good members have shared their stories on the *Listen, Learn & Love* podcast, offering other Latter-day Saints on this road vision, support, and hope. They are some of my heroes, and we should do everything we can to support them.

I hesitate, however, to highlight any of the specific journeys of these individuals because their stories may change in the future and they may choose to no longer walk this path. Further, many of these individuals are reluctant to be put on a pedestal or to have their story become a definitive illustration of how to be LG and a Latter-day Saint. While their stories give hope and perspective to others wanting to walk the same road, helping them feel less alone, Latter-day Saints who choose to remain in the Church and live a celibate life usually do not want their lives to become a prescription for all LG Latter-day Saints.

When the Church released its "Mormon and Gay" website in 2016,[1] it featured two stories of gay, celibate Latter-day Saints. By the end of 2019, however, both of those stories had been removed from the website because each person had chosen to pursue a relationship with a same-sex partner.[2] I point this out not to be critical of anyone but to share how difficult it can be for our LG members to remain single and celibate. Our younger Church members, especially, face decades of being alone, and what seems bearable at one time can often feel untenable as time goes on and loneliness persists.

That said, there are many LG members who are celibate and fully participate in the Church. We should not focus on the stories of those who leave and conclude all will leave. Many celibate LG Latter-day Saints live Church teachings and fully participate in the Church.

I also recognize the importance of organizations such as North Star[3] that give community, understanding, spiritual strength focused on the Savior, and direction for those who are celibate and want to continue to fully participate in the Church. I've attended North Star's annual convention and have felt an outpouring of Heavenly Father's love for His children. One of my celibate gay friends living in Europe told me he uses his annual savings to fly to Utah for the annual North Star convention—his only chance to have spiritual community with those walking a similar road.

I believe that an LG Latter-day Saints' probability of staying in the Church and being emotionally healthy increases when they feel comfortable coming out to their families and wards and developing a deep relationship with the Savior. Being honest and open about who they are relieves a burden and establishes a new framework from which they can find belonging. When people meet them with love and support, understanding the difficulty of their road, and withhold triggering questions about dating and marriage, they have an easier time feeling welcome in the Church community. We are one step closer toward becoming the full body of Christ.

DALLIN STEELE (GAY MAN)

The best thing is when they listen to me and they don't try to fix me or my situation. I am very lucky in my ward where most people are really good and ask honest questions. I got a new ministering brother, and we visited for over an hour with him just asking questions and being incredibly supportive. We even have an inside joke, and it's great!

Many in the ward have made sure I have space to speak and even exist. They make sure others know that too. Then I have a few who I can talk to, who listen to me when I open up about my struggles. They don't try to fix it. They listen and take a step back. I feel very blessed to be in my ward.

AUSTIN HODGES (GAY MAN)

I have had a lot of members ask me when I'm getting married to a girl, even after they are fully aware I am gay. That just brings up a lot of the pain I had growing up and feelings of inadequacy.

Right now in my ward, I have a family who has basically adopted me into theirs. They invite me over for Sunday dinner and Family Home Evening, check up on me, help me with projects, and invite me to sit with them at church. This has by far been the biggest help [in meeting] the difficulties of remaining a member. Their Christlike love and the charity they so freely give is an immeasurable blessing. They know I have a boyfriend; they invite him over too like he's part of the family. This is what being a member of the Church looks like. This is unconditional love. This is the goal of life—to love others selflessly. They are a miracle. I've been given a calling, assigned ministering families, and feel a part of the ward like everyone else. That is a huge help.

JOSEPH ELDREDGE (GAY MAN)

Don't force dating/marriage on me. Always check up on me and see what I want to do with my life and support me in it. Let me know that I am needed. Give me a calling and help me connect with other people. Give opportunities for me to speak in church, where my specific experience can be heard and (if there are other queer folk out there) to give hope to others. If I feel comfortable, see if I can help other queer people in the ward in their journeys.

JERRY CHONG (GAY MAN)

By being [Church members in] good standing, we can take the sacrament, we can have callings and assignments, and we can attend the temple and secure our personal salvation. This is what is taught and understood.

I remain obedient so that my voice can be heard. I do use my privilege as a Church leader to seek the chance to share information and understanding of inclusion of all people. Stake presidencies and bishops feel I can be trusted to speak on these matters and that I can be sensitive in my commentary so that people can process the experiences of others.

Not [every LGBTQ Latter-day Saint] is strong enough to tolerate comments spoken at church. We receive constant reminders that we do not fit in. We stay silent, putting on a brave front, uneasy of how people will react, especially in a classroom setting, if we show our emotions. I have gone home many Sundays asking myself, "Is it worth it? Why do I continue to try?" The answer is always, "Because the Savior and Heavenly Father love me, and I know it."

One tough thing LGBTQ members face is the need to explain their singleness to people at church, even to people who they have just met. They question why you are not married, why you are not dating, and they suggest possible companions for you. We do our best to answer these questions diplomatically. Why are they so concerned about our marital status? How does this affect their lives? If you ask, be prepared to hear the truth.

JOHN GUSTAV-WRATHALL (GAY MAN)

What the Church refers to as "celibacy" would more appropriately be called "sexual abstinence." Celibacy generally refers to a special vow that is taken as a form of self-consecration to God. It is usually connected to a particular kind of calling. That's how Roman Catholics generally understand and practice it. Celibacy, by definition, is not something that can be imposed on you just because you belong to a particular class of people, such as being gay or lesbian.

JAKE SHEPHERD (GAY MAN)

I have a little hesitation answering this question: is it possible to be celibate and live the teachings of the Church while being in a same-sex [nonphysical] relationship? My full opinion is yes, it is possible to live within this realm, though difficult for many reasons—but not entirely impossible. Some hurdles include no sexual activity, Church culture, and other liberties and freedoms given to those who are married.

Me and another guy, or my "boyfriend," if you will, have decided to date openly. We have a contract where we only do things which enable each other to live life fully in the gospel, meaning boundaries on chastity are clearly defined and kept. Many people see this as yet another gay relationship and that our ways are perverse.

... We as a couple have seen acceptance in each other's wards. As someone who has sought leaving the Church, I find my place within its walls to be much more peaceful.

Granted, as individuals, we won't have all the opportunities some might have if they are married to a spouse of the opposite gender. As a couple, we also do not see ourselves seeking marriage to each other. This means we will have a tougher time finding legal protection than heterosexual couples. Although we do plan to live together and spend our lives together like heterosexual couples do, celibacy is still in the plan.

We do not seek to change the Church's doctrine as a couple. We sustain the Prophet and his Apostles as seers and revelators. As I mentioned earlier, I find peace still within the walls of the Church. What I feel is important is to have members and especially leaders be understanding and accepting. Let the individual or couple find their place within the doctrine. Let those leaders counsel them [to help them] find the greatest peace with their sexuality and standing with their Heavenly Father. This is the job of the bishop, as a spiritual counselor. He should have spiritual tools to help counsel individuals who come to him, to help them find peace with the gospel. He should never chastise the individual.

I fully believe every facet of life exists on a spectrum and part of the plan of salvation is finding where we lie on the spectrum. Everything is possible with the grace of God, and He won't let us fail on our own plan of happiness.

BLAKE FISHER (GAY MAN)

In my ward, the most helpful thing people can do is to get to know me as I am now. Sit with me in the different tensions I find myself in. Help me find joy in living according to my current values, interests, and goals. Live mindfully in the present. Where do I see/feel light right now? And then express gratitude for it.

DAVID DOYLE (GAY MAN)

Give me callings and opportunities to serve. I want to feel like my being in church has a purpose and I make a difference. This can be a really lonely road. I really appreciate people who invite me over for game night or to see their kids act out the Nativity story. And also if they invite me to sit with them at ward activities because I don't like feeling that I'm imposing on your family by asking if there's an empty chair at your table.

If the lesson or activity is going to be about celestial marriage or dating or the latest general conference talk about homosexuality, please give me a heads up. Let me choose to participate or not. It's not fun to feel like I got surprised with something I wasn't prepared for. Or better yet, ask me ahead of time for some of my thoughts or ways to approach the subject in a sensitive way.

Don't ask about my future. I don't know. Plus, it can be depressing to think about growing increasingly lonelier as my nieces/nephews grow up. I'm here now—let's work on making today better.

VANCE BRYCE (GAY MAN)

My ward is great. Here's how they help: My bishop doesn't pretend to know the answers to everything. In fact, he often says he doesn't know. I know in my heart that the love from members in my ward for me is real. If I decided to bring a boyfriend to church, their friendship would not change. I have a calling, and I'm not babied. People listen to me during Sunday School and do not immediately disagree with me when my views challenge the status quo. People ask me questions and truly listen to my answers. I am asked to speak in church. I am asked to serve by cleaning the church and the temple. Nobody gets into my business about temple worthiness. When I am traveling or just need a break from church, nobody anxiously questions my activity. I am invited to dinner. I am part of the ward family.

Now for where they can improve: It's possible for single folk to be happy. Just because I don't have your life doesn't mean I'm not happy. Please don't set me up with single women or men. Single people have a lot to give. We have much more time on our hands.

We can take charge of big projects because we don't return home to spouses and kids. There is no difference between a married member and a single member. We are all holy children of God. You can ask questions about how celibacy affects me, but we better know each other pretty well first, and you should never pity me or assume that I'm miserable all the time. By expecting me to be miserable, you ask me to question the validity my happiness.

ODDBJØRN STRAND-ANGERMANN (GAY MAN)

I have never been without a calling in my home ward. I am in my eighteenth year as a clerk, [with] five bishoprics, and I have always been open about being gay. My bishops (and previously branch presidents) have never pretended to know all the answers, or tried to preach, but have been supportive.

Mixed-Orientation Marriage

A mixed-orientation marriage (MOM) is a marriage in which one or both of the spouses is not cishet. Many episodes of the *Listen, Learn & Love* podcast feature interviews with those in MOMs.[4] My friends Ricardo and Elizabeth Rosas are featured on the Church's website with a video and several related stories,[5] and have been on my podcast.[6] Ricardo, who has same-sex attraction, shares how his feelings of same-sex attraction are not what define him as a person or as a son of God. Rather, his experiences have provided him with tools that he can use to bless others as he continues to follow the Savior. The Rosas have helped me better understand that MOMs can be beautiful and authentic.

Some in a MOM don't like the MOM label, as it puts the focus on the label instead of the marriage. Further, some feel we give labels too much power in our identity—shifting the focus from our primary identity, which is a beloved son or daughter of Heavenly Parents.

Guests have shared several types of successful MOMs, including those in which one is gay and the other is straight, those in which both are gay but married to the opposite sex, those in which one partner is bisexual, and those in which one partner is transgender. Some told their partners about their orientation before being married, while others came out at some point during the marriage.

President Gordon B. Hinckley was the first General Authority to teach that entering a mixed-orientation marriage should not be seen as a way to overcome same-sex feelings. In 1987, he said, "Marriage should not be viewed as a therapeutic step to solve problems such as homosexual inclinations or practices."[7] In 2015, President Oaks added, "We definitely do not recommend [heterosexual] marriage as a solution to same-gender feelings. In times past, decades ago, there were some practices to that effect. We have eradicated them in the Church now."[8]

While the Church doesn't encourage this road and some of these marriages fail, mixed-orientation marriages can and do work for some. We should hope they succeed. Before I stepped into this space, the only MOMs I was aware of were those that had failed. I thus falsely concluded, from my limited sample size and understanding, that all MOMs failed. It was only after interviewing several couples in MOMs that my conclusion changed. I actually felt a rebuke from the Spirit during one of these interviews for my false conclusions. Now I understand these marriages can be beautiful and authentic love stories in which honesty, communication, vulnerability, power of and commitment to eternal covenants, and common eternal goals create a strong and healthy foundation. I also assume my awareness of successful MOMs is limited, as there are likely many couples who are not sharing this part of their lives with others, and there should be no requirement to do so.

I sometimes hear of a spouse in a MOM referred to as a "hero" for making the marriage work (in some cases, this refers to the cishet spouse and in others, to the LGBTQ spouse). I'm not sure we should judge who is more or less of a hero in a MOM. I'm not sure any of us understand the complexities of another's marriage to elevate one spouse over the other.

Many of these relationships succeed even if the LGBTQ spouse comes out after marriage. One may not come out before marriage because the individual was not fully aware of their sexual orientation or gender identity, was too afraid to acknowledge it, received counsel not to tell their future spouse, or believed that everything would be okay after marriage. These moments of open communication require courage from both spouses, but these marriages can succeed, especially if both partners have the same goals. In these instances, I've observed that complete honesty creates a foundation of trust and brings a couple closer together. I also feel the Atonement of Jesus Christ can provide hope, healing, perspective and power to help a marriage succeed.

I believe that many Latter-day Saints today recognize that they are LGBTQ before or during their dating years, helping them make more informed decisions and receive better personal revelation about marriage.

Some LGBTQ Latter-day Saints may choose to pursue a mixed-orientation marriage and start to date. While I wouldn't universally recommend this path, I also wouldn't universally recommend *against* this path. When advising LGBTQ Latter-day Saints, I do not prescribe a definitive course by pointing either to a MOM that is working or to one that failed. I do not receive personal revelation for another person and therefore cannot know what the best choice would be for them. Listening to stories of both failed and successful MOMs, however, could be helpful in providing LGBTQ individuals with several perspectives, helping them make a knowledgeable choice about their own path forward.

A few episodes of the *Listen, Learn & Love* podcast feature guests in a MOM that ended in divorce.[9] When we learn of a MOM marriage ending, we should not assume it ended because of one partner's sexuality. There could be multiple reasons the marriage ended. I have interviewed the LGBTQ spouse, both former spouses (and the straight person's new husband), and an adult child of parents who were in a MOM. I would never produce one of these podcasts with the goal of trying to end a marriage or to communicate that these marriages are not authentic and will fail. However, these episodes teach principles such as keeping communication lines open and finding common ground, especially when children are involved. Listening to these stories may help others considering this road make a more informed decision and have better tools for a successful MOM. Good information can lead to better questions and allow for clearer personal revelation.

In the interest of building honesty and trust, it is important for an LGBTQ person who is considering a MOM to share that information with those they date, which takes great courage. This doesn't need to happen on the first date, but as the relationship becomes more serious, issues of sexual orientation, gender identity, and the possibility of a MOM should be discussed. These conversations should happen before getting engaged. If the cishet person in the relationship feels this is not the right path for them, this may cause the relationship to end, but it's also possible to bring the couple closer together. Each person in the relationship needs to receive personal revelation for their individual path. I also remind my LG friends who feel their path is a MOM that while some potential cishet spouses will not feel this is their path, the "right one" may conclude this is their path. Yes, entering into a MOM—like any marriage—has some unknowns. But a partnership based on trust, vulnerability, and the Savior can bring two people together in a beautiful marriage.

Some MOMs fail just like some straight marriages fail. As in any divorce situation, we should mourn the marriage's end and resist placing blame on either partner or concluding it was because of one's sexual orientation or gender identity. While we may have a natural tendency to try to discover why a marriage fails and who is most at fault, I encourage us to resist this. Maybe finding those reasons is our way of assuring ourselves that our marriages will not fail, but it may also prevent us from fulfilling our baptismal covenants to not judge and to mourn, bear, and comfort.

Maintaining any marriage can be difficult. And while those in a MOM have the goal of creating and maintaining a successful marriage, outside voices can make their journey especially difficult. Some people will share stories of failed MOMs and tell those in MOMs that they are not being authentic, not living their truth, or are fooling themselves. These messages create unneeded doubt and may cause them to lose sight of their goals. Let's create messages and share stories that support those who want to enter into and keep their mixed-orientation marriages together.

During the summer of 2019, a husband and father in a prominent Utah family came out as gay, and his marriage ended.[10] I was sad to see the marriage end. Many observers made negative comments on social media and elsewhere. But as we strive to not judge, we follow the counsel of Elder Uchtdorf:

> Stop it! It's that simple. We simply must stop judging others and replace judgmental thoughts and feelings with a heart full of love for God and His children. God is our Father. We are His children. We are all brothers and sisters. I don't know exactly how to articulate this point of not judging others with sufficient eloquence, passion, and persuasion to make it stick. I can quote scripture, I can try to expound doctrine, and I will even quote a bumper sticker I recently saw. It was attached to the back of a car whose driver appeared to be a little rough around the edges, but the words on the sticker taught an insightful lesson. It read, "Don't judge me because I sin differently than you."[11]

Travis Steward, a former mission president and a gay man in a MOM, serves as an example of following Elder Uchtdorf's counsel to not judge:[12]

> To all my friends, I feel to share this article [about the failed MOM mentioned above] with you all today and invite you to consider a couple of things as you process this. I feel so deeply and believe I

know something of their pain and suffering. Please know that there are so many very real and difficult complexities to this situation that have led to such gut-wrenching decisions. It can be hard for us to make sense of things that we do not experience personally. God isn't asking us to understand everything; we can't; there is only One who does. He does, however, ask us to love unconditionally and leave the judgment to Him. He does ask us to have compassion for all, . . . not just for those we can understand. Perhaps that is what these experiences are all about, to help us practice loving unconditionally. I am no poster boy for what [this family] should be doing, and I believe he would not want to be the poster boy for what I am expected to do. I hear and honor his need to be open and honest about his difficult journey and invite you to do the same.

Margaret Steward shared a similarly loving post around the same time:[13]

I invite the same compassion that my husband has called us to while also offering one insight. I have been at his side for years now, hearing him share his story. One of the first things he shared with me that tender morning he first opened up was his fear of everyone's judgment and agenda for him if he openly shared his experience. I have witnessed that play out over and over again. He often says: "I am too gay for some and not gay enough for others!" . . . If individuals need to talk about any difficult or perplexing aspect of their lives, it usually isn't because you or I need to hear it. It's because they need to say it. They need to own it for themselves. They need witnesses for their real life. There are many who for their own reasons do not share their feelings or thoughts, and that's fine too. I have found that making room for my discomfort with others' experiences that I don't understand, while withholding judgment, creates a space for learning and for love.

The theme of both comments is to withhold judgment since none of us can fully understand the "difficult complexities" of someone else's situation.[14]

Same-Sex Marriage

While same-sex marriage is outside of the teachings of our Church, I understand that some of our LG members do choose this path. Bryce and Sara Cook, active Latter-day Saints and parents of two gay sons, spoke on my podcast of the "double-bind" their gay sons face. Here is how they describe it:

> Our LG members have the same basic human need or desire that most of us have: to fall in love with that special someone we are attracted to and, ultimately, to share our life together as a couple. In addition, if our LG members were raised as faithful Latter-day Saints (or later converted to the Church) and have testimonies of the gospel, they also desire to actively participate as members in full fellowship in the Church they love. But for our LG members who fall in love with someone of the same sex, these two major life paths are mutually exclusive. If they choose to legally marry the person they love who is of the same sex, they must give up full fellowship in the Church; if they choose full fellowship in the Church, they must give up the person they love and a core part of their human experience. For those of us who are straight, can we imagine having to face that kind of choice when we were dating and falling in love? If we are now married, can we imagine having to choose between our spouse and the Church? We are so fortunate to not have to face that kind of choice, but that is the choice imposed on our LG members—that is the double-bind.[15]

Ben Schilaty helped me better understand the difficult road he and other LG Latter-day Saints walk, particularly in choosing to stay in the Church or pursue a same-sex marriage. His story also makes me want to follow the example of his mother, to support LG Church members if they decide to step away.

> At thirty years old and seven years [since coming out to my parents], I was sitting on the same couch that I had sat on when I came out to them, and I just spewed seven years of experiences. I couldn't keep them in anymore. They included the pain of being gay and a Latter-day Saint, wondering what my future would look like, and a hole in my heart that just couldn't seem to be filled. Church materials used words like *affliction*, *temptation*, *inclination*, and *struggle* to describe experiences like mine. I felt like I had been tried to the point of breaking. I just couldn't struggle with my "affliction" anymore.
>
> After listening for quite some time, my mom seemed to grasp how hard the last seven years had been for me. She promised, "Ben, we're not just on your side. We're with you one hundred percent. If you need to leave the Church and marry a man, you and he will always be part of our family." My dad nodded his head in agreement. I didn't know how much I needed to hear that from my mom. I had felt trapped in a doctrine and culture that seemed to have no place for a gay man like me, wedged between wanting to be in a same-sex relationship and wanting to stay in the Church. Hearing my mom tell me that it was okay to

> leave set me free. She honored my agency just as my Heavenly Parents do. She also reassured me that if I made a choice that was outside of our doctrine, I wouldn't be outside of our family. I couldn't do anything that would remove me from my family. My mother gave me life and then gave me the freedom to live it.
>
> The Lord revealed to Joseph Smith, "All truth is independent in that sphere in which God has placed it, to act for itself" (D&C 93:30). My mother acted within her sphere of influence, as the matriarch of our family, to let me know that I would always be part of the family. She used her agency to give me a supernal gift.[16]

Some LG Latter-day Saints will decide to stay in the Church; others choose to leave the Church to reduce their pain and loneliness and improve their emotional health, opening the option of seeking romantic companionship.

From a pragmatic perspective, there are many ways LG individuals can live their lives if they choose to leave the Church. Some ways are more responsible than others. One less responsible approach is a road with multiple partners, drugs, and alcohol—a road where fewer gospel teachings are still being lived. This road usually results in less long-term stability and direction; may result in addiction, disease, or death; and be less likely to include a consistent relationship with Heavenly Father.

A more responsible approach is a long-term, committed, monogamous same-sex marriage—a road where perhaps more gospel teachings are still being lived. In my experience, many of those in committed same-sex marriages are doing well in their lives. Marriage gives them the stable foundation to move forward, have meaningful careers, stay away from risky behaviors, have better emotional health, give back to society, and often have a relationship with Heavenly Father.

Many Latter-day Saint parents spend time in fasting and prayer that their LG child who has chosen to step away from the Church will make responsible choices that will keep them safe. Many are deeply worried about their emotional health with fear their LG child will die by suicide to end their pain and loneliness. Some pray their child will find a life partner who will bring out the best in their child, help them make thoughtful choices, have a relationship with Heavenly Father, and find stability in their lives. Yes, this is a path outside the teachings of our Church, but these parents, recognizing the reality of their family situation, still want the best for their LG child.

In July 2019, my podcast featured Luke Warnock, who had recently graduated from a Salt Lake area high school, where he had come out as gay. He had served as the student-body president and a key member of the state championship basketball team. Luke, who is not a Church member, is attending college and hopes to marry a man.[17]

The month after I interviewed Luke, I attended my forty-year high school reunion. As part of that reunion, we watched a tribute of all those from our graduating class who had died—including a few who were gay. In 1979, it seemed many LGBTQ individuals left Utah for major cities where there was more acceptance and a feeling of belonging and support. Among the deceased was one of the finest from our class, but I never became his friend since I felt uncomfortable around gay people and wasn't sure how to navigate the situation as an active Latter-day Saint. As I sat in our auditorium, I felt sad that this good man was gone and not there to enjoy the reunion. I thought about his parents and siblings and their sadness at his passing and how society would have been brighter with his contributions.

I then reflected on my friend Luke and the support he is receiving as he moves forward in his life. Luke and one of his friends, Andrew Heath from his basketball team, visited with me at my home. Andrew, who is preparing for an LDS mission, reported that nothing changed when Luke came out as gay. Andrew didn't withdraw his friendship. He already knew he didn't need to choose between supporting his gay friend and being a committed Latter-day Saint. As I sat there in my high school reunion, looking at the picture of my gay classmate who had died, I wished I'd had the tools that Andrew has to extend this kind of friendship and kindness forty years ago. Could I have made a difference for good in his life?

I believe that in forty years, Luke will attend his high school reunion, be warmly welcomed, and be making significant contributions to society (Luke wants to be a therapist). On some level, I feel at peace that legal same-sex marriage is a possible road for Luke. Though it is outside the doctrine of our Church, that path could give Luke vision and hope to make responsible and safe decisions as he continues through life.

Some LG Latter-day Saints who desire a same-sex relationship or marriage fear the criticism and judgment that could come from other Church members. One celibate gay Latter-day Saint told me he was concerned that if he went down this path, he would go from being the hero (staying in the Church, remaining celibate) to the villain (leaving the Church and pursuing a same-sex relationship). If he decides to choose that road, he hopes people would still see him as the same person he is today, with the same Christlike attributes, trying to do his best in the "double-bind" Bryce Cook earlier described, and contributing to society. He hopes we don't make him the poster boy for what is wrong in the world.

I feel my straight marriage can stand on its own merits. I don't need to talk negatively about those in same-sex marriages to validate my marriage. Further, if we extend kindness to those who enter same-sex marriages and keep our family and friend circles together, they may not feel the pain of rejection. Some who step away from the Church feel anger, a secondary emotion to pain, that is often directed at family, friends, or the Church. Of course, not everyone who steps away feels angry at the Church; many still want the Church and its individual members to succeed. Perhaps we can help more people who leave feel this way by offering our kindness and support, and honoring their agency.

The following individuals are active Latter-day Saints who share their thoughts about those who choose a same-sex marriage.

VANCE BRYCE (GAY MAN)

I feel like I can understand someone who has left the Church to have relationships. Of course I do. If I receive personal revelation to do that, then I'll be one of them. I have utmost respect for my friends who have made that hard choice. They are some of my favorite people, and they are some of the best children of God I've ever met. They are in tune with their souls, and they know what they need, and they risk mocking and scorn just to be themselves. I refuse to be someone who sees a person as less-than just because they don't choose to live their lives exactly the same as I do. I expect the same from them.

KYLE FRIANT (GAY MAN)

I am happy for [those in same-sex marriages]! I am glad . . . when they find a loving, committed partner. I would dread it if my choice to stay in the Church were used by an active member to disparage someone who chooses to [leave]. Our experiences are all different, and each person deserves to be validated in their journey and life choices.

DALLIN STEELE (GAY MAN)

In my life I have come to understand that each person . . . needs to follow their own path and make their own choices. I am always happy when someone chooses to do something that makes them happier. It is a path to healing.

I believe that before we came to earth, I fought for their right to choose what path they would follow, whatever it was. I don't want to live a life full of sadness just because someone makes a different choice than me.

I understand why they leave. Many, if not most, people desire that deep connection with that special someone. We all desire to feel loved, wanted, and important, and that manifests in different ways.

TEMBER HARWARD (GAY MAN MARRIED TO A WOMAN)

[When I saw people leave the Church to pursue a same-sex marriage], I was sad in the sense that I know they're distancing themselves from fully having the Spirit in their lives and the blessings of the ordinances of the gospel; however, I also believed that their choice may have been necessary to their journey, to learn for themselves the good from the bad. I also understood, as one who lived that way before, that it's extremely painful living single and celibate, and the need for companionship is immense; so I was empathetic to why they left.

BRIANT CARTER (GAY MAN)

My perspective is from the other end of the road as I am sixty-five and have been active [in the Church] all my life. By making that choice, I have been blessed with amazing experiences and met lifelong friends. That could not have happened . . . as a non-member of the Church. In [choosing to stay in the Church], there is a part of me that has been set on a shelf, dormant, since I have never been in a close, committed relationship. Burying these parts of me has been detrimental to my health on several levels. As things currently stand, there is a sacrifice required in choosing either direction—damned if you do and damned if you don't. I am always thrilled when two people decide they want to spend the rest of their lives together and honor that decision.

BOB VERSTEGE (GAY MAN WHOSE HUSBAND DIED)[18]

I would be happy for [a couple in a same-sex marriage]. [My husband] and I experienced a great love. I want everyone to experience that connection; this love ultimately brings people closer to God.

JERRY CHONG (GAY MAN)

When I hear of an LGBT member who has found someone to call their spouse, my heart becomes full of warm emotions. I am happy for them and for the commitment they are about to make to each other. I respect the desire to find someone. I wish I could find someone to spend time with, to laugh with, and to be romanced by. I know firsthand how hard it is to remain active, faithful, and celibate. This combination . . . leaves my heart empty, and I push through it by keeping busy in my callings and in providing service. I have lost myself in advocacy work for LGBTQ members in our congregations by arranging to meet with my local stake presidencies to discuss inclusion and sensitivity training. I know that the potential to educate local leaders and bishops is facilitated by the callings that I have held and by my faithfulness and obedience. I have sacrificed my own possibility of companionship to help the next generation have an easier time coping and being accepted in their congregations.

CALVIN BURKE (GAY MAN)

I've never felt anything but compassion and love for [those in same-sex marriages]. I know how challenging this path is, and I do not fault anyone for making the choice to leave [the Church]. Rather than dwelling on our differences, I continue to have them in my life because it is important for me to support all of my friends and loved ones on their spiritual journeys, no matter where those take them. More importantly, I also need encouragement and support in my own journey—so I keep my friends around for that too!

RJ RISUENO (GAY MAN)

I think that life is so complex and unique that on both sides, it would be so beneficial to just look into each other's eyes knowing that each step we take on our journey is our own. And we know what's best for us.

Suicide prevention

As heart-rending as it is, some LGBTQ individuals consider another option: suicide. My efforts—the *Listen, Learn & Love* podcast, LGBTQ visits, social media messages, firesides, and this book—are a response to the suicide of Stockton Powers, a gay Latter-day Saint, in the hopes of preventing further suicides.

Brené Brown gives insight into how some LGBTQ Latter-day Saints feel, the toll on their emotional health, and why some consider suicide: "The most terrifying and destructive feeling that a person can experience is psychological isolation. This is not the same as being alone. It is a feeling that one is locked out of the possibility of human connection and of being powerless to change the situation. In the extreme, psychological isolation can lead to a sense of hopelessness and desperation. People will do almost anything to escape this combination of condemned isolation and powerlessness."[19]

The possibility of suicide for LDS LGBTQ youth is well illustrated by Jane Clayson Johnson in her recent book *Silent Souls Weeping* published by Deseret Book. Clayson tells the remarkable story of Tammy and Kayden Maxwell.

WHEN SUICIDE FEELS LIKE THE HAPPIEST OPTION:
KAYDEN'S STORY

No conversation about depression and suicide would be complete without sharing the challenges of Church members who identify as gay or are otherwise part of the LGBTQ+ community.

Suicide rates for children ages twelve to eighteen are frighteningly high. A 2015 study by the Centers for Disease Control (CDC) reported that 8.6 percent of high-school students had attempted suicide (17 percent had considered it). For adolescents who identify as lesbian, gay, or bisexual, however, the percentage was *more than triple* that (the study did not look at those who identify as transgender): 29.4 percent of LGB students had attempted suicide and 42.8 percent had seriously considered it. Just over 60 percent of LGB teens had reported feeling "so sad or helpless every day for 2 or more weeks in a row that they stopped doing some usual activities." Undoubtedly, there are a number of Latter-day Saint LGB youth included in these percentages.

Kayden was one of them. Though his story does not provide answers to the questions many gay and lesbian members have about their place in the Church, it is a peek into a life experience that few of us adequately understand. By age fourteen, Kayden recognized that he did not have the same feelings for girls as other boys his age did. At first, he didn't comprehend exactly what that meant for his future. In fact, he initially thought, "I'll just take care of it with the bishop, one on one . . . and fix myself and then no one else would have to know."

But Kayden fell into a deep depression as he realized that he would never be able to live the life he had always dreamed of. "You sing songs about it in Primary, you learn lesson after lesson about how to have a happy family. . . . It's a beautiful plan and it's wonderful, and I would've done anything to hold to that. [But] as soon as you accept that you're gay, it suddenly complicates things dramatically."

In his journal, Kayden made a list of pros and cons regarding the four paths he believed he could take: (1) leave the Church, gain the opportunity to have a companion and children—but feel like a sinner; (2) marry a woman and together strive for the ideal family life he wanted—but feel like a fraud; (3) remain celibate and wait for the afterlife—when, as he'd often been told, "everything would all work out"; or (4) end his life immediately to hasten the outcome of option three.

Kayden's conclusion after reviewing the pros and cons of each path is heart wrenching: the fourth option.

JANE: "You felt like suicide was the only answer?"

KAYDEN: "It wasn't the only answer, but it was the happiest one. I was suffocating just looking at my own future and what was lying in front of me. It just started to feel like I had nothing to look forward to in this life."

Kayden's mom, Tammy, describes the struggle that ensued, "the depth of self-hatred. . . . He just really thought the best thing was for him to move on to the next life. . . . He believed that God had made a mistake."

The years that followed were fraught with worry and despair for both Tammy and Kayden. They talked openly to one another about *everything,* which allowed Tammy to gain insight into Kayden's feelings while also keeping him as safe as she could. He saw a therapist who helped him work through many things. At times, Kayden felt supported by his Latter-day Saint peers at school, but at other times he felt bullied by them. His depression worsened during his senior year. Though Kayden had previously been a straight-A student, he stopped going to classes and almost didn't graduate.

Tammy tearfully recalls the terror of those days, the constant fear that her son would not survive his deep depression. "There were times I feared going downstairs to his bedroom because I didn't know what I would find. I didn't want to send his younger brother and sister down without me because I didn't want them to find him."

> Tammy may not have realized it at the time, but the younger children she was protecting were also the reason Kayden did not take the fateful final action.
>
> JANE: "Why didn't you do it?"
>
> KAYDEN: "My little siblings, actually. I just really couldn't leave them behind. I love them so much."
>
> Tammy still worries about getting a call informing her that Kayden has taken his own life. Perhaps she always will. Her fear for her son's well-being and feelings of helplessness have precipitated her own depression, which she continues to battle. "He wants to belong so bad. It just breaks my heart over and over and over. . . . I can't get over the loneliness that I feel for him that I know he feels—that just wanting to belong."
>
> Today, Kayden hopes that the worst crisis has passed. He left the Church for a different faith community not long after a gay acquaintance died by suicide, but he says he isn't hostile. "I had a really positive experience with the Church. My ward was so welcoming and my bishop was so kind, and I didn't leave because people were cruel to me; I left because I did not feel comfortable with the options that lay ahead of me. . . .
>
> "Every single story we read about [Jesus Christ], He's extending love to people who don't feel like they deserve it and He's reaching out an arm to people that society has cast out.
>
> "I know my intent and God knows my intent . . . and that's all right."[20]

I'm grateful for Tammy and Kayden for sharing their story. They are two of my heroes. Their story helps us better realize the difficult road for many LGBTQ Latter-day Saints and why some consider suicide. Tammy reports that Kayden is doing much better, is an excellent college student, and moving forward in his life.

They also help us understand that talking about suicide helps prevent it. Sister Reyna I. Aburto, second counselor in the Relief Society General Presidency, father died by suicide and teaches the importance of talking about suicide: "It was only recently that I learned talking about suicide in appropriate ways actually helps to prevent it rather than encourage it."[21] If you'd like to get some basic suicide training to better see warning signs and how to respond, I suggest taking a QPR course—usually a one- to two- hour educational program available in many areas.[22]

Let's be unified in our efforts to encourage those considering suicide to not choose this path. If you are suicidal, please get professional help and open up with family and friends who love you. In addition to seeking help, we have many podcasts on this subject.[23] Perhaps listening to these stories will give you more tools, vision, and an increased desire to stay—or help you better help others.

This world is a better place with you here. I believe your best days are ahead of you and you will look back and be glad you stayed. In March 2020, I asked on Twitter advice from those who were once suicidal to those who are currently suicidal. Here are some of their responses:[2]

> Take things one day at a time. Every day you make it is another victory. You are loved by those around you. You'll look back down the road and be so glad you stayed.
>
> No matter what, no one is ever better off without you. Even if you've made huge mistakes. The world needs what YOU have to offer.
>
> Breathe. Take a walk. Play with puppies. Do anything but get out of your head. Reach out. Please stay. Someone needs you. You need you.
>
> It's worth it. There are brighter days ahead amidst the darkness.
>
> I'm glad I didn't do it. It took about 2 months after that day for life to start improving and another 3 years for things to become something approaching normal, but I have a really, really good life now.
>
> Get a psychiatrist, be brutally honest.
>
> Depression lies. And it gets better. It gets better. Hold on. These seem so simple, but every time it gets too hard I just hold on a little longer.
>
> I still struggle with suicidal thoughts, but I'm glad to still be here. Tell people how low you are so you can get help. Staying is worth it.
>
> If you are feeling a wave of suicidal thought right now—get up, jog in place, crank up the music and dance the biggest dance you can. If you can't stand - wave your arms above your head, roll your eyes around your head, blink and open, blink and open. Deep breaths.
>
> Something my dad told me . . . Don't make a permanent solution for a temporary problem. It's always stuck with me.

Text help to 741741 to talk to a crisis counselor, 24/7.

Whatever motive you need to stay alive is worth it. It can be something like family or pets, but it can also be spite or you want to see what meme the internet comes up with next week. It doesn't need to be big and meaningful because living is living no matter the reason.

I tried. I'm so glad I failed. It was hard. At first, I thought it was just something else I'd failed at. Over time, I learned that I was loved. You too are loved. All of you. You are enough. You are complete. You are exactly who God designed you to be.

You may think that no one will miss you or even care that you're gone. That's what I thought. Then one of my friends took his life last year and I got to see the other side. It sucks. You're NOT alone and people WILL miss you! Reach out before you give in.

You are loved by so many people you haven't met yet.

We can choose 2 live 4 the sake of loved ones & the small joys of life. The waves of despair r real, but they also subside. Please stay 2 witness the rest of ur life's painting. There r deep shades, but countless beautiful colors await as well. Ur going 2 b alright! Ur not alone.

ENDNOTES

1. "Church Updates Official 'Mormon and Gay' Website," Newsroom, The Church of Jesus Christ of Latter-day Saints, October 25, 2016, newsroom.churchofjesuschrist.org/article/official-update-mormon-and-gay-website.
2. Both individuals reported working closely with the Church to have their stories removed from the website and were treated with kindness, support, and understanding.
3. See northstarlds.org/.
4. For *Listen, Learn & Love* podcasts that deal with mixed-orientation marriages, seelistenlearnandlove.org/mixed-orientation-marriage-podcasts.
5. "Ricardo's Story," The Church of Jesus Christ of Latter-day Saints, accessed April 6, 2020, churchofjesuschrist.org/topics/gay/videos/ricardos-story?lang=eng.
6. See episode 67 of the *Listen, Learn & Love* podcast.
7. Gordon B. Hinkley, "Reverence and Morality," *Ensign*, May 1987, churchofjesuschrist.org/study/ensign/1987/05/reverence-and-morality.

8. Dallin H. Oaks, interview by Jennifer Napier Pearce, Trib Talk, *Salt Lake Tribune*, January 29, 2015, YouTube video, 17:39, youtube.com/watch?v=UIJ6gL_xc-M&t=619s.
9. For *Listen, Learn & Love* podcasts that discuss mixed-orientation marriages that ended, see listenlearnandlove.org/marriages-that-ended.
10. Dennis Romboy, "Ed Smart, Father of Elizabeth Smart, Announces He Is Gay," *Deseret News*, August 15, 2019, deseret.com/2019/8/15/20807894/ed-smart-father-of-elizabeth-smart-announces-he-is-gay.
11. Dieter F. Uchtdorf, "The Merciful Obtain Mercy" (general conference address, Salt Lake City, April 2012), churchofjesuschrist.org/study/general-conference/2012/04/the-merciful-obtain-mercy.
12. Travis Steward, "To all my friends," Facebook, August 16, 2019, facebook.com/travis.steward.908/posts/2489309821305315.
13. Margaret Steward, "I invite the same compassion," Facebook, August 16, 2019, facebook.com/margaret.b.steward/posts/10216838886858187.
14. Margaret and Travis Steward, who presided over the Texas Houston Mission from 2015 to 2018, share their story of being in a mixed-orientation marriage in episode 177 of the *Listen, Learn & Love* podcast. It is one of our most listened-to episodes, helping many to understand this possibility for LG Latter-day Saints and how a MOM can be successful.
15. See episode 116 of the *Listen, Learn & Love* podcast.
16. Ben Schilaty, "Agency and Same-Sex Attraction," *Ben There, Done That* (blog), June 24, 2019, benschilaty.blogspot.com/2019/06/agency-and-same-sex-attraction.html, italics in original.
17. See episode 159 of the *Listen, Learn & Love* podcast.
18. See episode 118 of the *Listen, Learn & Love* podcast.
19. Brené Brown, *Daring Greatly: How the Courage to be Vulnerable Transforms the Way We Live, Love, Parent, and Lead* (New York: Gotham Books, 2012), 140.
20. Jane Clayson Johnson, *Silent Souls Weeping: Depression – Sharing Stories, Finding Hope* (Salt Lake City: Deseret Book, 2018), 156-8.
21. Reyna I. Aburto, "Thru Cloud and Sunshine, Lord, Abide with Me!" (general conference address, Salt Lake City, October 2019), churchofjesuschrist.org/study/general-conference/2019/10/31aburto?lang=eng.
22. See qprinstitute.com/
23. For *Listen, Learn & Love* podcasts on suicide prevention, see listenlearnandlove.org/suicide-podcasts.
24. @Papa_Ostler (Richard Ostler). "For those of you that have been suicidal and are now OK, what would you say to those reading this thread who are suicidal? Please stay." Twitter, March 23, 2020, 1:52 p.m., twitter.com/Papa_Ostler/status/1242147102773243904.

CHAPTER 10

WHEN A FAMILY MEMBER LEAVES THE CHURCH

The purpose of this chapter is to give peace and hope to Latter-day Saint parents who have a child who has left the Church.[1] When a child leaves, it can be difficult to know what to do and how to feel.

In periods of self-reflection, some parents may feel the fault is with them. Attending church may become harder as they hear other parents share stories about their active children, causing them to conclude that their own parenting didn't measure up. Those feelings of shame are only heightened when other Church members stop asking about the child because they are unsure of what to say.

Sometimes I think we envision parenting as a vending machine—we put a series of coins into the vending machine and press C3, which represents a desired outcome as our children grow into adults. We are a little anxious until the lever starts to turn, releasing the requested product. But have we ever pressed C3 and received D4 instead? Perhaps we blame ourselves, thinking we didn't put in the right coins or inserted them in the wrong order or didn't press the correct button. We might see someone else at another vending machine put in coins, press C3 and get C3. We conclude that we must have done something wrong.

When a child steps away from the Church, parents (especially, in my observation, mothers who have consecrated their lives to their children) may spend hours upon hours self-reflecting, contemplating what could have gone wrong. This can quickly turn into a downward spiral of over-analysis that is emotionally unhealthy. I don't believe Heavenly

Father wants us to go down this road. He didn't ask us to be perfect parents, only to try our best. I don't think Heavenly Father wants us to tie our self-worth to outcomes beyond our control. He wants us to focus instead on things within our control like our relationship with Him and the Savior. We need to abandon this vending machine mentality. As parents, we can only do our best and then leave the rest at the Savior's feet.

Parents worry (rightly so) about their child's eternal welfare and about their family being together in the next life. Some parents experience greater emotional turmoil when a child leaves the Church than when losing a child to early death. To some this reaction may seem harsh or unbalanced, but it stems from our doctrine of the eternal family. Latter-day Saint parents believe they will be reunited with their deceased children in the afterlife, but many parents are less sure of their eternal relationships with family members who leave the Church.

When a child steps away, we mourn a future outcome that Jon Ogden has called a "sad heaven." Sad heaven occurs when we mourn "empty chairs around the table in the next life."[2] We conclude today that our child will not be with us in eternity and that there will permanently be an empty chair. This conclusion leads to deep sadness, which I don't think Heavenly Father wants us to feel. To use a sports analogy, this is like my beloved Los Angeles Dodgers losing in next year's World Series in game 7—an event that hasn't happened yet—and me feeling all that emotional pain and sadness now. Yes, we mourn. We care. We pray. We put our children's name on the temple prayer rolls. But our understanding of the plan of salvation and of loving Heavenly Parents, who want to do everything they can to help Their children return, can give us peace in this life and hope for the future.[3]

My brother David Ostler (former mission president and stake president) has adult children who no longer believe in the doctrines of the Church, and published a book on ministering to those with questions.[4] Regarding empty chairs, David gives this counsel: "At our house, my wife and I still talk about no empty chairs, but we [also] talk about having no empty chairs at the dinner table, around the pool, on a vacation, at their life events, and in all the chairs from our children's lives."[5] I like his vision which concentrates on things that are within our control and turning the things we can't control over to Heavenly Father.

In an article published by *LDS Living*, David gives six tips for parents of adult children who do not believe in the Church:[6]

1. Don't preach or lecture.
2. Listen to understand and validate.
3. Use words that affirm; don't use labels.
4. Accept and love them fully.
5. Remember agency and the love of our Heavenly Parents.
6. Take care of yourself.

Affirming David's first point, President Ballard teaches, "Please don't preach to them! Your family member or friend already knows the Church's teachings. They don't need another lecture! What they need, what we all need, is love and understanding, not judging. Share your positive experiences of living the gospel."[7] Those who want more helpful suggestions on how to talk to those leaving the Church can also refer to the website of Dr. Julie Hanks, an active Latter-day Saint, who shares twenty-five things not to say and twenty-five things to say to a loved one stepping away from the Church that help keep communication lines open and family circles together.[8]

Several General Authorities have given us guidance this subject. Elder Uchtdorf, for instance, humanizes and gives us increased understanding of those who step away:

> One might ask, If the gospel is so wonderful, why would anyone leave? Sometimes we assume it is because they have been offended or lazy or sinful. Actually, it is not that simple. In fact, there is not just one reason that applies to the variety of situations. Some of our dear members struggle for years with the question whether they should separate themselves from the Church. In this Church that honors personal agency so strongly, that was restored by a young man who asked questions and sought answers, we respect those who honestly search for truth. It may break our hearts when their journey takes them away from the Church we love and the truth we have found, but we honor their right to worship Almighty God according to the dictates of their own conscience, just as we claim that privilege for ourselves.[9]

Emphasizing the importance of love and empathy, Elder Quentin L. Cook teaches specifically about how to treat LGBTQ individuals who leave the Church: "As a church, nobody should be more loving and compassionate. Let us be at the forefront in terms of expressing love, compassion, and outreach. Let's not have families exclude or be disrespectful of those who choose a different lifestyle as a result of their feelings about their own gender."[10]

I don't believe saying kind things about those who step away from the Church results in more people leaving. Rather, having and expressing empathy for those who separate themselves from the Church increases the chance of our families and friendships staying together.

Love is also the theme of Tom Christofferson's story. When he left the Church, his parents welcomed him and his partner into their home. In his book *That We May Be One*, Tom writes how his parents taught their children and grandchildren to respond to Tom and his partner with this statement on love: "The only thing we can really be perfect at is loving each other. The most important lesson your children will learn from how our family treats their Uncle Tom is that nothing they can ever do will take them outside the circle of our family's love."[11] Elder Uchtdorf similarly teaches:

> Because love is the great commandment, it ought to be at the center of all and everything we do in our own family, in our Church callings, and in our livelihood. Love is the healing balm that repairs rifts in personal and family relationships. It is the bond that unites families, communities, and nations. Love is the power that initiates friendship, tolerance, civility, and respect. It is the source that overcomes divisiveness and hate. Love is the fire that warms our lives with unparalleled joy and divine hope. Love should be our walk and our talk.[12]

Our love for one another doesn't need to be motivated only by a desire for someone to return to the Church. Harper Dawn Forsgren, a returned missionary, tweeted: "We as members of the church need to stop focusing on 'We need to love people because our love will bring them back to the church' and instead focus on 'We need to love people because people deserve to be loved.'"[13] I agree with Harper. Love with no agenda is the kind of love that keeps friendships and families together. In my experience, people on the receiving side of this kind of love are the most likely to open up if their feelings change or they need help.

In addition to love, we can try to approach those who leave the Church with a measure of understanding, acknowledging that only God knows people's hearts and is the only one who can judge them. I love the words in Elder Gay's talk "Taking upon Ourselves the Name of Jesus Christ," which cautions us against judging someone's standing with God:

> A few years ago my older sister passed away. She had a challenging life. She struggled with the gospel and was never really active. Her husband abandoned their marriage and left her with four young

> children to raise. On the evening of her passing, in a room with her children present, I gave her a blessing to peacefully return home. At that moment I realized I had too often defined my sister's life in terms of her trials and inactivity. As I placed my hands on her head that evening, I received a severe rebuke from the Spirit. I was made acutely aware of her goodness and allowed to see her as God saw her—not as someone who struggled with the gospel and life but as someone who had to deal with difficult issues I did not have. I saw her as a magnificent mother who, despite great obstacles, had raised four beautiful, amazing children. I saw her as the friend to our mother who took time to watch over and be a companion to her after our father passed away. During that final evening with my sister, I believe God was asking me, "Can't you see that everyone around you is a sacred being?"[14]

We do not understand all things, and we each have our own unique struggles. These words of Elder Gay give us insight into God's love for all His children and encourage us to treat everyone as sacred beings, even when we can't understand their choices. As we show faith in our Heavenly Father, who shares the same hopes we have for our family members who have stepped away from the Church, and trust in His plan of salvation, we can find peace in mortality, leaving everything at the Savior's feet.

ENDNOTES

1. There is a Facebook group for active Latter-day Saint parents with children who have left the Church: facebook.com/groups/BridgesLDSParents/.
2. Jon Ogden, "Op-Ed: Belief in 'Sad Heaven' Hurts Relationships in Era of Mormon Doubt, *Salt Lake Tribune*, August 8, 2016, archive.sltrib.com/article.php?id=4190887&itype=CMSID.
3. The question of a person's ability to progress between the kingdoms of glory in the next life has not been made clear by the prophets. From the secretary to the First Presidency: "The brethren direct me to say that the Church has never announced a definite doctrine upon this point. Some of the brethren have held the view that it was possible in the course of progression to advance from one glory to another, invoking the principle of eternal progression; others of the brethren have taken the opposite view. But as stated, the Church has never announced a definite doctrine on this point." Ambiguity leaves open the possibility that our loved ones who have left the Church could be with us in the afterlife. I point this out to give hope to parents with children who have stepped away. See *Dialogue: A Journal of Mormon Thought* 15, no. 1 (Spring 1982): 181–83.

4. David Ostler, *Building Bridges: Ministering to Those Who Question* (Salt Lake City: Greg Kofford Books, 2019).
5. David Ostler, "6 Tips for Parents of Adult Children Who Don't Believe in the Church," *LDS Living*, June 8, 2019, ldsliving.com/6-Tips-for-Parents-of-Adult-Children-Who-Don-t-Believe-in-the-Church/s/90940.
6. Ostler, "6 Tips for Parents," *LDS Living*, June 8, 2019.
7. Marianne Holman Prescott, "Elder Ballard Tackles Tough Topics and Gives Timely Advice to Young Adults," *Church News*, The Church of Jesus Christ of Latter-day Saints, November 14, 2017, churchofjesuschrist.org/church/news/elder-ballard-tackles-tough-topics-and-gives-timely-advice-to-young-adults.
8. Dr. Julie de Azevedo Hanks, "25 Things NOT to Say to a Loved One Leaving the Church," accessed March 31, 2020, drjuliehanks.com/2020/02/20/25-things-not-to-say-to-a-loved-one-leaving-the-church/.
9. Dieter F. Uchtdorf, "Come, Join with Us" (general conference address, Salt Lake City, October 2013), churchofjesuschrist.org/study/general-conference/2013/10/come-join-with-us.
10. "New Church Website on Same-Sex Attraction Offers Love, Understanding, and Hope," Church News, The Church of Jesus Christ of Latter-day Saints, December 6, 2012, churchofjesuschrist.org/church/news/new-church-website-on-same-sex-attraction-offers-love-understanding-and-hope; "Let Us Be at the Forefront," Same-Sex Attraction, The Church of Jesus Christ of Latter-day Saints, video, accessed February 19, 2020, (churchofjesuschrist.org/topics/gay/videos/let-us-be-at-the-forefront).
11. Tom Christofferson, *That We May Be One: A Gay Mormon's Perspective on Faith and Family* (Salt Lake City: Deseret Book, 2017), 19.
12. Dieter F. Uchtdorf, "The Love of God" (general conference address, Salt Lake City, October 2009), churchofjesuschrist.org/study/general-conference/2009/10/the-love-of-god.
13. Harper Dawn Forsgren (@harperforsgen), "Sunday Thoughts," Twitter, June 24, 2018, 4:21 p.m., twitter.com/harperforsgren/status/1011011450960109568.
14. Robert C. Gay, "Take upon Ourselves the Name of Jesus Christ" (general conference address, Salt Lake City, October 2018), churchofjesuschrist.org/study/general-conference/2018/10/taking-upon-ourselves-the-name-of-jesus-christ.

CHAPTER 11

THE FUTURE

I feel that we as Church members have more work to do to fully meet the needs of LGBTQ Latter-day Saints. Indeed, I believe President Ballard taught this when he said, "We need to listen to and understand what our LGBT brothers and sisters are feeling and experiencing. *We must do better than we have done in the past* so that all members feel they have a spiritual home where their brothers and sisters love them and where they have a place to worship and serve the Lord."[1]

Thomas McConkie, an active Latter-day Saint, framed the need to *do better* with these words: "I feel that the LGBTQ issue/tension/challenge is the defining challenge in our church right now. I don't mean to say that authoritatively, but more impressionistically. I can't think of a more profound turning point in our history or opportunity to really come together and practice Christian love. My heart aches for what is going on right now."[2]

As we move into the future, each of us has the responsibility to *do better than we have done in the past* so our LGBTQ members feel welcome, valued and a sense of belonging.

Ongoing Restoration

As we know, the Restoration is on-going as taught by President Nelson: "We're witnesses to a process of restoration. If you think the Church has been fully restored, you're just seeing the beginning. There is much more to come. . . . Wait till next year. And then the next year. Eat your vitamin pills. Get your rest. It's going to be exciting."[3]

One day as I was pondering on this concept, a metaphor came to my mind, which captures the need to better support LGBTQ Latter-day

Saints and their families. I visualized a forty-chapter book. In this book, we have already moved past earlier chapters, and we still have more chapters to write—representing the on-going work of the Restoration. It is our responsibility to keep asking and pondering—improving the book until we reach the end.

In using this metaphor, I don't want to infer that Church doctrine will change. It is instead a framework for assessing where we have been, where we are, and things we can do in our wards and families to implement President Ballard's words.

The Past

The earlier chapters of this forty-chapter book are the past teachings and practices of our Church and of society that are no longer taught and that may have caused pain for LGBTQ Latter-day Saints and their families (the belief that sexual orientation is a choice and that people can change their sexual orientation).

If someone opens up about their "early-chapter" experiences and we dismiss their words, I believe they will be less likely to stay in our church, heal, and put the experiences behind them. No one should have to prove their pain. We should just accept it and be willing to sit with them in their pain. Dismissing it usually results in more pain, anger, and a lower likelihood that one will feel safe opening up again.

As committed Latter-day Saints, we may feel that our job is to defend the Church and that thereby we cannot listen to other people's stories. We may be tempted to dismiss their feelings, or be reluctant to validate their experiences. But I feel we can both listen to and validate others and support the Church. It is not an either-or proposition—but part of our baptism covenants to mourn, bear, and comfort.

Though society in general probably influenced some of the Church's past teachings, some Church members feel we should have done better. If you feel this way, your feelings are valid. I hope the affirming words of Elder Uchtdorf are helpful: "To be perfectly frank, there have been times when members or leaders in the Church have simply made mistakes. There may have been things said or done that were not in harmony with our values, principles, or doctrine. I suppose the Church would be perfect only if it were run by perfect beings. God is perfect, and His doctrine is pure. But He works through us—His imperfect children—and imperfect people make mistakes."[4]

I am one of these imperfect members Elder Uchtdorf described. I made mistakes during my service in a YSA ward and in other Church assignments. Even now, as I'm trying my best to support the Church and our LGBTQ members, I'm sure I will say, write, or do things that I will look back on later, armed with new understanding, and cringe because of the pain I caused others. I apologize for my mistakes.

Perhaps these past chapters are similar to what Elder Bruce R. McConkie said in 1978 in explaining Church leaders' past statements about why the priesthood was once withheld from Black Latter-day Saints: "Forget everything that I have said, or what President Brigham Young or President George Q. Cannon or whomsoever has said in days past that is contrary to the present revelation. We spoke with a limited understanding and without the light and knowledge that now has come into the world."[5]

In sharing this quote by Elder McConkie, I don't want to infer our teachings will change. Rather, we need to look at the past and humbly recognize we sometimes spoke with limited understanding.

My biggest Book of Mormon hero is Nephi. One of the reasons I love and respect him is his honest statements about his own weaknesses (see 2 Nephi 4). His honesty didn't diminish his prophetic ministry but showed his human side and has given me more hope as I follow his example to improve, "know[ing] in whom I have trusted" (2 Nephi 4:19).

These words from Elder McConkie and Nephi build my faith in our church. Our leaders are not perfect and may speak at times with limited knowledge. Understanding this can give us hope for the future and encourage us to extend grace to our leaders in their demanding assignments. This is a more sustainable approach, especially as we try to follow the words of President Ballard to "do better than we have done in the past."

I firmly believe our leaders, whom I sustain and support, are doing their best—and it's not my job to determine whether or not they have a full understanding about Heavenly Father's plan for His LGBTQ children. I do not claim to have more understanding than our leaders. I can only receive personal revelation for me, my family, and the people I serve.

Current Adjustments

Sometimes I see something that feels like a new chapter, or adjustment, helping to implement President Ballard's vision. For example, the Church's website on this subject has developed and expanded over the years. The original website launched in December 2012 as mormonsandgays.lds.org and was generally well received.[6] A revised website, launched in 2016, had new content and a new title, "Mormon and Gay," a subtle change that reflected the notion that a person doesn't need to choose between these two identities. One can, in fact, be gay and an active Latter-day Saint.[7] In February 2020, the site was moved to churchofjesuschrist.org/topics/gay, and for the first time, a dedicated section for transgender Latter-day Saints was added at churchofjesuschrist.org/topics/transgender.

Several adaptations are occurring at BYU. In April 2017, the first LGBT-specific campus-wide event was held by the BYU NAMI (National Alliance on Mental Illness) club.[8] In March 2018, BYU Student Life hosted the first LGBT campus event, and more than six hundred people attended.[9] That summer, the Office of Student Success and Inclusion was created when President Kevin J. Worthen invited Dr. Vern Heperi to serve on the president's council as an assistant to the president. Soon after accepting the position, Dr. Heperi hired a gay Latter-day Saint to work full-time as an inclusion advisor.[10] In May 2019, BYU Women's Conference held its first LGBTQ focus session, in which LGBTQ Latter-day Saints shared their stories.[11] In December 2019, BYU held an LGBTQ+ Christmas event.[12] In January 2020, BYU presented a panel on faith and sexuality, which included Ben Schilaty, an honor code administrator and gay Latter-day Saint.[13] Also in January, BYU allowed same-sex dance partners for outside competitors at the U.S. National Amateur DanceSport Championships held at BYU.[14]

I believe that BYU will continue to set an example for how to minister to our LGBTQ members, embracing their contributions, and in amplifying their voices. We can model what is happening at BYU and other Church settings as templates for our local congregations and our families.

In June 2018, I was pleased to read an article in the *Deseret News* about the Tabernacle Choir at Temple Square singing with the San Francisco Gay Men's Choir. It included a picture of Elder Donald L. Hallstrom of the Seventy and Ron Gunnell, assistant president of the Tabernacle Choir, visiting with Dr. Timothy Seelig, artistic director and conductor of the Gay Men's Choir. Tabernacle Choir President Ron Jarrett said: "Music affects people in many ways. This is a great opportunity to bring two cultures, if you will, to the center of things and to build bridges, to make friends, and to make an enjoyable experience for everyone through music."[15]

In that same month, I was impressed by the remarks of former Utah Senator Orrin Hatch, an active Latter-day Saint, on the Senate floor of the U.S. Capitol. His comments on LGBTQ issues reflect increased education and understanding. "No one should feel less because of their orientation," Hatch said. LGBTQ people "deserve our unwavering love and support. They deserve our validation and the assurance that not only is there a place for them in this society but that it is far better off because of them. Regardless of where you stand on the cultural issues of the day, whether you are a religious conservative, a secular liberal or somewhere in between, we all have a special duty to each other. That duty is to treat one another with dignity and respect. It is not simply to tolerate but to love." Hatch added that a person's gender identity is not a choice and "these young men and women deserve to feel loved, cared for, and accepted for who they are."[16]

Other new efforts to respond to the needs of LGBTQ members occurred in 2019. I became aware of several stakes that started LGBTQ family home evenings, at which LGBTQ Latter-day Saints and allies could meet together to better support LGBTQ members and their families. And in December 2019, FamilySearch.org (owned by the Church) launched a new function that allows users to build same-sex family trees on its free website.[17] Paul Nauta, FamilySearch's public affairs manager, spoke about the change: "We're adding functions that allow people to document family relationships as they exist." During Christmas of 2019, I was glad to see the Gay Men's Chorus of Washington, DC, perform at the Washington, DC, Temple visitors' center as part of the center's annual lineup of holiday concerts.[18]

And finally, at the time of this writing, in January 2020, with Church support, Utah banned conversion therapy.[19] In all these examples, no one had to give up anything, no church doctrine changed, and we all benefitted by coming together as members of the same human family.

Each of these changes may seem small on their own, but all together, they signal significant progress and shifts in attitude. The Restoration is an ongoing process as taught in the ninth article of faith: "We believe all that God has revealed, all that He does now reveal, and we believe that He will yet reveal many great and important things pertaining to the Kingdom of God."

I look forward to seeing future chapters, or adjustments, on how we can continue to find ways to come together to better love and support our LGBTQ members.

The Future

I've thought a lot about what the end of the book, chapter forty, might look like. For me, all Latter-day Saints, both cishet and LGBTQ, equally feel the balm of Gilead in our church. One example is a Latter-day Saint mother of an LGBTQ child having the same hopes in this life and the next that the mother of a cishet child does. I don't claim to know what chapter we are in, but in our current chapter, Latter-day Saints parents usually experience a great deal of fear when they first learn their child is LGBTQ. In chapter forty, that fear is gone.

I believe in Jesus Christ's doctrine that "all are alike unto God," which suggests that all His children should experience the same hope, peace, and belonging in our church (2 Nephi 26:33). I feel we can be confident enough in our restored gospel to realize we have more work to do and pray for and support our leaders who have stewardship to wrestle with and address these complicated churchwide issues.

Some ask me if certain aspects of our doctrine will have to change before we get to chapter forty. I don't know. I don't feel it's my place to answer this question since I don't know Heavenly Father's will and I am not a leader in our church. Many LGBTQ Latter-day Saints (and their families) have told me that the ninth article of faith gives them hope for the future. I like things that bring hope. Perhaps Heavenly Father has more adjustments—future chapters—to help our LGBTQ members and their families fully feel the balm of Gilead.

On the local level, I hope that we as members in our wards and families can do our part to get us to chapter forty so that all, regardless of their sexual orientation or gender identity, will feel understood, valued, and welcomed. All are children of our Heavenly Parents and our brothers and sisters. If we can get over our prejudices, stop judging, and learn more compassion, we can help our LGBTQ members feel like they belong. We can listen, learn, and love and create a more compassionate and understanding culture for everyone.

Honoring Stockton

Alyson Paul's brave Instagram post discussed in chapter 1 about her gay son Stockton shared her grief with a very specific invitation: "I lost my son yesterday to suicide. He is a beautiful young man with so much to give. My son is gay. He was a square peg trying to fit in a round hole and as such suffered immensely. We can do better recognizing differences and loving others unconditionally. My challenge to you all is to choose love."

In accepting her message to choose love, we honor Stockton's memory—and the memory of all LGBTQ individuals who have tragically died by suicide—by loving and ministering to others in the Savior's way. He loves and lifts each person, one by one. All are alike unto God, and all should be alike unto us. Let's act on our impressions about things we can do within our circles of influence.

And as we act on those impressions, we are following the words of our popular Latter-day Saint hymn "Love One Another":

> As I have loved you,
> Love one another.
> This new commandment:
> Love one another.
> By this shall men know
> Ye are my disciples,
> If ye have love
> One to another.[20]

ENDNOTES

1. M. Russell Ballard, "Questions and Answers" (devotional address, Brigham Young University, Provo, Utah, November 14, 2017), speeches.byu.edu/talks/m-russell-ballard/questions-and-answers/, emphasis added.
2. See episode 157 of *Listen, Learn & Love* podcast.
3. "Latter-day Saint Prophet, Wife and Apostle Share Insights of Global Ministry," *Newsroom*, The Church of Jesus Christ of Latter-day Saints, October 30, 2018, ewsroom.churchofjesuschrist.org/article/latter-day-saint-prophet-wife-apostle-share-insights-global-ministry.
4. Dieter F. Uchtdorf, "Come, Join with Us" (general conference address, Salt Lake City, October 2013), churchofjesuschrist.org/study/general-conference/2013/10/come-join-with-us.
5. Bruce R. McConkie, "All Are Alike unto God" (devotional address, Brigham Young University, Provo, UT, August 18, 1978), speeches.byu.edu/talks/bruce-r-mcconkie/alike-unto-god/.
6. "New Church Website on Same-Sex Attraction Offers Love, Understanding, and Hope," *Church News*, The Church of Jesus Christ of

Latter-day Saints, December 6, 2012, churchofjesuschrist.org/church/news/new-church-website-on-same-sex-attraction-offers-love-understanding-and-hope.

7. "Church Updates Official 'Mormon and Gay' Website," *Newsroom*, The Church of Jesus Christ of Latter-day Saints, October 25, 2016, newsroom.churchofjesuschrist.org/article/official-update-mormon-and-gay-website.
8. Jennifer Dobner, "LGBTQ Students Discuss Challenges Faced at Mormon-Owned BYU in First-Ever Forum," *Salt Lake Tribune*, April 29, 2017, archive.sltrib.com/article.php?id=5230363&itype=CMSID.
9. Jennifer Ball, "BYU Student Life Hosts LGBTQ and SSA Forum," *The Daily Universe*, March 15, 2018, universe.byu.edu/2018/03/15/byu-student-life-hosts-lgbtq-and-ssa-forum/.
10. "New Assistant to the President for Student Success and Inclusion," News, BYU, January 26, 2018, news.byu.edu/news/new-assistant-president-student-success-and-inclusion.
11. Kaitlyn Bancroft, "LGBTQ Outreach Members Encourage Faith in Christ, Not Outcomes," *The Daily Universe*, May 3, 2019, universe.byu.edu/2019/05/03/lgbtq-outreach-members-encourage-faith-in-christ-not-outcomes/.
12. Jennifer Weaver, "BYU Office of Student Success and Inclusion Hosts LGBTQ+ Christmas Party on Campus," KUTV, November 13, 2019, kutv.com/news/local/byu-office-of-student-success-and-inclusion-hosts-lgbtq-christmas-party-on-campus.
13. Whitney Bigelow, "LGBTQ and Ally Perspectives Shared during Campus Panel on Faith and Sexuality," *The Daily Universe*, January 16, 2020, universe.byu.edu/2020/01/16/lgbtq-and-ally-perspectives-shared-during-campus-panel-on-faith-and-sexuality/.
14. Courtney Tanner, "BYU Will Allow Same-Sex Dancing at Annual Competition," *Salt Lake Tribune*, updated January 22, 2020, sltrib.com/news/education/2020/01/21/first-time-ever-byu-will/.
15. Jason Swenson, "It's All about the Music: San Francisco Gay Men's Chorus Performs with Mormon Tabernacle Choir," *Deseret News*, January 26, 2018, deseret.com/2018/6/26/20647875/it-s-all-about-the-music-san-francisco-gay-men-s-chorus-performs-with-mormon-tabernacle-choir#members-of-the-san-francisco-gay-mens-chorus-including-steve-gallagher-front-in-purple-and-rocky-sharma-second-row-in-purple-sing-with-the-mormon-tabernacle-choir-during-soundcheck-at-the-shoreline-amphitheatre-in-mountain-view-calif-on-monday-june-25-2018.
16. Thomas Burr, "In Passionate Speech, Sen. Orrin Hatch Urges Compassion for the Gay Community, Help for Suicide Prevention," *Salt Lake Tribune*, updated June 14, 2018, sltrib.com/news/politics/2018/06/13/in-passionate-speech-sen-orrin-hatch-urges-compassion-for-the-gay-community-help-for-suicide-prevention/.

17. Tad Walch, "FamilySearch Completes Project to Allow Same-Sex Family Trees," *Deseret News*, December 10, 2019, deseret.com/utah/2019/12/10/21004733/familysearch-same-sex-family-trees-lgbtq-geneology; "FamilySearch Now Provides Ability to Document Same-Sex Family Relationships," *Newsroom*, The Church of Jesus Christ of Latter-day Saints, December 10, 2019, newsroom.churchofjesuschrist.org/article/familysearch-document-same-sex-family-relationships.
18. A.J. Jano, "Gayety at the Temple: Gay Men's Chorus of Washington Performs at D.C. Temple Visitors' Center," Blog, Affirmation, December 18, 2019, affirmation.org/gay-mens-chorus-washington-performs-dc-temple-visitors-center.
19. Dennis Roboy, "Utah Becomes 19th State to Ban Conversion Therapy for Children," *Deseret News*, January 22, 2020, deseret.com/utah/2020/1/22/21077104/conversion-therapy-lgbtq-mormon-lds-church-ban.
20. Luacine Clark Fox, "Love One Another," *Hymns of The Church of Jesus Christ of Latter-day Saints*, (Salt Lake City: The Church of Jesus Christ of Latter-day Saints, 1985), 308.

about the author

Richard H. Ostler, a former YSA bishop, speaks at firesides and conferences about how to more fully embrace LGBTQ Latter-day Saints, see their gifts and contributions, and better understand their unique road. He is the host of the *Listen, Learn & Love* podcast (listenlearnandlove.org) which provides a platform for LGBTQ Latter-day Saints to share their stories.

He is deeply committed to The Church of Jesus Christ of Latter-day Saints and to creating more understanding and support for LGBTQ members—a goal started during his service as a YSA bishop as he learned to set aside past assumptions to better fulfill his stewardship responsibility to meet the spiritual needs of LGBTQ ward members.

In addition to serving as a YSA bishop, he has served as a temple ordinance worker, stake young men's president, high counselor, and ward mission leader.

He has a BS from the University of Utah, an MBA from Brigham Young University, and is a small business owner. Richard and his wife, Sheila, live in Salt Lake City, Utah. They have six wonderful children and several grandchildren.

contributor index